TEMPERED STEEL

Col James H Kasler

TEMPERED STEEL

THE THREE WARS OF TRIPLE AIR FORCE CROSS WINNER JIM KASLER

Perry D. Luckett and Charles L. Byler

Potomac Books, Inc.
Dulles, Virginia

Library of Congress Cataloging-in-Publication Data
    Luckett, Perry D.
        Tempered steel : the three wars of triple Air Force cross winner Jim Kasler / Perry
    D. Luckett and Charles L. Byler.—1st ed.
            p.   cm.
        Includes bibliographical references.
        ISBN 1-57488-834-X (hardcover : alk. paper)
        1. Kasler, James H.   2. United States. Air Force—Officers—Biography.
        3. Fighter pilots—United States—Biography.   I. Byler, Charles L., 1943–
        II. Title.

    UG626.2.K373L83   2004
    358.4'092—dc22   2004008148

Hardcover ISBN 1-57488-834-X
(alk. paper)

Printed in Canada on acid-free paper that meets the American
National Standards Institute Z39-48 Standard.

Potomac Books, Inc.
22841 Quicksilver Drive
Dulles, Virginia 20166

First Edition

10   9   8   7   6   5   4   3   2

CONTENTS

FOREWORD

A MAN is playing golf early in the morning—the silence, the great stretches of grass, the tall trees. He swings. The shot is good, but there is something strangely awkward about his movements, even his walk. He replaces the club in the bag and goes on.

James Kasler is the man, now in his seventies, partly crippled, but indomitable, absolutely singular. Like those depicted in *The Greatest Generation* or *Never in Doubt*—and he was also a member of that generation as a B-29 tail gunner in World War II—Kasler is one of those men there are never enough of. He became a pilot after the war, then a fighter pilot, married with children, and in Korea in 1952 established his legend. Laconic, supremely able, gaining experience as he went, he shot down six enemy MiGs and became an ace.

The Air Force became his life. He went to Vietnam, of course, and there distinguished himself even more as a leader of air strikes against targets far to the north—in Hanoi and its industrial surroundings. These strikes were in F-105s—heavy, fast, loaded to their limits, and unable to make the trip to target without refueling in the air on the way in or out. The air defenses were formidable. Unlike in Kosovo or Iraq, many planes and pilots were lost. Although only a major, Kasler was so outstanding that he was known by name in the War Room of the White House itself. Kasler led the mission against the oil storage tanks today, President Johnson might be told, or Kasler has a flight in the area and has been alerted.

Some of the most aggressive pilots, some of the most courageous—John McCain and Robbie Risner among them—despite their skill were shot down, and Kasler had to bail out of an F-105 going more than 550 miles an hour, his leg trapped against the side of the cockpit, deep in North Vietnam. The leg was shattered. He was captured and went days without medical attention, paraded through villages on the way to prison in Hanoi. There he gave his greatest performance of all.

The prisoners in Hanoi lived in insect-tormented filth under the strictest discipline. Not knowing whether they would live or die, having no contact with the war or the outside world, continually beaten, interrogated, commanded to confess, they might easily have given up hope. Some did. Kasler represented the opposite. He endured everything; he gave nothing.

Kasler was twice operated on under primitive conditions. The surgical wounds swelled, filled with pus; he believed he would lose his leg and die. In this condition he was tortured to unconsciousness and beaten. He gave nothing. He was the spirit, the leader of those who had no hope. One year passed, two . . . then three, five, and finally more than six years. Jane Fonda came to Hanoi; shootings occurred at Kent State; riots raged in the streets.

Country, family, God—not necessarily in that order—along with a sense of duty and something he had exhibited from the very first, something that people recognized and that enabled him to go on despite everything. How much one admires it, how impossible it is to fake, how difficult it is to define.

Kasler had already won two Air Force Crosses, the second highest U.S. decoration, just below the Medal of Honor, and extremely difficult to win. For what he had shown in Hanoi, he received a third. No other individual, alive or dead, has done that or come close.

In this era of false celebrity, entertainment, and pursuit of wealth, Kasler touches a feeling that most people recognize as primary—an unmediated feeling. This biography offers the opportunity to know the man who fostered it, a chance to experience the deeds and thoughts of a remarkable hero and a great American.

JAMES SALTER
Author of *The Hunters* and *Burning the Days*

ACKNOWLEDGMENTS

SPECIAL thanks go to Col. James H. Kasler, Martha Kasler, and their three children for their openness and willing support of our effort. Colonel Kasler was indefatigable in providing original documents, personal testimony, photographs, and encouragement. Martha's warm spirit and sharp insights inform many parts of the narrative. Colonel Kasler's son, Jim (the Younger, as we learned to call him), coordinated the family's involvement, helped us with contact information, and offered enthusiasm and support during months of writing and editing. Daughters Suzanne and Nanette consented to interviews that deepened our understanding of James Kasler and his family relationships.

Thanks also to James Salter (one MiG credited, one damaged)—a warrior turned author who flew the F-86 with Kasler in Korea, then wrote *The Hunters* as a fictional account of flying with the Fourth Wing in that war. We appreciate his recognition of Kasler as the "nonpareil" in his recollection *Burning the Days*, his advice and aid to this project, and his foreword, which beautifully captures the essence of James Kasler.

Among the many who took time to write and talk about Colonel Kasler are Medal of Honor recipients Vice Adm. James B. Stockdale and Col. "Bud" Day. We particularly appreciate having Admiral Stockdale's thoughtful, honorific afterword, as well as his inspiration for our book's title. Hoa Lo, the name of the prison known to Americans as the "Hanoi Hilton," translates from Vietnamese to English as the "fiery furnace." In his preface to *A Vietnam Experience: Ten Years of Reflection*, Admiral Stockdale writes, "But there were many of us who were able to use the fire which was meant to destroy us as a saving fire, as a cauterizing agent, as a temperer of what became our steel." Thanks also to NAM-POW and three-war veteran Col. Lawrence Guarino for his comments on the book jacket, as well as for his time responding to letters.

Four retired Air Force officers graciously agreed to interviews, sometimes on short notice: Maj. Gen. Hoyt Sanford Vandenberg Jr., Brig. Gen. Cecil "Bud" Crabb, Brig. Gen. Robinson Risner, and Col. John Brodak. General Vandenberg and Colonel Kasler shared several duty assignments during their careers, beginning when Kasler was Vandenberg's gunnery instructor at Nellis Air Force Base. We're especially grateful to the general for several personal stories concerning their time together and for his comments on the book jacket. Col. John Brodak was cell mate and caregiver to Colonel Kasler during some of his darkest days in Hanoi. Kasler candidly states that he owes his life to Brodak.

Among those who contributed from the Korean War era (besides James Salter) are "Casey" Colman, a WWII ace who also had four credited MiG kills in Korea, and the late Martin Bambrick, fighter pilot and photographer par excellence, who granted permission to use his photograph of Kasler painting a star to mark the latter's fifth kill.

John G. Hubbell, author of *P.O.W.: A Definitive History of the American Prisoner-of-War Experience in Vietnam, 1964–1973*, granted permission to use the raw transcripts of his 1973 interviews with Colonel Kasler. We closely followed those transcripts and several chapters of Hubbell's published book to reconstruct Kasler's experiences as a POW.

Many people deserve acknowledgment as readers of the manuscript at various points during its writing. Aviation writer Robert F. Dorr heads this list, which includes novelist David Chacko, as well as Dutch aviation writer and F-105 historian Theo W. van Geffen.

Col. Frederick Kiley read the entire manuscript early and late, then responded with excellent suggestions concerning its structure, section headings, and areas for improvement. Kiley's book *Honor Bound: American Prisoners of War in Southeast Asia, 1961–1973* (with Stuart I. Rochester) was also a vital source of information about the prisoner-of-war experience in Southeast Asia. Equally important was his experience with the publishing process: he was largely responsible for finding Brassey's, Inc. as the publisher of this biography.

Medical doctors who read the manuscript include the late Air Force Brig. Gen. Charles W. Delp Jr. of the Pennsylvania National Guard's Medical Corps and Wayne Miller, MD, of the Mayo Clinic.

Donald Davidson of the Hall of Fame Museum at the Indianapolis Speedway was at the 1973 Indianapolis 500 when Colonel Kasler was honored there. He read the relevant pages and provided historical and technical insights concerning those events.

F-105 Thunderchief historian and author Lt. Col. W. Howard Plunkett provided much historical information and detail, including microfilm of the Fourth Wing's unit history for the Korean War during Colonel Kasler's service. This history was vital to documenting the victories that made Kasler an ace. Colonel Plunkett provided other historical material and proofread the manuscript.

Irene Luckett contributed many hours of original research, helped interview James and Martha Kasler, and read and suggested changes to the book. Her gentle nudging also helped us remember that, as the poet John Donne put it, "no man is an island entire unto itself"—that James Kasler's story is closely connected to Martha and to his children. Thanks to Irene for expanding our understanding of Colonel Kasler's role as husband and father.

We're especially indebted to James Joyner, our editor at Brassey's. His insightful reading of our manuscript and astute suggestions sharpened our style and coverage of events. Moreover, his patient handling of contractual details, permissions, and production issues smoothed *Tempered Steel*'s progress to its present form. Our production editor, John Church, deserves similar praise for guiding the book through its final stages. Much of the credit for this book's quality goes to Joyner, Church, and others mentioned here. Any errors in its content or misinterpretations are, of course, our own.

PERRY D. LUCKETT
Colorado Springs, Colorado

CHARLES L. BYLER
Boyertown, Pennsylvania

PRELUDE

MAJ. James Kasler joined his flight in close formation, flicked on his radar, and picked his way between the thunderstorm cells. His timing had to be exact, so he had selected a prominent river junction in Laos as his starting checkpoint. As luck would have it, Jim's flight broke out at a small hole in the clouds, directly over the point of departure. He was three minutes ahead of schedule, so he made a 360-degree tight turn to use up time before setting course to the north.

When Jim passed the initial point at the end of Thud Ridge, he called the flight to push it up and started a turn south toward Hanoi. As he turned, the fog bank faded away beneath him and his flight broke into the clear. At that same instant, flak began bursting around them. Jim glanced to the right toward Phuc Yen airfield and could see the flak guns blinking at them. With his flight running only three hundred feet above the ground to avoid surface-to-air missiles (SAMs), the Vietnamese had leveled their heavy 85mm and 100mm guns and were firing almost horizontally. This meant the shells were killing their own people as they struck the ground—reflecting how important the Hanoi petroleum, oil, and lubricants (POL) complex was to their war effort.

Jim's flight was moving parallel to the northeast railroad that leads into the city of Hanoi. It was North Vietnam's most important supply link with the People's Republic of China, so flak guns of every caliber and description protected it. Ahead, Jim could see two gray smoke columns rising, one on each side of the Hanoi POL field the 388th Wing had just struck. But they hadn't hit a major fuel tank. The sky was dotted with hundreds of white, gray, and black puffs—the remaining traces of flak shells that had been fired at the departing Korat aircraft. Thus, Jim had a good idea of what was awaiting him over the target.

Jim approached slightly left of target, called for afterburner, and began his pull-up. He climbed through eight thousand feet and started a slow turn to the right until he reached his roll-in point near eleven thousand feet. He cut his afterburner, dropped dive brakes, and rolled into the bomb run. As he was turning in, he could see three ten-gun, 85mm batteries on the Gia Lam airfield frantically firing at him and his flight. Ignoring them as much as he could, Jim continued his run. He could hardly believe his eyes— big, fat fuel tanks filled his view. He pushed his pickle button to release his bombs and made a rolling pullout to the right. When he cleared the smoke, he turned gently to the left around the target complex. The huge fuel tanks were erupting one after another, sending up immense billowing fireballs.

By the time Jim had circled to the target's southwest corner, each of his flight members had also made the bomb run and rejoined him. The smoke now merged into one huge, boiling, red-and-black pillar—an unbelievable sight. As Jim circled back, he could see flames leaping out of the smoke thousands of feet above him. He swung around to the north toward Phuc Yen airfield. He had seen two MiGs on the end of the runway when they began their dash toward Hanoi and had thought he might get a shot if either got into the air. But Jim changed his mind about looking for MiGs when he saw the intensity of the flak bursting around them. He banked his Thunderchief to the south and looked at the ground; so many guns were firing, the valley reminded him of a desert city viewed from the air at night. But it was daylight, and those winking "lights" were thousands of shots fired at them in anger.

After Jim crossed south of the Red River, the flak diminished as the gunners apparently switched their attention to the fighter-bombers behind his flight. He headed west, searching the roads for targets of opportunity. As he approached Hoa Binh on the Black River, he noticed a new road had been cut up the side of a high plateau that extended east back toward Hanoi. He popped over the rim of the plateau and dropped his nose to investigate. There, directly under his gun sight pipper, was a truck. He squeezed the trigger, and 20mm cannon projectiles tore into the truck, setting it on fire. Jim and his flight found twenty-five trucks on the plateau. They set twelve on fire and damaged at least six others.

As Jim pulled out of one of his strafing passes, he looked back at Hanoi thirty-five miles to the east. It was a windless day, so the black smoke formed a perfect pillar reaching above thirty-five thousand feet. By now their fuel was running low, forcing them to head for home.

This Hanoi POL strike was one of the most successful missions of the Vietnam War. The F-105s destroyed more than 90 percent of the complex. In fact, it was one of the few targets in North Vietnam that never required a restrike because the Vietnamese abandoned the facility altogether. For planning and leading the famous mission, James Kasler received his first Air Force Cross.

CHAPTER 1

The Child Is
Father of the Man

BUT this extraordinary man's story doesn't start with his service in Vietnam. It begins forty years earlier with his birth in a small Midwestern town to an ordinary family that prepared him for a life of service to his country.

James Helms Kasler was born on May 2, 1926, in South Bend, Indiana, the second of Rex and Inez Kasler's three children. His middle name is his mother's maiden name. His parents were typical Hoosiers: solid, hardworking people who brought up Jim and his two brothers in the church (see fig. 1). (Brother Richard was a year and a half older than Jim; Tom is two years younger.) They taught the children values and instilled in them a love of country. Jim's father wasn't a strict disciplinarian, but his mother was. She chased him around the living room table to catch and punish him whenever he did something bad. The exercise kept her in great condition because he was a typically rambunctious boy with a penchant for mischief.

At the same time, Jim was an exceptional worker, so his grandparents H. B. and Minnie Kasler often requested that he come stay with them during the summer to work on the farm in Liberty Center, Indiana. Although he worked hard at home and on the farm, he found ways to entertain himself with whatever was available.

He spent a lot of time in his homemade car (see fig. 2) and enjoyed most things mechanical, but he was happy to try anything adventurous. For example, when Jim was six or seven, he thought riding pigs was great fun and often competed in his own porcine rodeo. The pigs weren't as fast as the fighter jets he would ride as an adult, but no one could fault their maneuverability.

Like the famous flier Charles Lindbergh, Jim was terrified of heights as a child. To overcome his fear, he often challenged himself to climb to the top of the silo on his grandfather's farm, which was upwards of seventy-five feet high, as well the windmill just outside the back door of the farmhouse that was used to pump water for the household. One day, he and brother Dick got the bright idea of trying out a parachute with a chicken as the parachutist. They made the parachute out of old cloth and string, climbed up the windmill, tied the chicken to the parachute, and dropped it. The experiment was unsuccessful, as they discovered when the chicken splatted—dead on contact—at Grandma Kasler's feet. But all was not lost: they ate the chicken for dinner, and Jim received an early lesson about what can happen when a creature that can no longer fly has to depend on a parachute for survival.

During those early years, Jim was already interested in history, war, and warriors. His ancestry may have contributed to this inclination. Grandfather Kasler descended from a Hessian soldier who had settled in America after the American Revolution. Grandmother Minnie Kasler was half Miami of Ohio Indian. The Indians had captured Minnie's mother when she was a girl and had given her to an Indian brave as his mate. The warrior's bloodlines therefore continued from Minnie Kasler, through Jim's father Rex, into his own makeup. Rex Kasler had served during World War I as Billy Mitchell's chauffeur and carried supplies to Eddie Rickenbacker. Rex's framed discharge paper still hangs on the wall of Jim's home office in Momence, Illinois. Both of Jim's brothers and his cousin William also served in World War II.

Besides the direct influence of his family, Jim found other heroic models in fiction. His favorite fictional hero was Prince Valiant. After all, how could one expect more than to battle every Sunday and survive? Grandfather Helms, who lived in Bluffton, Indiana, saved the Sunday editions each year, so Jim could read all the Prince Valiant comic strips when he visited Bluffton in the summer. He enjoyed the tales of knightly honor and battle, seeing in them the stalwart qualities he would carry forward into his own adulthood.

From age eight to thirteen, Jim lived in Birmingham, Alabama. There and in nearby Homewood, Jim enjoyed exploring the many caves of Red Mountain, where his friends and he contemplated vague horrors. A risk taker even then, he enjoyed the imagined perils. He always carried a garbage can cover and a wooden sword in case he had to dispatch a threatening wild animal or an alien cave creature. Jim's interest in explosive ordnance also began early. He and his friends went out to a nearby fishing pond and built a cannon out of shells. His father began bringing gunpowder to the pond so the boys could stuff the makeshift cannon with wadding paper and powder, torch it off, and blow toy ships out of the water.

During his quieter hours, Jim painted hundreds of individual lead soldiers in appropriate, realistic uniforms. He made the entire basement of his parents' home a battleground for these soldiers— complete with hills and trenches on which he carried out a lengthy, complex war. At the same time, he assembled very sophisticated, detailed model airplanes that flew. While trying them out, he began to build an interest in flying and in combat aviation, though not yet imagining he would become a fighter pilot.

After Kasler's family moved to Louisville for his junior high school years, he maintained his interest in warfare and fancied himself a commander. The Kaslers' home was next to a large open field, with an abandoned racetrack at the end of the street—a perfect place for military maneuvers. Jim recruited kids in the neighborhood to build imaginary military lines, threatening them and making them dig trenches. They covered the trenches with boards, on which they placed stove-turret vents to signify military towers. Jim was a ruthless commander, continually rallying his "troops" against enemy soldiers (large reeds) that stood in the adjacent lot. They spent many hours charging the reeds, whacking them down with wooden swords, and sometimes dying a heroic death.

At times, the "war" was on hold for new recruits or better weather. These housebound days were a perfect chance for Jim to pound a set of snare drums that his parents thought he had acquired to drive them crazy. After a number of practice sessions, he became confident that he could be a drummer. One day, he was sitting in class when he heard the junior-high band marching down the street, drums thumping. He jumped up, ran over to look out the window, and thought, *Why aren't I in that band? Why am I not playing?* So he persuaded his teacher and the bandmaster to let him join the band and practiced with them a few times. When they had a big parade in downtown Louisville, in which Jim's little band was to march next in line to a huge band from Emanuel High School—the largest high school in Louisville—Jim was the only drummer who showed up. All the others had a sudden touch of "chicken fever." So Jim played and marched down the streets of Louisville, beating the drum well enough to carry the band through their performance.

At the same time that Jim was expressing his martial and musical abilities, he extended the artistic flair he had shown in painting his toy soldiers. He began building miniature log cabins out of toothpicks that were little works of art. They also exhibited meticulous, enduring construction because Jim still has them today—more than six decades later. They presaged his interest in landscape and scene painting, which he took up as a young adult.

Jim was a second-semester freshman in high school before the family moved from Louisville back to Indiana in 1941, this time to Indianapolis. Japan bombed Pearl Harbor later that year and drew the United States into World War II. As time dragged on, Jim was worried that the war would end before he could be a part of it. Meantime, he read everything he could about the war and was especially fascinated with the Germans' Stuka dive-bomber and with tank warfare. He closely followed news about the major air and sea battles as well. He even intentionally graduated a half year early in January 1944, hoping to get into combat before the fighting was over. He admits that although he was patriotic, he was motivated more by a desire to test himself as a fighter and to become famous for his exploits. Many of his schoolmates had the same feelings.

Thus, at seventeen and a half and deeply imbued with a warrior's spirit, Jim went with a friend to join the Army Air Corps's aviation cadet program early in 1944 at an armory just south of Indianapolis. Two hundred boys were in the armory, stripped naked, each carrying a clipboard in front of him with his information on it. When Jim finished the physical, he had to go see a psychiatrist, who asked him a lot of what he considered to be silly questions. He thought his friend had obtained a much better grade than he did on the general test. "What's a cam?" he asked the friend. Being a mechanic, the friend knew the answer, so Jim started worrying that he had failed the test. When the results came back, though, his friend had failed, and Jim had passed.

Still, the doctors had some concerns about Jim physically. They thought something was wrong with his kidneys—that he was holding too much water. They called him "Pits" or "Bags" because of the bags under his eyes. He had to go back once a week for a month to have his urine specimens checked. Fortunately, nothing was wrong with him. Eight days after his eighteenth birthday, on May 10, 1944, he was called into the service. He boarded a train for a three-day ride from Indiana to Fort Thomas, Kentucky, during which he endured a standard battery of inoculations. To receive them, he had to sit naked, straddling a bench with seven or eight other young men and sliding forward to get his shots. The medical corpsmen jabbed needles in both of his arms at the same time. Jim wasn't certain, but he didn't believe they sterilized the needles between injections.

After a brief stop at Fort Thomas, Jim rode the train another three days to Sheppard Field (Wichita Falls, Texas) in order to complete basic training. Basic was miserable in Texas, with temperatures already above one hundred degrees in mid-May. The drinking water was so bad they had to pool money from their meager allowances, buy jugs of water from stores, and ration it to the people in their barracks. The recruits went out to the dry-firing range, lay there in the sand, and clicked their rifles for hours. "Meat wagons" (ambulances) hauled off hundreds of people who passed out from the heat and humidity every day. One day, a general officer was supposed to inspect the troops, so the sergeants put them all in formation and kept them standing in the sun for an hour and a half. Finally, everyone started passing out, but Jim just kneeled down on the ramp to wait, illustrating what would become his legendary high tolerance for heat, cold, and nearly unimaginable pain.

The stupidity of some of the training paled compared to other kinds of petty harassment and invasions of privacy that were typical of Army life in those days. For example, the commanders were obsessed with making sure none of the troops contracted a disease, so they routinely conducted surprise "personal inspections." At 4:00 A.M., the sergeants rousted them out of bed and ordered, "Put on your raincoats." They went outside and stood in line. The next order was, "Okay. Milk it back and shake it down," after which a medic walked down the line looking at their genitals to make sure they didn't have the clap. No element of privacy could survive basic training.

EIGHTEEN-YEAR-OLD TAIL GUNNER

After Kasler graduated from basic training, he discovered the aviation cadet program had been closed to new candidates. Instead, he was given a choice between navigator or gunnery school. He knew it would take a long time to go through navigator training and he wanted to go into combat, so he signed up for gunnery school. They made him a tail gunner because he could fit in the tail gunner's compartment better than a bigger man. He was five feet four inches tall at the time and weighed only about 135 pounds. But he didn't stay small long. He grew an inch that first year and then topped out at over six feet and 185 pounds by age twenty.

Jim and other gunner prospects went to Buckman Field in Fort Meyers, Florida, which was out in the backwoods at that time. The trip took three or four days by train because they did a lot of switching and sitting on side rails. Jim got off the train at Buckman carrying a duffel bag and all his gear, dragging a footlocker behind him. As he and the other recruits approached a tent city set up around the airfield, men came running out of the tents yelling, "Go back! Go back!" They were trying to rattle the recruits—a time-worn military tradition—so Jim paid no attention. Still, by the looks of things, he thought he should go back: the place had very few signs of civilization.

Jim started flexible gunnery training the next day. He began by learning to field strip the .45-caliber pistol and the machine guns. He spent many hours on the skeet range shooting at clay birds or riding around an oval track on the back of a truck with a shotgun mounted like the handheld machine guns on bombers. He fired from twenty different stations around the track. The practice later paid off for him in Korea, where he had to use the gun sight on his F-86 Sabrejet in a fixed position.

Jim also trained in B-24 bombers, firing at targets towed by B-26s, which Women Air Force Service Pilots (WASPs) flew. These women served in civilian status and wore made-over men's uniforms. At least twenty-seven were killed in the line of duty while ferrying bombers and P-38 fighters across the country or towing targets. Jim always thought they received too little credit for their service, especially because some gunners were inaccurate enough at first to put the tow plane in danger from stray fire. Yet, when men became available to fill the flying jobs, the women went home with little more than an official thank you. It was 1977 before Congress passed a bill, introduced by Sen. Barry Goldwater (R-Arizona), giving the WASPs honorable discharges and declaring them to be veterans.

The gunners also fired rubber bullets at "pinball machines," their name for P-39s rigged so the nose of the fighter plane lit up if they scored hits on the leading edges of the wings or the nose. They actually shot down one of the P-39s with rubber bullets, but fortunately the pilot walked out of the forest two days later.

Right after Kasler finished flexible gunnery training, he moved to "S" shipping squadron. There, he got in a row with his sergeant and pushed him around a bit. So the lieutenant called Jim into his office and said, "What do you want: three days of KP (kitchen police) or seven days of ordnance?" Jim thought, *I'm no fool. Ordnance is heavy. I'll take the three days of KP.* So they put him in the cadet barracks area and assigned him to cleaning pots and pans, after which he quickly reevaluated his decision. He was miserable trying to get the burned grease off the cookware. He had to throw the pots into the fire and scrape them in order to get them clean. He decided—given a choice—he would never take KP again.

Jim soon had a chance to exercise his resolution because he got into another little scrape just two days after he finished KP. He had to sign a disciplinary-action report, which the Army called a Form 104. Again, he went before the lieutenant, who said, "Ok, three days of KP or seven days of ordnance?" Jim chose seven days of ordnance, then spent the week throwing 114-pound ammunition boxes around and dipping .50-caliber ammunition tips with nondrying paint to shoot at the towed flags they used for aerial gunnery practice.

All together, Kasler signed six Form 104s at gunnery training. Every time, he chose seven days of moving ordnance over cleaning pots and pans. After he signed the fifth form, he had to go before an officer who had risen from the rank of lieutenant to major in seven weeks. The officer had returned from overseas duty and was very happy to be stateside. After combat, he figured Kasler's infractions were pretty small stuff and seemed to understand Jim's temperamental nature. Rather than getting angry with him, he just sent him out on detail. Jim went out to the range before sunrise, moved and stacked ammunition boxes all day, and came back after dark.

One evening, when Kasler came in from the range, someone told him, "Hey Jim. Your name is on the shipping list. You're going to Laredo, Texas, to be a gunnery instructor."

"The hell I am," Jim said. "I'm not going to be an instructor. I'm going to combat. I want to get on a bomber crew as a gunner."

The next morning, Kasler went back out to the range. When he came in again that night, other trainees said, "Jim. They're really looking for you."

Jim said, "I don't care. I'm going back to the range."

The following day, Jim was back working on the range at 4:00 A.M. About 9:00 A.M. he looked across the flats and saw dust rising off of the ground from a vehicle speeding his way. It was the first sergeant, who screeched to a halt and said, "Get in this jeep!"

Jim said, "I have to check in with the sergeant because I'm working here."

The first sergeant shouted, "Get in this jeep, you son of a bitch!" So Jim climbed into the jeep, and they roared back to the barracks.

The first sergeant threw Jim's clothes into a duffel bag, pulled all his gear together, and hauled him to the processing line for Laredo and gunnery-instructor duty. After about thirty minutes, the processing sergeant said, "There's no way we can get him processed in time." So the first sergeant took Jim in front of the major again to sign another Form 104. The major said, "Kasler. If you come in here one more time, I'm going to take your PFC [Private First Class] stripe away from you." Jim started laughing, and the major did, too. By this time they had developed a rapport, so the major just sent Jim back to the range and the ever-present ammunition boxes.

About a week later Kasler received orders to join a bomber crew, and the Army sent him home for a week's leave. Jim was amazed to find how desirable he had suddenly become to a few girls in his neighborhood who had never looked at him before. He surmised that the uniform had something to do with it (see fig. 3). Or perhaps it was the muscles he had developed slinging around those ordnance cases at the flight line. Of course, he had to admit, the field had shrunken considerably since so many young men had left for the service. Whatever the reason, though, he found their attention delightful.

After his short leave, Kasler went with other future combat gunners by train to Lincoln, Nebraska, where the Army had a bus to meet them. It was midnight and about thirteen degrees below zero when they arrived in Lincoln. The driver hauled them to the base, where they stood waiting outside for a long time. Finally, sergeants came out and marched them to a barracks building that had no windows, bedding, blankets, or heat. They had only bare mattresses on which to sleep. Jim said to a buddy, "We can't hack this. It's freezing." So the two went down to an open mess hall and asked the sergeant if they could sleep in the corner where it was warm. The sergeant let them stay through the night and even gave them something to eat. Jim learned early that a trooper must provide for himself in the United States Army Air Corps.

Jim joined a crew in Lincoln and then went down to Alamogordo, New Mexico, to start flight-crew training with B-29s. He didn't care at the time that he was riding in the wrong end of an airplane. The war was on, and he was going to be in it if his training didn't go on forever. Training missions consisted of runs on the practice bombing and gunnery range. The B-29 was far advanced over the B-24 and the B-17. It was faster, flew higher, could fly farther with a heavier bomb load, and featured remote-controlled guns, rather than the handheld ones that had been on the earlier bombers. Back in the tail Jim had two .50-caliber guns. His gun sight had two wheels on it—one on the side and one on the top. The wheel on top swiveled the pair of machine guns left and right, whereas the side wheel (which had a trigger on it) pivoted them up and down. Despite these advances, however, the training airplanes still had old Wright Cyclone engines, so an engine or two blew on nearly every mission. Oil poured out of the planes as they limped home.

Jim encountered no real surprises in New Mexico until he finished gunnery training at Las Cruces. There, while waiting to ship overseas for combat, he witnessed a historic event. On July 16 at 5:30 A.M., he was walking to the mess hall in total darkness. Suddenly, the sky flashed as bright as daylight. Jim had no idea what was happening. Later he learned he had seen the blast from the first atomic bomb detonation at Trinity Site. As he was to discover while flying combat in the Pacific, it would not be the last time he found himself near a historic atomic blast.

From Las Cruces, Kasler's crew was scheduled to travel to Sacramento, California, where they would pick up their B-29, *Twentieth Century Limited*. But they had to exercise a bit of resourcefulness to get away as scheduled. Although fighter pilots have a wild reputation, bomber crews have always had some characters as well. The certified character on Jim's crew was Jesse Flores, their engineer, who was supposed to start the engines for flight. Every weekend while they were training at Las Cruces, Flores would get a bottle of Bulldog gin and a bottle of tequila and drink both bottles himself.

The morning they were due to leave for Sacramento, Flores had been out whooping it up. He returned, became belligerent with his crewmates, and wanted to fight. But Jim rifled a shot to his jaw, easily coldcocking him, and the crew carried the unconscious engineer onto their airplane. The navigator knew something about starting the engines, so he got them under way. They headed out over San Francisco that night with Flores still sobering up in the cockpit. After landing in Sacramento, they eventually flew to Hawaii, then went on to Wake Island, Kwajalein, and Guam, which was central headquarters for Twentieth Air Force. B-29s were stationed on Guam, Tinian, and Saipan in the Mariana Islands. By far the largest air base in the world at that time was on Tinian, an island about five miles wide by twelve miles long.

Kasler's B-29 carried a crew of eleven. As tail gunner, Jim had to start the auxiliary power unit in the back and then go down the ladder in the aft section and help pull restraining chocks from the wheels. To keep the correct weight position and balance for takeoff, Jim sat in the tail. He went up a little chute into the tail gunner's compartment, closed his hatch (which was round like those on a submarine), turned around, pulled down his seat, and sat on it. Jim's small size at the time perfectly suited the compact space. Plexiglas surrounded his tail gunner's compartment, which was pressurized and separated from the rest of the crew by thirty or forty feet. When they no longer needed pressurization after a training mission, Jim could open the hatch and go up into the center section of the plane on the way back home.

Although the B-29 had an altitude advantage over earlier bombers, crews didn't use that advantage very often in the Pacific. B-17s and B-24s headed for Germany were training at thirty thousand feet or higher, if they could get up there. But General LeMay, commander of the Twenty-first Bomber Command, had the B-29s flying at eight thousand to twelve thousand feet because wind drift made high-altitude bombing ineffective. At first, crews thought the low-altitude patterns would expose them to murderous enemy fire, but Jim discovered that bombing at low altitudes was much more accurate and not as dangerous in the Pacific as one might think. Although the Japanese had flak, they didn't have as much as Allied airmen encountered over Germany. The Japanese Zeros (fighter planes) also weren't as formidable as Germany's Me-109s because typically B-29s could outrun them. The United States lost some B-29s to Japanese fighters, but they were usually damaged or straggling airplanes.

Kasler flew six of his seven combat missions to Japan in the *Twentieth Century Limited*. By way of preparation, the crew ran two practice missions over Marcus Island in July 1945 before they flew regular missions over Japan. The United States's landing forces had bypassed Marcus, so it was still in Japanese hands and remained a threat. In fact, the Japanese shot down another B-29 during Jim's second practice mission.

Jim's first combat mission was a July 26 raid on Tokuyama. The B-29s circled at a checkpoint over the ocean until their time came up. Staggered between eight thousand and twelve thousand feet with a one-thousand-foot vertical separation, the groups kept circling, and then ran in one at a time. Back in the tail, Jim looked down and forward, and he could see a horrendous firestorm coming up off of Tokuyama. About that time, the searchlight picked up their B-29. Jim felt as though the enemy was looking right at him and sensed his remaining moments on the planet might be numbered. It was the only time he felt anxiety—not really fear—going into combat.

When their aircraft hit the thermal wave coming up from the city, it nearly flipped onto its back, wrenching Jim's hands from his guns and slamming a shoulder rudely against the canopy. He thought they'd "had the stroke"—his phrase for a fatal blow—but the pilot was able to recover, get back into their run, and drop their bombs—a mixture of hundred-pound demolition and incendiary bombs (white phosphorus). The Allies had discovered Japanese cities were very susceptible to firebombs because they contained so much paper and wood. The B-29s destroyed far more property and people in those conventional firebomb raids than they did with nuclear weapons at the end of the war.

Although Jim felt some heightened anticipation before a combat mission, he never feared enemy fire, even as a teenaged gunner. He had an inherent faith that a higher power would protect him but didn't offer any explicit prayers for his safety. Other members of his crew took a more direct approach. For example, both blister gunners on the crew were Roman Catholic. After their first combat mission (and every other one), Jim came out of the tail to discover rosary beads all over the floor. He figured they must have carried several backup sets on each mission and worked them hard while under fire. Although Jim wasn't a Catholic himself, he was glad for any help the blister gunners could provide him.

Kasler's second and third missions were also to urban areas: Uji-Yamada and Nagaoka. On August 7 his B-29 hit the naval arsenal at Toyakawa. After they had flown two or three missions, Iwo Jima—closer to Japan—opened as a B-29 landing field and refueling site, which meant they could start carrying heavier bomb loads. Jim's B-29 recovered there two or three times while Marines were still fighting Japanese on the island. Jim was utterly amazed at what he saw: American ships sunk in the harbor. Hundreds of them! The Japanese had fought fiercely there and were still fighting on Mount Suribachi, causing the United States Marines the worst casualties in their storied history.

On Jim's next mission to the Marifu Railroad Yards on August 14, the Japanese ground gunners shot up their aircraft a bit. Their radio operator for that mission, Stevens, received a Purple Heart for a shrapnel scratch. They started losing fuel and couldn't make it back to Iwo Jima, so they diverted to Okinawa. The *Twentieth Century Limited* became the first B-29 to land there, even though the runway wasn't quite finished. After they landed, they walked over to the edge of the field where Marines were sitting along the strip up on a hill, eating lunch. Right below, fifty yards away, other Marines were spraying napalm into the caves and firing their weapons. A Marine looked at Kasler's B-29 and said to Jim, "I sure as hell would never fly on that thing."

Jim replied, "Hey, it's a lot safer than what you are doing, buddy!" He was grateful to be well above ground, despite the dangers of combat flying.

Jim believed the tail gunner's job was important and had its exciting moments, but it still wasn't the same as being at the controls, taking an aircraft through its paces. He had begun forming images of himself in the pilot's seat, rolling into bombing runs and taking on the enemy's ace fighters. Then, coming back from one of their raids on Japan, he had a moment that defined his future. He was out of the tail in the right blister gunner's seat, looking out over Saipan as they cruised home, when a P-51 fighter came swooping up and popped right in beside them. The pilot waved at him, then peeled off in a roll. Jim thought, *Now that's the way to fly!* From that moment, Jim knew he wanted to be a fighter pilot.

HIROSHIMA AND FLYING IN THE PHILIPPINES

The atomic bomb came to Tinian in great secrecy. Kasler had no "need to know," so he learned nothing about its deployment. But he knew something unusual was happening because the far west end of one runway was closed off with a high chain-link fence around the entire area. Soon, some of the "Big Bertha" bombs, which had been used to destroy submarine pens in Europe, arrived. These huge bombs were a good smoke screen for the atomic bomb, whose large size required cutting out the B-29 bomb bay's center section. When the Big Berthas first arrived, Jim couldn't imagine what kind of target in Japan would need such a powerful weapon.

Right after the atomic bomb fell on Hiroshima and the day after

the Nagasaki raid, Kasler's B-29 went to Saipan and loaded supplies they would drop to Allied prisoners of war (POWs) in Japan.
Before the war had officially ended, they were flying over Japan
looking for prison camps. In Yawada, the Japanese housed prisoners next to the steel mill with "POW" painted on the roof—their
way of trying to protect an industry critical to their war effort. On
the first drop Jim's group made, the packages weren't very secure.
When the chutes opened, a lot of them slipped out of the harnesses,
and their contents spilled over the ground. A day later, they went
back over Japan and dropped more supplies. This time, the packages remained intact as they landed.

As Jim's B-29 flew over Nagasaki and Hiroshima at a few hundred feet, he sat in the side door and used a large K-9 cocking
camera to snap pictures. The Army released these photographs to
the media in order to show ground zero. Jim kept copies, but someone stole them from him later when he was stationed in the Philippines. Losing the photographs distressed him because they were
a firsthand historical record of these stunning events. Even as a
youngster, he understood the issues concerning the use of such
devastating force. But his personal observations led him to believe,
as many analysts have determined, that the atomic bombs may
have saved lives. As his B-29 flew all over Japan, Jim saw dozens of
airstrips, with hundreds of Zeros and Betties lined up under the
trees waiting for the Allied invasion. (He took photographs of
them, but they disappeared with the others in the Philippines.)
Had the Allies been forced to invade Japan, a horrible number of
lives would have been lost on both sides.

Jim earned the first of his eleven Air Medals for his World War
II missions, but he also received an injury that would haunt him
for decades. Before a mission, he was climbing up the ladder after
pulling the chocks when a rung broke and he fell, catching his right
knee on the bottom rung. Though he didn't know it at the time, he
had punched a hole in his kneecap. Not wanting to miss a combat
mission, Jim climbed up the ladder and flew with the injury and
pain. The hole filled with calcium over time, causing the knee to
stiffen and then to lock up. Two wars later, the same knee would
grind into the canopy rail of his crippled F-105 when he ejected
over North Vietnam. Eventually, Jim would have four operations
on that kneecap—and finally, a knee replacement in 2002.

The standard tour in World War II was thirty-five missions, far fewer than the one hundred that the Air Force would require in Korea or Vietnam. Still, because of limited time in the service, only a few people on Jim's crew had enough points to go home. Jim had only seven missions, so he was ordered to Clark Field in the Philippines.

While on Tinian, Jim had often climbed three hundred feet down a cliff to a cove, where he could swim in the ocean just off the Tinian deep. Out a little way, the ocean floor drops off thousands of feet, but a coral reef runs up close to the shore. Jim waded to the end of the coral, swam out to the point, and then rode the waves up and down right up to a ledge. One day, he was swimming to the point when suddenly a huge black shape slid under him—an enormous black manta ray. He was seldom frightened, but that ray scared the hell out of him. He had never seen a creature so large in his life. Later he learned that his fear was misplaced: manta rays aren't dangerous, unless one kills someone with a flipper by accident.

Not long before Jim was due to leave for the Philippines, he was lying on his private beach sunbathing. By chance, he looked down toward the cliff at one end of the cove. A truck was plunging off the cliff into the water, followed by jeeps and more trucks. Men were dumping hundreds of vehicles into the ocean because the U.S. government didn't want to saturate the market in the United States by returning them as surplus. Recognizing an opportunity, Jim's crew "borrowed" two jeeps destined for burial at sea. They cranked them up into the bomb bays of their airplane—a perfect fit—and took them to the Philippines with them.

When the crew arrived in the Philippines, the Army put Jim in charge of the motor pool—slightly ironic for a young man who hadn't known what a "cam" was when he took his exam for entry into the Army Air Corps. By this time he was a buck sergeant (three-striper). Jim had five Japanese men working for him, and he got along very well with them. They didn't mind being in the Philippines after the war. They were worried about going home to Japan because they had surrendered, which the Japanese—as a matter of honor—were not supposed to do. Although Jim's main job was running the motor pool, he still had to log four hours of flying time monthly to earn his flight pay. So he trundled out regularly to fly in a B-17, which was like a Ford Model-T compared to the B-29.

After two months or so, Jim had the option of going home on a troop ship or waiting to fly back on a B-29. He decided to wait and fly home, but his crewmates, Cavanaugh and Banet, took the ship. A month later, what remained of his crew took a B-29 to Hawaii and then caught a passenger plane (probably a C-54) to San Francisco. Jim eventually reported to Camp Atterberry, Indiana, to be discharged. About six hundred men were in the auditorium, when a sergeant stood up and said, "We would like you to stay in the service. Or at least sign up for the inactive reserve because the United States needs to maintain a large reserve force." He explained that the reserves were necessary because of early signs of trouble around the world, especially with the Russians. Out of those six hundred, however, Jim was the only one who signed up for the inactive reserves. The sergeant explained that if he ever decided to come back into the service, it would count as longevity time, and so forth. Even then, Jim planned to come back in and become a fighter pilot, but first he wanted to go back home to Indianapolis and, perhaps, to college.

CHAPTER 2

Two Loves:
Martha and Aviation

MARTHA Lee Rankin grew up in tiny Macomb, Illinois, where at five years old she could walk across the entire town, know everybody along the way, and never feel threatened by anyone. Her mother was a kindergarten teacher who enrolled Martha at an academy on a college campus at Western Illinois State Teachers College. When Martha completed the seventh grade, her family moved to Indianapolis, Indiana, where she attended eighth grade at Public School 66 and then moved on to Shortridge High School. Coincidentally, Jim Kasler also was enrolled at Shortridge, though Martha barely noticed him at the time.

Martha graduated from Shortridge High in 1946, so she had the summer off before moving on to Butler University. Of course, Jim had graduated early, gone off to war, and returned at age twenty with vague notions of attending Butler, as well. Through a mutual friend, Mott Groom, Jim expressed interest in dating Martha. He had noticed she was pretty and personable, with just a hint of the charming shyness that went with being a small-town girl. But Martha remembered Jim from high school, when he was five feet four inches tall. She told Mott she didn't want to date "a little guy" and refused to go out with him. Some time later, Jim came one night to pick up a girl at Martha's club meeting. When Martha saw him, she didn't recognize the broad-shouldered six-footer, now 185 pounds, tanned, blond, and very good-looking. "Who's that?" she asked.

Her friends said, "That's Jim Kasler . . . the guy we wanted to fix you up with."

And she said, "Okay. Maybe I will go out with him."

On their first date Jim and Martha went to a drive-in movie with two other couples on a very warm summer evening. The boys wanted to go to a drive-in, but not for the usual reasons—they needed an outdoor theater so they could listen to a Joe Louis fight on the radio. From that date, Martha knew immediately Jim was not the high school type she was used to. He had been away to war, was ready to make up for lost time, and had a feisty personality. By Jim's own admission, when he came home from World War II, he was a big man with a runt complex. His fuse was short, so he had little tolerance for others who tried to get under his skin. Thus, he was continually in fights—always poking someone in the nose for something and apologizing later.

That temper emerged around Martha, too. One night, she went with Jim to a theater in Indianapolis. After the movie, Jim discovered he had locked the keys in the car. Without hesitation, he picked up a brick, broke the side window, and unlocked the door. That was Martha's first experience with Jim being the decisive, but volatile, person he was and continued to be. On another evening, Jim was supposed to have a date with Martha, so he called her to tell her what time he was coming. Martha said, "Jim, you know, I just honestly don't think I like you well enough to go out with you. I don't think you should spend your money on me."

Jim said, angrily, "I'll be right over!" and slammed down the receiver. He was so mad that he threw the family's telephone through the window, which didn't please his mother.

When Martha saw him roaring around the corner toward her house, she said, "Okay! I'll go! I'll go! I'll go!" Despite Martha's subsequent discouragement, Jim kept calling and asking for dates.

Even then, Martha knew Jim was special, but she wasn't in a hurry to get serious over him. She was only seventeen years old and dating several boys at the time, so marriage was the farthest thing from her mind. On the other hand, Jim's intentions were clear by their third date. He thought Martha was a "cute little gal" with a trim figure, a great personality, and a sharp mind—the perfect package for a lifelong partner. He talked her into going on a canoe ride on the White River. By then, he was completely enamored of her and, at one point, was chasing her around the canoe for a kiss. When he caught her, Jim told her he was thinking about marrying her. Martha thought that was outrageously funny, so she laughed heartily. Her refusal made Jim mad, and Martha still believes he thought at the time, *By God, I'm going to get her. I'm going to make her fall for me and then I'll just dump her.* He kept on asking for dates that summer, but Martha limited them to about twice a month so Jim wouldn't assume she was becoming serious over him.

COLLEGE

In the fall of 1946, Jim and Martha started Butler University together. Jim attended under the G.I. Bill, but he wasn't a very good student because he was too busy having fun and had no incentive to study. Back then, one didn't need a college education to be a pilot—many World War II pilots didn't have one. At the end of the war, most of them left the military, but some came back and were often senior in rank because they had received very rapid promotions in combat. Thus, the Air Force had a shortage of officers in the lower grades to go into the strategic, tactical, and airlift squadrons. Because only a small percentage of these officers were coming out of the service academies at West Point and Annapolis, the Air Force had to depend on aviation cadets with, at best, two years of college or the equivalent. Graduates of the aviation-cadet program were commissioned when they received their wings.

Eventually, when a college degree became necessary to be a military officer of any sort, Jim would earn his degree. For the time being, though, he found social life much more interesting than studying. He owned a blue 1938 Ford convertible with a rumble seat, and he always had it loaded with girls. Jim and his brother Dick pledged Sigma Chi fraternity with some of their buddies. But pledging didn't work out well because they were so much older and more independent than the fraternity members who were trying to initiate them with dumb pranks. Finally, the fraternity kicked them out. Later, when its officers reconsidered and asked them to come back, Jim and the others decided fraternity life wasn't for them.

On the other hand, Martha immediately pledged a sorority, Pi Beta Phi, and found instant support for a small-town girl transitioning into college. For Martha, it was an interesting first year, with the new experience of being on campus and all the young men returning from World War II. At the same time, she couldn't forget about Jim because he had taken a job as a busboy at her sorority (even then a great strategist), and she kept thinking, *He is cute . . . very cute.* She decided to take a longer second look at Jim when he came to the sorority house to pick up one of her best friends, Mary Jo Pierce. She said to him, "I hear you've quieted down a bit."

Jim said, "What? Well, maybe a little bit."

"Then I might consider going out with you again." *After all,* Martha thought, *he is good-looking and might yet have some potential.*

Jim and Martha dated off and on over the next three years, gradually determining they would be married. At that point, Martha quit school and took a job as a receptionist and switchboard operator at the Prudential Life Insurance Company. One day, Jim bought a diamond ring, went to Martha's office, and proposed. They were engaged for a while before they married on April 9, 1949 (see fig. 4). Jim was still enrolled at Butler University, working three jobs and going to school at the same time.

Jim also was playing semiprofessional football with a team called the Tyron All-Stars. Every weekend, they went off to a football game in a neighboring town, and the players were ruthless. After each play the wives would look around to see whose husband was lying on the field injured. Once, when they were in Cincinnati, Ohio, Jim was on the ground with a broken arm after one play. But he still worked shoveling gravel for a construction company while he had his arm in a cast. Today, given what Jim has endured, Martha can understand how he did that, but at the time, it seemed almost impossible.

PILOT TRAINING IN WACO, TEXAS

Jim was supporting Martha and himself by selling asphalt driveways for several asphalt companies and driving a truck for a construction company. But he had no intention of doing that kind of work long term, so he needed a career. One day, he read in the newspaper that the Air Force's aviation cadet program was closing to married men in September 1949. He went down to the recruiting office at Fort Benjamin Harrison, gathered all of the program brochures, took them home, and spread them around their apartment.

That was Jim's way of telling Martha he wanted to sign up, but she paid no attention to him. Because he had talked before about looking for diamonds in South America and other crazy schemes, she thought it was a big joke. But Jim recognized it was now or never, so he applied to the program. Soon, they notified him to come to Fort Benjamin Harrison for a physical and an interview. He passed the tests and was accepted in 1949. Then, during January 1950, he was told to report to Waco, Texas, for pilot training in the T-6. Martha was pregnant with their first child, but he had to leave for flying school, so he settled her with her sister in Indianapolis and went to Waco alone.

As a cadet in those days, Jim was confined to the base for the first three months. He couldn't get off base for any reason, married or not. After three months he found a place in Waco for Martha to live and sent for her. He was making only seventy-five dollars a month, and he rented a place for fifty-five, so Martha had to survive on the remaining twenty dollars a month. She frequently came out to meet Jim at the base, where he could bring her a piece of chicken or something else that he had taken from the mess hall. She lived on peanut butter for a long time.

When Martha arrived in Waco, she was about eight months pregnant. The base allowed Jim to go home at noon on Sunday, but he had to be back by midnight. Meantime, his first baby was ready to be born. He went in to see his commander, a major, and said, "My wife's in the hospital having a baby. I'd like permission to go there."

"Why? What are you going to do when you get there?" the commander asked.

"Well, I just think I should be there," Jim replied.

They went back and forth for a while, but finally the commander let Jim go. Martha had the baby, and they named her Suzanne. Jim thought Suzanne was beautiful, but at the rate they were losing pilots in training, he wondered if he would ever see her grow up.

Whatever the danger, however, Kasler was meant to be a pilot. He was the first in his class to solo in the T-6. Years later he learned that his instructor, Captain Searle, considered him the finest pilot he had ever put through a class. Because of his apparent skill and leadership qualities, they made him one of the cadet squadron commanders. Captain Searle thought he should go into P-51s first and then move on to jets. But Jim knew the future was in jet air-craft, so he asked to go directly into the jet program. The Korean War had begun, and he decided that if the war lasted, he would need jet skills to fly in combat.

FIGHTER PILOT WITH FAMILY

Because Kasler was at the top of his class, the Air Force let him go straight to F-80 jet training at Williams Field in Mesa, Arizona. Virgil "Gus" Grissom, a fellow Hoosier, was one of his classmates there. Jim, Martha, and Suzanne lived in a place called Wingfoot Village. The houses were new, but small, built like house trailers expanded on each end with a bunk bed on each side and a little living room and kitchen combination. Fifteen cadets and their wives all lived in the same area.

Flying in faster aircraft exhilarated Jim: the T-6 had cruised at 135 knots, whereas the F-80 could hit 600 knots. At Williams they had only two T-33s, the two-seater training version of the F-80. As a result, prospective pilots took just one backseat ride before they soloed in the F-80. Again, Jim was the first in his class to solo, and he ended up as the cadet commander of the entire class (see fig. 5). At that time, flying jets was essentially experimental and fraught with danger. In a pregraduation speech their group commander, Col. Leon Gray, said, "Look at the two men sitting next to you. Within one year, one of those men is going to be dead." One year later, twenty-two of their graduating class of eighty-two were dead. It took only about eighteen months to kill the one-third Colo-nel Gray had predicted.

Despite the family's hardships while Jim was training, they did have some good times and funny experiences. Once when Suzanne was just a baby, but old enough to recognize her dad, they went on a family picnic to a local lake. While they were sitting there, water-skiers came by who turned out to be friends of the Kaslers. They pulled up and asked Jim if he would like to ski. Of course, Jim said yes, even though he had never skied before.

Because Jim didn't have a bathing suit with him, he stripped down to his boxer shorts, got in the water, and put on the water skis. The boat took off with Jim squatting down, hanging onto the rope. When it came around the next time, he was still squatting down. He couldn't get up on the skis. Finally, as they went around again, he came up out of the water. But his shorts were down around his ankles, and all that the others could see was his bare bottom going off into the distance. The next time they swung around, he was bent over with one hand hanging onto the rope while trying to pull up his shorts with the other. Martha laughed hysterically, but little Suzanne cried because she thought her daddy was being hurt. The only thing hurt was his pride.

After Jim graduated, he and Martha needed to go home to Indianapolis on leave before continuing to Luke Air Force Base for gunnery school. They didn't have a car, so their friend, Danny Llewellyn, offered to take them home. When the Kaslers arrived back in Indianapolis, they bought a car—a 1947 Buick—from a friend who was a used-car dealer. It was a monster car with a powerful "straight-eight" engine: very stable on the road. In May 1951 they started back to Luke Air Force Base in Phoenix, Arizona, so Jim could go through gunnery school in the F-84B and F-84C.

During World War II, Luke had been the largest fighter training base in the Air Corps, graduating more than twelve thousand fighter pilots from advanced and operational courses in the AT-6, P-40 Warhawk, P-51 Mustang, and P-38 Lightning aircraft. By February 7, 1944, pilots at Luke had achieved a million hours of flying time. After the base was deactivated on November 30, 1946, combat developed in Korea, so the Air Force reactivated it in February 1951 as Luke Air Force Base under the Air Training Command.

Kasler began flying at Luke during the summer of 1951, when temperatures in Phoenix typically soared over one hundred degrees. By 10:30 or 11:00 A.M., they had to stop the training sorties because the F-84 couldn't get off of the ground when it was that hot. Even under normal air temperatures, it needed a lot of runway to take off, so it became the butt of many bad jokes. One had it that the F-84 was equipped with a sniffer to detect the end of the runway—that it wouldn't lift off until it smelled the dirt just beyond the pavement. In fact, a line in a ribald fighter pilots' song went, "Don't give me an F-84, for she's just a ground-loving whore." Besides problems with air temperature and a long roll for takeoff, engines failed and flight-control surfaces folded up. Kasler's operations officer, who was a bit crazy, had a little book that listed by tail number every F-84 built. Every time one crashed, he giggled and crossed it off his list. By the end of 1951, he had crossed off an alarming number of aircraft.

More bizarre than the limit on training time, however, was that pilots at Luke didn't have pressurized g-suits. On takeoff or during other maneuvers, the forces exerted on a pilot are several times greater than the force of gravity, or g. These g-forces push blood from the head to the feet and therefore can quickly make a pilot black out if not countered by a pressurized suit. So every time Jim went down on a dive-bombing run, he would pull up and black out. Down range, he would regain consciousness and then plunge toward the ground again.

The F-84's gun sights also weren't very good, so the pilot had to do a lot of manual computing to line them up correctly on target. Here, Jim's experience as a tail gunner came in handy because he was used to computing coordinates on the B-29.

After gunnery training on the F-84, Jim's class received orders and left Luke in September 1951. Many went directly to Korea, but they sent Kasler, Gus Grissom, and six other pilots to Presque Isle, Maine. Although Presque Isle was about as far as Jim could go from Luke without leaving the United States, the trip was worth it because he was able to check out in the F-86E—the Air Force's hottest new fighter.

Jim had just one problem with the F-86: he couldn't get enough flight time in it because he started on an air-base version of musical chairs right after arriving at Presque Isle. He logged only two rides before the base said they were going to close the runway for repairs and sent the pilots to Dover, Delaware. Martha, Jim, and toddler Suzanne packed up and moved. They lived off base at Dover for about three weeks while Jim stood alert twenty-four hours a day. Then Dover decided they were going to do some repair work and sent the Kaslers to Rome, New York. They had been at Rome only a few weeks when Jim received word to go back home to Presque Isle. *Finally,* Jim thought, *a chance to get in some regular flying time.*

As soon as the Kaslers arrived back at Presque Isle, however, he received orders to go to Eglin Field, Florida, for gunnery training in the F-86. He flew down to Eglin, where he was supposed to have three or four weeks of gunnery work, but after one week they ordered everyone back to Presque Isle. Meantime, Jim had rented Martha a house in Caribou, Maine, and she and Suzanne were living there. They didn't have any furniture—just cots to sleep on—because their household goods shipment hadn't caught up with them. When Jim landed back at Presque Isle, the wing commander climbed up on the side of the airplane and said, "Jim, you're going to Korea." He had fewer than forty hours of flight time in the F-86.

Jim's itinerary on the way to Korea allowed him a short stop in Indianapolis to settle Martha and Suzanne there during his absence. But they faced a complication: Martha was pregnant again and, on their way home, her water broke. Jim first checked her into the Methodist Hospital in Indianapolis, but they couldn't afford civilian medical care. Fortunately, a Red Cross lady arranged for Martha to go to the maternity ward at Camp Atterberry, where she was in and out of labor six times. Meanwhile, Jim was supposed to be at San Francisco checking in for departure to Korea, so he sent messages explaining why he had to delay. Finally, he just couldn't wait any longer. His only recourse was to leave Martha in the Camp Atterberry hospital because they couldn't tell how long it was going to take for her to deliver.

When Jim arrived late in San Francisco, they demanded to know where the hell he had been. "I sent you messages," Jim said. Luckily, they found the messages that had explained why he was late, processed him hurriedly, gave him the immunizations he needed, and rushed him out to the ship—the USS *Sitkoh Bay,* a World War II small carrier built by Kaiser Industries. All the F-86s from Presque Isle were lashed to the deck because the ship's elevators were too small to handle them below. About six hours out to sea, the ship developed engine problems, so they had to go back to port. They were there a few more days for repairs before they steamed out again. The crossing itself took eighteen days. The old carrier creaked and rolled, top-heavy with sixty airplanes on deck. In fact, the captain threatened to throw the F-86s overboard to save it. Had they encountered any kind of heavy storm, they would have been in serious trouble.

Jim had no news about Martha and the imminent birth of their twins. He fretted about leaving them behind but could do nothing about it. His first news came when he was about halfway across the ocean: he received a telegram saying the second baby had died after four or five days. He consoled himself by thinking, *At least one survived.* But a day or two later, he received another telegram saying the first baby had been stillborn. That's how he learned they had lost a set of twins. Fortunately, though grieving the loss, Martha was physically all right. She went to live with Jim's parents in Indianapolis partly to recuperate, but also because Jim's first lieutenant's pay still wasn't enough to support Martha and daughter Suzanne living on their own, even with his flying allotment.

CHAPTER 3

Korean War Ace

DOWNTIME AND DOGFIGHTS
(KIMPO, KOREA, 1951–1952)

KASLER'S ship finally arrived in Yokohama, Japan, in November 1951. From there, Jim went on to the 335th Fighter Interceptor Squadron of the Fourth Fighter Interceptor Wing at Kimpo, Korea, twenty miles south of the demilitarized zone (38th Parallel). Kimpo also was known then as "K-14." The 335th flew the F-86A model, not the more recently built F-86E (see fig. 6). The perceived threat at that time in the United States was the Soviets' nuclear arsenal, and it was Air Defense Command's job to ward off that threat. In most people's minds, Korea was just a "police action." Thus, the "E" models were in the United States and the "A" models were in Korea. Furthermore, most new fighter planes on the drawing boards then were pure interceptors or multirole fighters with interceptor ability, but they hadn't been built yet. The F-86 was what the Air Force had available, and there just were not enough of them to match the MiG numbers.

F-86 pilots in Korea were hopelessly outnumbered by the MiG-15s—far more than the British Royal Air Force had been at the Battle of Britain. The Allied forces were so short of aircraft, they had to use World War II propeller planes, such as the P-51 Mustang and the Navy's F-4U Corsair. Of course, these propeller planes

27

were mostly for ground attack, but Navy lieutenant Guy Bordelon, flying a Corsair, did become an ace in Korea—the only U.S. ace who didn't fly the F-86 Sabrejet. He shot down five of the enemy's "Bedcheck Charlie" propeller-driven aircraft.

Kasler had not flown the F-86A when he arrived in Korea, so he had to adapt to some of its differences from the "E" model. He had very little time because the flight instructors put him through what was called "clobber college." They gave him three rides and then let him practice near Seoul before turning him loose in combat. Fortunately, Jim talked to a pilot at Kimpo about the "A" model before he took one up. One key difference was that it had wires or cables running to the flight-control surfaces, whereas the "E" model used hydraulic controls. When Jim had gone to supersonic speed with the F-86E, he just punched on through the sound barrier. He produced a sonic boom, of course, but had no problems. Jim asked the pilot if the "A" could go supersonic.

"Yes," the pilot said, "but use the trim tab to get it out of a supersonic dive, or you'll just be stretching the cables to the flight controls when you pull back on the stick."

On the second day, Jim took an "A" model up to forty thousand feet, rolled it over into a dive, plunged toward the ground, and went supersonic. But when he pulled back on the stick, nothing happened. As the other pilot had warned him, he was just stretching the control cables. So he thumbed the trim tab a couple times to pull out of the dive. But the aircraft snapped up sharply, and Jim's head pitched forward so quickly that his helmet pressed against the stick and stayed there. The airplane was rolling around the sky, and Jim couldn't lift his helmet and head off the stick because of the g-forces. Finally, he came out of it, but if the stick had hit under his helmet, it might have bashed a hole in his skull. The g meter was pegged at fourteen. Jim swore silently, wondering what had happened.

After Jim landed and taxied in, he looked out at the crew chief, whose mouth was hanging open as he stared wide-eyed at the airplane. Jim climbed down from the cockpit and looked back to see the plane's right elevator folded completely down. Metal skin was hanging off of the wings, which obviously were bent. The right flap was thoroughly torn. In short, the airplane was a wrinkled mess that had to be written off of the inventory. The wing commander couldn't figure out how Jim even landed the airplane in that condition. Jim explained that it had wrinkled when he tried to go supersonic, something he had done before in the "E" model without any problem and had heard he could do with the "A" model. The commander seemed to understand. Kasler was certified for combat after his third flight, and his short matriculation in clobber college was over.

Despite Jim's experience with that one F-86A, most of the time he preferred the "A" model in combat because the "E" was a much heavier airplane. Jim could get another four to five thousand feet of altitude from the "A," which he needed because the MiG-15 could reach higher altitudes than any F-86. After the war, he learned why. The British had given an Orenda engine to the Russians as a "goodwill" gift, and that Orenda design was superior to the F-86's best engine. The Russians copied it and put it in every MiG. Furthermore, the F-86 was up to two tons heavier than the MiG, mostly because of safety devices, such as an extra set of parking brakes or emergency landing gear, which experienced fighter pilots didn't use. Although MiGs came over the 38th Parallel as many as one hundred at a time, they were always above the F-86s, so Jim couldn't reach them. Rarely did an F-86 pilot catch one at or below his altitude. He and his squadron mates had to fly around, waiting to see if the MiGs would come after them.

When Jim first arrived at the Fourth Fighter Interceptor Wing, pilots could fly only the airplanes assigned to their respective squadrons. They had squadron-level, rather than wing-level, maintenance on their airplanes. That wasn't good news for Jim because his squadron, the 335th, had the worst aircraft maintenance of the three fighter squadrons in the Fourth Wing. The other two squadrons were readying fifteen or sixteen airplanes for a mission, whereas the 335th was lucky to have five or six ready out of twenty. With fewer airplanes to fly, the pilots were slower in completing their required one hundred missions. For instance, Kasler's old friend, Gus Grissom, had arrived shortly after him and was in one of the other squadrons. Grissom finished his one hundred missions in about four months and left, but Jim had logged only thirty missions at the time. Jim stayed in Korea nearly nine months to complete his one hundred missions—more than twice as long as Grissom.

Although he was frustrated with not flying regularly, Jim learned valuable lessons about how not to run an organization— fighter squadron or business. His squadron commander, "Bones," was a fighter ace, but had a disastrous management style. The commander insisted on running everything, including aircraft maintenance. If a pilot wanted to go on leave, for instance, he would sit down and type the orders himself. That sort of thing would never work, Jim recognized. A good leader has to learn how to pick subordinates well and then trust them to do the job without micromanaging them. "Bones" would soon learn this lesson, as well.

At Kimpo the F-86 pilots lived on a hill in renovated barracks the Japanese had built in World War II. One day, Jim was walking back up the muddy road from the operations office to the barracks after a mission. That same day, their new wing commander, Col. Harrison Thyng, had tried to fly a mission with their squadron. Two planes aborted before takeoff, and two more aborted early in the mission with mechanical problems. Thyng was not happy. He came by in his jeep as Jim was walking along, stopped beside him, and said, "Jump in. I'll give you a ride." Jim's squadron commander was in the front seat, so he climbed in the back. As soon as Jim was settled, Thyng turned to the commander and said, "Bones, you pack your bags, get a flight, and get off my base. You are no longer squadron commander." From that day forward, Jim recognized Colonel Thyng was special—as a fighter pilot and as a leader. Thyng knew when a problem existed and solved it directly.

Jim's squadron was assigned a more effective commander then, and they started to shoot down more MiGs. One reason may have been the influence of Capt. Philip "Casey" Colman, who had transferred into their squadron from F-80s at his own request (with help from Colonel Thyng). Colman was already an ace from World War II, but he very much wanted to be a jet ace in Korea. Colman became Jim's flight commander and designed the patch for their squadron. They were called the "Mach Riders" because they could fly supersonic. The patch had an enlarged caricature of Casey's profile, complete with a cigar-clenched-in-teeth grin and a big sombrero on his head, riding on top of a miniature F-86 in flight. Colman's nickname, "Casey," was a takeoff on the name of the old railroad engineer Casey Jones. Although Colman disputes the details, he ran out of fuel on one mission, landed wheels up, and slid his F-86 in on a set of railroad tracks—right into the squadron's scrap yard. His F-86 was indeed scrap at that point.

Dogfights on Casey's wing were always exciting, but even his aggressive style couldn't guarantee a kill. For example, after Jim had been flying for a while in Korea, he and Colman—just the two of them—tangled with eighty MiGs. They were up and down and on the run, shooting at everything they could, but the MiGs kept running at them. Amazing as it seemed, they fired a lot of ammunition and consumed plenty of fuel, but neither man shot down a MiG.

In April 1952, however, the war started to heat up for Kasler. On the first day of the month, thirty-six of the F-86s tangled with nearly eighty MiGs near the Yalu River. Lieutenant Dobbs of their squadron shot down one MiG, and Lieutenant Carl of the 336th Squadron damaged another. *Still nothing for me*, thought Jim. But they had plenty of flying time left. Later that same day, after flying an escort mission for an RF-80 reconnaissance plane with no action, he flew north to the Sonchon area. Two MiGs jumped their flight, but they reversed direction, and Jim's lead pilot knocked one down. Jim hammered away at the fuselage of the other, scoring numerous hits. Finally, black smoke billowed out of the MiG as it went down just northeast of Sonchon. Jim had his first credited kill.

Near dusk, thirty-eight of Fourth Wing's F-86s engaged fifty or more MiGs throughout MiG alley. Captain Love was credited with one kill. Lieutenant Carl racked up a "probable," and they had four or five more listed as "damaged." Just east of Sinuiju, Kasler and his wingman reversed on two more MiGs and fired at them, but could get only a damaged score on both. That same day, Major Asla damaged two more MiGs in fending off an attack by six of the enemy on his element (two aircraft).

April 21 was another eventful day for the wing and for Kasler. On a mission southeast of the Yalu River, Jim was leading an element that attacked a flight of four MiGs. He opened fire on the number-four man, who rolled over and plowed into the ground near the Chosin Reservoir. That was Jim's second confirmed MiG kill.

On May 4, Casey Colman and Kasler each scored MiG kills. Casey was flight leader when they spotted eight MiGs crossing the

Yalu at six thousand feet. They dived steeply on them. Casey scored hits on a MiG and the pilot bailed out, but Casey also had a MiG on his tail that was raining ammunition on him. Jim yelled, "Break." He reversed on the MiG, and fired at it. When its fuselage exploded, and it went down, Jim had his third confirmed kill—and needed just two more to become an ace.

Four days later, Jim damaged another MiG, which should have been a credited kill. He was flying with 2d Lt. James Low as his wingman, covering fighter-bombers at Pyongyang, when he spotted trucks rolling down a road. They hadn't seen any MiGs, so Jim went down and strafed a few trucks. He and Low were getting ready to pull out and head home because they were low on fuel. Suddenly, a MiG jumped Jim, but he broke left, reversed direction, slid in behind the MiG, and started blasting his left wing. The MiG's left landing gear fell out of its well, and its left wing was full of holes. But Jim ran out of ammunition because he had used so much strafing the trucks.

Jim looked around for his wingman, but he was gone. As Jim closed on the crippled MiG, he could see its T-tail sticking up, and he was tempted to clip it off with his wing. He dearly wanted to do that. But he thought better of it, pulled up, and flew alongside the MiG in close formation on his right wing. Jim could see the pilot's leather helmet and mask hanging loose. The pilot was looking away from Jim at his left wing, no doubt surveying the damage. Jim thought, *The stupid bastard. He should have known somebody was shooting at him.* Suddenly, the pilot turned and looked at Jim, wide-eyed with surprise.

Jim was down to about three hundred pounds of fuel and a long way from home. If he had had enough fuel, he would have tried to make the MiG pilot go with him. He had to leave him there, but he believed the MiG never made it back to base. It was streaming something—probably fuel—and he couldn't have landed with a damaged left main gear hanging out of the wheel well. Jim climbed to altitude and was on a smooth ride back home when he ran out of fuel, necessitating the first of three successful dead-stick landings he was to make in jet aircraft during his career. In addition, after another combat mission in Korea, he ran out of fuel after he landed, but before he could turn onto the taxiway—not an official dead-stick landing, but definitely cutting it close.

On the ground Jim chewed out his wingman, Lieutenant Low, for abandoning him. Low had a story about spotting another MiG and going after it, but that was a good excuse only if the other MiG posed a danger to Kasler. A wingman's first responsibility is to protect his leader's back in case an enemy aircraft attacks from behind. That responsibility becomes especially critical when the leader already is concentrating on a dogfight. Also, Low's claim concerning the other MiG remained unconfirmed by a gun camera's film or other means, so Jim was skeptical about the story, figuring Low was off hunting something to shoot at. Ironically, if Low had stayed on Jim's wing as he was supposed to, he could have finished off the MiG Jim had shot up and claimed a kill of his own.

In May 1952 the wing began using their F-86s as dive-bombers to destroy ground targets. On May 13, Jim was flying cover to guard the fighter-bombers from possible MiG attack during one of their bombing runs, but he saw no action. During that mission, however, Col. Walker "Bud" Mahurin—a World War II ace—was flying his F-86 on his third bombing mission of the day when he called in that he was on fire. Mahurin had three credited MiG kills, as well as one probable and one damaged, but that was to be the end of his action in the Korean War. He and Francis Gabreski, another celebrated World War II ace, were credited with having established the tactics that had allowed the heavily outnumbered F-86s to maintain a ten-to-one kill ratio against MiGs in Korea. Mahurin was held prisoner and released after the war.

Meanwhile, maintenance continued to be a major problem for all three squadrons of the Fourth Wing. They had about eighty aircraft in their inventory, but they were hard put to get forty airplanes in the air at one time. Their technicians had trouble getting parts to maintain and repair the airplanes. They were also short of drop tanks, which carried the extra fuel they needed to reach the enemy near the Yalu River. They knew more than five hundred MiGs were stationed just north of them, and they often saw "bandit trains" eighty to one hundred MiGs long. Something had to be done about getting more F-86s into action.

After exhausting normal channels, Colonel Thyng put his career on the line when he went straight to the Chief of Staff of the Air Force, Gen. Hoyt S. Vandenberg, to complain about the lack of airplanes and parts. Fortunately, General Vandenberg responded correctly. He ruffled some feathers, though, when he took F-86s away from Air Defense Command in the United States and sent them to Korea, while rotating F-80s back home. Although it may seem obvious that a war would demand the most modern equipment, leaders continued to see Russian nuclear bombers as the main threat to the United States, so they wanted the best F-86 interceptors in Air Defense Command to protect the homeland.

THE DAY KASLER MADE ACE
(YALU RIVER AREA, MAY 15, 1952)

Despite those early problems with supplies and maintenance, Kasler's squadron alone eventually had one-half of all the aces in Korea. Colonel Thyng decided they should have a flight standing alert at dawn every day, ready to intercept MiGs. Jim's flight was one of the first to pull that duty. His flight commander was still Captain Colman. Casey's wingman was James Low, later to become the youngest jet ace of the war, although he had just one MiG credited at the time. Jim was an element leader, still needing two MiG kills to become an ace. His wingman, 1st Lt. Albert Smiley, had one MiG.

On May 15, 1952, they set up their aircraft on alert and left Smiley bunked at the ready Quonset hut near the end of the runway. His job was to man the phone while the others went out to get warm in the rising sun. Eventually, they heard the phone ring several times, and Casey asked if someone was in the hut. Jim ran in and found Smiley leaning on one elbow, lying on a bunk looking at him. Jim demanded, "Why in the hell didn't you answer the phone?"

Smiley said, "Oh, I knew someone would."

Jim snatched up the alert phone, and a voice demanded, "Where the hell have you been? Scramble! Scramble!" He hit the klaxon alarm and said to Smiley, "I'll fix you when we get on the ground, you SOB." They took off and headed straight for the Yalu River. As they got closer, the ground radar controller kept directing them farther up the river, away from Antung, the huge MiG base in China, just across the Yalu. The controllers told them the MiGs had turned. Then, a few minutes later, the controllers said they had lost radar contact.

Two days earlier Jim had visited the radar site near Kimpo that was controlling his flight. They told him they could pick up MiGs over Antung only above fifteen thousand feet. With that in mind, Jim broke his element away from Colman's and dived toward Antung. He said "Albert" into the radio, and when Smiley looked over at him, Jim punched off his drop tanks to get lighter for combat. Smiley did the same. The rules of engagement didn't allow them to cross the Yalu or to attack the MiG bases, but they found ways to bend those rules while in "hot pursuit." Sometimes, they just ignored them.

Kasler and Smiley caught the MiGs just as they were pitching out to land at Antung. Jim dropped his dive brakes and did a "split-S" maneuver to get in behind the lead MiG. At twelve hundred feet he opened fire, and the MiG immediately started flying apart. When Jim pulled up on its left wing, the canopy was gone, and the pilot was sitting in a pool of fire. The MiG fell to the right and scorched a wide, fiery trail across the air base.

Next, Jim looked out to the right and saw a MiG firing at Smiley, who had just torched another MiG. Smiley was admiring his work so intently that he didn't notice the MiG on his tail, hosing him with lead. Jim shouted for him to break as he went after the MiG on Albert's tail. The MiG dropped to the deck and flew right down the runway at Antung. The sky around the MiG was black with flak as ground gunners hammered away at Kasler, but Jim chased it about fifty miles on the deck until they reached the sea.

At one time during the pursuit, Casey Colman dropped down between the MiG and Jim, who had just fired a burst that lit up the enemy aircraft. Casey bounced back up, out of the way, and said, "Come on, Kas. You have your five."

"Negative," Jim replied. "Smiley got one of them. This one's mine."

When they reached the sea, the MiG pilot pulled up into an Immelmann—an aerial maneuver named after World War I German ace Max Immelmann that pulls an aircraft up through a half-loop and then rolls it level, thus simultaneously gaining altitude and reversing direction. But Jim stayed with him and as the MiG started down again, scored with another burst. By this time, he had closed to within five hundred feet as they dived down over the coastal mudflats. Morning haze over the flats made forward visibility impossible, but he could still see straight down. They both were doing about five hundred knots in a sixty-degree dive when the MiG suddenly splashed into the mud—Jim's only clue that he was in grave danger of augering into the ground.

The instant Jim saw mud shoot up around the MiG, he dropped his dive brakes, grabbed the stick with both hands, and pulled back as hard as he could. He kept waiting for the impact, certain that he was going to join his opponent in a muddy tomb. The haze became darker and darker as he neared the mudflats. Jim grunted aloud, "This is it!" Then, just as suddenly, the F-86 grabbed some air, leveled out, and turned slightly upward. The sky ahead started to lighten, so Jim pulled in his dive brakes and eventually broke into the sunlight at four thousand feet. He didn't know exactly how close he had come to the mud, but he estimated it was only ten feet. He flew back to base with splatters of mud on his aircraft—thrown up by the MiG's impact.

Immediately after seeing the sunlight again, however, Kasler wasn't thinking about escaping death. Over the radio he said, "Casey, I'm an ace." Even Smiley was off the hook for not answering the alert phone because Jim was so thrilled about making ace and living to tell about it. Although Jim didn't know it at the time, one of his kills that day may have had added significance. About a month later, an intelligence officer in Tokyo told him that Mao Tse-tung's son had been shot down on May 15 and that the three MiGs Kasler and Smiley got were the only ones downed that day. One or the other took out Mao's progeny, but they never learned which one. Coincidentally, Jim became the United States's fifteenth jet ace for shooting down his fifth MiG-15 on the fifteenth day of May (see fig. 7).

Early in the morning on May 25, Kasler nailed his sixth and last MiG-15, five miles northwest of Sonchon. A lone MiG jumped Albert Smiley. Jim yelled, "Break," and reversed to get on the MiG's tail. When the MiG pulled up, Jim came after it, fired, and saw it start smoking. He was still firing when the pilot ejected. Jim could see strikes on the back of his seat, and the chute never opened. He guessed that he had hit the pilot when he came out of the airplane in his ejection seat. That same day, Lieutenant Moore of Jim's squadron and Capt. Frederick "Boots" Blesse, operations officer of the 334th Squadron, both chalked up MiGs. (Blesse ended up a double ace with nine MiGs and one LA-9 propeller plane to his credit, went on to fly in Vietnam, and retired a two-star general.)

After another month of uneventful missions, Kasler was flying with James Low as his wingman again on June 26, 1952—his ninety-seventh mission. Jim was just about to head for base when he spotted a MiG and gave chase. The mountains made the air turbulent, so Jim couldn't get his airplane settled down enough to put his gun sight on the enemy. He stayed focused on the kill, though, because he knew his allotted missions—and his chances for another MiG—would soon be up. By some instinct, he looked back to check Low's position and discovered a MiG on his own tail instead. He had to break off the attack in order to avoid taking fire.

Back at the base, Low claimed a probable kill on the mission. After this second incident in which Low abandoned his wing, Jim went to Colonel Thyng to ask that he ground him. Although Jim recognized the man's skill, he was concerned that his penchant for chasing the enemy might kill a squadron mate who was depending on his cover. But the wing commander took no action against Low, perhaps because the latter continued to be a skilled MiG killer whenever he engaged the enemy in combat. Years later, as a POW in North Vietnam, Low would again desert Jim and the rest of the POWs by seeking and accepting early release. The Air Force separated him involuntarily from the service for cooperating with the enemy.

During Jim's last three missions, he saw no action. He completed one hundred missions in July 1952 and returned home. An article that appeared in the July 7, 1952, *Life* magazine cited Jim as one of the seventeen jet aces from Korea who had become "a new and deadly addition to the ranks of air warriors." His picture appeared with the likes of Col. Francis Gabreski (33.5 kills in WWII, 6.5 in Korea) and Maj. George Davis (fourteen kills in Korea). As a side note, despite the popular image of the jet pilot as a young "hot rock" with a roving eye for the ladies, the Korean War aces averaged nearly thirty years old, were losing their hair, and were extremely cautious because few "hot rocks" lived to that average age. Thirteen of the men were married, they had twenty-three children among them, and most had eyes only for their wives and the MiG-15.

Jim hadn't shot down the most MiGs or led the most missions in Korea, but at least one other famous flyer considered him the best pilot in the wing. James Salter, also in Kasler's squadron, had graduated from West Point at the end of World War II and flown with Jim in Korea as James Horowitz. When Counterpoint Press reprinted his novel *The Hunters* in 1997, Salter placed a photograph on the dust jacket that showed him standing with Kasler in front of an F-86 in Korea—a tribute to the impression Jim had made on him during the war.

That impression of Jim as a peerless fighter pilot emerges even more strongly in *Burning the Days* (1997), where Salter says, "We had many aces . . . For me, though, for reasons I cannot fully explain, Kasler was the nonpareil." He goes on to say,

> [Kasler] had dignity, from what I don't know. It had been given to him, I believe, just in case. Skill, of course, a great natural as well as acquired skill together with nerve, and a furied patience like that of a lion lying flattened in the tall grass. Crowning it all was the unsentimentality of a champion. . . . He was an obscure lieutenant when he came. He left renowned.

Jim appreciates Salter's high opinion of him but remembers that he seldom talked with Salter about flying. Instead, they had long discussions in Korea about writing and books. Salter's favorite book at the time was Hemingway's *A Farewell to Arms*, which Jim had read three times.

CHAPTER 4

Testing, Training, and Danger

NELLIS AIR FORCE BASE

AFTER Korea, Kasler came home to Indiana for a month's leave (see fig. 8). Then, in July 1952 Jim, Martha, and daughter Suzanne traveled to Nellis Air Force Base, Nevada, where he would spend three years. An episode on that trip illustrates a key aspect of Jim's character. At one point, when they came to a marked detour in the road, Jim said, "No. We aren't going to take a detour. Let's go see what's ahead." His experience with detours was that they were often unnecessary and always time-consuming.

Jim kept going straight on, and soon they came to a washed-out bridge over a wide, dried-up riverbed. Jim stopped the car, went down into the riverbed, and tromped around to make sure it was dry. Back in the car, he roared down the slope and into the bed. Just about halfway they got stuck—really deep, all the way up to their fenders—and not a soul around. Jim stepped out of the car. Luckily, he spotted a farmer riding on a horse, hailed him, and struck up a conversation. Before long, Jim climbed up on the horse with the farmer, and they rode off into the distance—leaving Martha and two-year-old Suzanne inside the Buick, sitting in the middle of the riverbed.

A short while later, Jim came riding back with the farmer on his tractor. They hitched the car to the tractor and pulled it across to the other side of the riverbed. Jim thanked the farmer, started the car, and silently continued down the road. Martha observed that traveling in a straight line wasn't always the most convenient approach. But Jim assumed Martha and Suzanne were resilient enough to endure occasional mishaps and adventures, which certainly were part of being an Air Force officer's family. Besides, although the "stop" had been inconvenient, Jim estimated he hadn't used much more time than if he had followed the detour—maybe less. Moving in a straight line had become his modus operandi and would remain so to the present day.

Once in place at Nellis, the Kaslers encountered a terrifying situation. Flying was a slaughterhouse in those days. Pilots and their families called the base "Nellis cumulus" during 1952 because one often could look toward the range area and see huge black clouds of smoke billowing into the air above the airplane crashes that splattered the landscape. Of course, ejection seats kept them from losing as many pilots, but the human cost was staggering: fifty-four fatalities in one year. The threat to Jim was even keener. Of eighteen pilots who lived on Erwin Street (the Kaslers' location) at Nellis—fourteen died in crashes.

The crashes and fatalities were particularly tough on spouses. Whenever a puff of black smoke marked another plane crash, an ominous quiet fell over the housing area. Most women went inside but kept peeking out a window, watching, trying to act busy, praying a husband hadn't crashed. When they saw the chaplain and the wing commander coming through the housing area, they wrung their hands or bit their nails, and some ran and hid because they didn't know whose house the officers were going to approach. Then the condolence team moved solemnly to a front door to tell a wife that her husband was dead. Just that quickly, lives were devastated. Some of the women couldn't take the stress, so they simply left, preferring divorce or separation to the daily menace of watching a husband go down in smoke and flames.

The strain extended to other members of the family. On one occasion, Jim's parents came out to visit and were standing in his backyard when an F-86 crashed right on the runway, exploding into a huge fireball. His parents asked, "What's that black smoke up in the valley there?" When Jim told them the cause, they were visibly shaken. Although they knew flying was risky, they hadn't connected the risk so graphically to its typical outcome: charred remains and molten metal.

The deaths scared some pilots, too. After weighing the esprit and thrill of flying against the very real danger of sacrificing themselves in training, they went into other lines of work. For those who remained, close friendships made a single loss everyone's tragedy. One of the fatalities was Billy Dobbs, a close friend who had four credited MiG kills while flying in Jim's squadron during the Korean War.

The rampant crashes had a number of key causes. In general, the early days of jet aviation were risky because equipment, tactics, and pilots were often untried. While Jim was in Korea, for example, they called one graduating class of pilots "49 Crash." This class had a 75 percent loss rate—so bad that the surviving remnant was sent back for retraining. Of Jim's own graduating class of 126, only 38 were still alive and even fewer still flying for the military three years later.

Besides the general risk of jet flying, Nellis and Luke were part of Air Training Command, which was into the "Tiger" program in 1952. Their motto was "Every man a tiger," and this policy was killing pilots like slow flies in a cloud of DDT. The Fighter School commander, Clay Tice, even had the Tiger patch with that saying, along with the phrase "Over 500 MiGs destroyed by Nellis-trained pilots," painted on the nose of his personal aircraft. Anything went—the more rambunctious the better—even though they saw planes spinning into the ground nearly every day.

Pilots also were expected to be combat-ready, no matter what plane they drew. Kasler flew at least nine aircraft types and, on any one day, might fly four different aircraft. In fact, Jim's first flight at Nellis was in an F-80, a type he hadn't flown for a year. His briefing consisted of assigning him an airplane and having the crew chief review how to start the engine. The next day, Jim was attached as number four to a flight going to the gunnery range. As they were ascending after takeoff, a flight of F-86s jumped them and engaged them in a twenty-minute dogfight in the Nellis corridor below five thousand feet. After the fight, they didn't have enough fuel left to go to the range. That sort of low-level, high-risk fighting was commonplace in the Tiger program.

Then, too, no one thought properly about flying safety in those days. They piled up hours and pushed limits without regard for pilots or machines. For example, Jim was assigned as a flight instructor at Nellis in the combat crew training squadron. But a pilot needed 750 flying hours to instruct, and Jim had fewer than 570 hours. Every day, flight operations gave Jim an airplane and had him tag along with another flight to the range. During the weekends, he took any fighter he could find and flew. His squadron commander would say, "Go put twenty hours on this plane this weekend." That is a lot of hours in a jet fighter, especially with no midair refueling, which meant plenty of takeoffs and landings to complete nine or ten one-hour missions a day. No pilot would do that anymore because fatigue leads to errors and losses.

Jim went on that way for a long time, just plugging along, building up flying hours so he could become an instructor. If he wanted to go to the West Coast or back home to see his mother, he could file a flight plan and go. He often took an F-80 and went cruising down the Grand Canyon, sometimes coming closer than he should have to the walls of rock in front of him. Once, he nearly crashed when he flew too far down into the canyon and started back up too late. He kept pulling on the stick and finally had to ease down the flaps to help him just clear the wall. He admits that wasn't too smart, but it did give him a lot of experience and knowledge about what the aircraft could do.

Occasionally, Jim filled in time by flying the B-25 bomber to tow targets for other fighter pilots—an unusual bit of cross training that scared the hell out of the B-25 crew chiefs. Of course, Jim wasn't above adding to their fears by getting into the cockpit and saying, "I'm going to start this son of a bitch up and see what it will do." Then he would take the bomber up, tow targets, roar back to the airstrip, pitch up the nose, and land it just like a fighter. As soon as he touched down, Jim could see the crew chief hustling toward him to see what this crazy fighter jock had done to his airplane.

While Jim coped with the stresses of flying, Martha Kasler had to deal with her first experience living on a base and being a "real" Air Force wife. Nellis was an accelerated education for her, in part because it was a particularly exciting place to be. At least six jet aces who were friends of the Kaslers (see fig. 9) were stationed there from 1952 to 1953. The producers of a movie called *Sabre Jet*, which starred Robert Stack, invited the aces and their wives to

Hollywood to see the premiere. Robert Cummings, a famous comedic actor, invited them to his home, and the owners of a harness-racing track received them as honored guests for a day at which the races were named after the aces.

An Air Force officer's wife also had to learn the standard social codes and behaviors. In retrospect, some are hard to believe. As soon as the Kaslers arrived on base, they were expected to call on the commanding officer and his wife. Martha's duty was to understand the parameters for this social obligation: visit between certain hours, have calling cards to leave (separately printed for herself and Jim), place the calling cards correctly on a little silver tray near the commander's front door, and (for Martha) always wear white gloves and a hat. The Kaslers had to attend every social function to which they were invited. Having an outside job was socially unacceptable and nearly impossible because being an officer's wife was a full-time occupation. Besides, Martha had a second full-time job: mother of Suzanne and, beginning in 1953, their newly born twins, Jimmy and Nanette.

Fortunately, by the time the Kaslers' twins arrived, the immense stress caused by the Tiger program had begun to dissipate. The number of fatalities and airplane losses had become intolerable. Jim's commander was fired for "supervisory error"—for failing to control his pilots—and was replaced by Brig. Gen. James Roberts. When Roberts came to the base, he talked seriously with every pilot. "Every man a tiger" was a dead program, he said. The Air Force came out with standard operating procedures for flying safety and produced the first flying-safety posters. Yellow, black-edged safety signs appeared on the walls. Commands started handing out error reports to pilots and supervisors. Suddenly, supervisors were nailed for what was going on in their squadrons, and many commanders lost their jobs (as they should have, under the circumstances).

As a result of these changes, the accident rate plummeted while training actually improved. Fighter pilots still took chances. They overstressed the airplanes and performed all the maneuvers necessary to aerial combat, but they were smarter about it. By the end of 1953, fatalities at Nellis had dropped to twenty-eight (and falling), and the wing was losing far fewer airplanes.

Students assigned to Kasler's flight in 1952 quickly discovered he was a tough, no-nonsense instructor, but most were thrilled to be learning from a Korean War jet ace who could give them the "hot skinny." Lt. Hoyt Sanford (Sandy) Vandenberg Jr., whose father was the Air Force Chief of Staff during the Korean War, was one of those students, having just graduated from basic pilot training at Williams Air Force Base. Vandenberg always had the feeling he was assigned to Jim's flight because the latter was one of the Air Force's best instructors, but Jim never showed whether he knew if Sandy's father might have influenced the assignment or suggested it made any difference to him. He treated Vandenberg like any other student pilot.

Jim's style was laconic but demanding. He said little and never suffered foolish questions. But he also didn't overmanage students or give them too many details before a flight. Instead, he gave them the basics and then let them go out and practice. When they screwed up, he came down on them hard because he believed a good "ass-chewing" was always preferable to crashing or getting shot down as a result of a foolish error. That's how the students learned.

Vandenberg was on the receiving end of Jim's "direct instruction" during a gunnery mission in F-80s against a banner towed by a B-26 at twelve thousand feet. The F-80s carried no drop tanks and had only two of the guns loaded. Each pilot in the flight had a different color of nondrying paint on the tips of his bullets to identify hits on the target banner. They started a firing run at an entry point above the target. Jim led them up there, then peeled off, reversed direction, and fired on the banner. The student pilots were to follow in turn.

Vandenberg was number four behind a lieutenant colonel who was experienced in propeller planes but unable to get the hang of flying in jet aircraft. On each pass at the target, the man never got into the proper starting position, so Vandenberg kept getting stacked up behind him. Kasler and the number-two pilot, "Curly" Reder, went down in good position and made excellent firing passes. But by the time the lieutenant colonel went in, lagging badly behind Reder, he pushed Vandenberg even farther back in the formation. Jim was becoming more and more upset, unable to believe they could be so far out of position. Of course, he couldn't see everything that was going on at the entry point.

When they landed and debriefed, Jim tore into Vandenberg about his sloppy flying and poor position. That upset Sandy because he strongly believed it wasn't his fault. He tried to defend himself, but Jim was so distressed that he leaped up and stalked out of the briefing room. Vandenberg and Reder went off to the officer's club for lunch. After they sat down, Sandy saw Jim in the cafeteria line and decided he was going to talk to his instructor again. He walked over, stepped into the line with Jim, and said "Lieutenant, I want you to know that there wasn't a damn thing I could do up there on the perch (entry point) because I was following the colonel." For a moment, the silence was deafening, while Sandy thought, *I've just taken on my instructor, which is the same as talking back to God.* Jim just kept pushing his tray along and said without looking up, "I know that. What the hell do you expect me to do about it?"

That honest response, which was typical of Jim once he had cooled down, made things okay for Vandenberg and became a major turning point in his training. Following the inept flier around in the air remained difficult because he never completed an aerial maneuver. For example, Jim would bank right into a cloud and then turn inside the cloud to see if the flight could follow. The prop jockey would always shoot right up through the top of the cloud. Yet, after the episode in the officer's club, Sandy was content knowing that Jim knew what the problem was and that it wouldn't affect his own evaluation.

Although Jim decided he could contend with the old-timer's lack of skill, his fuse was very short when he experienced outright incompetence. For example, at Nellis the flights armed their aircraft in front of the tower. One day, Jim's flight pulled into the arming area, where the armorers charged the guns and pulled out the safety streamers. Jim then called for a channel change on the radio, going from ground to tower for taxiing instructions. They all went over to the other channel except the errant lieutenant colonel.

Each flight leader within the squadron had a fish name as a call sign, so Kasler was "Gar," and the flight was "Tiger-Gar Flight." Jim said, "Okay, Gar, check in." On that day, the older pilot was "two," but he didn't respond. Curly Reder was "three" so he said, "Three's here." Vandenberg immediately said, "Four!" They all looked over at two. He had his head in the cockpit, obviously having missed Jim's instruction, and was on the wrong channel. Jim changed over to the guard channel and said, "Gar two, come up on channel five." No response. The fellow still wasn't looking around, so he couldn't see that Jim was trying to reach him on the radio.

Suddenly, Jim took off his helmet, jammed it on the control stick, shut down his engine, crawled out of the airplane, and strode into the snack bar in base operations. There the three students sat, with engines running but without a leader. Obviously, Jim wasn't going to return, so they taxied back to the line, contemplating the importance of clear communication and competency for readiness.

Rarely, Kasler's students were able to turn the tables on him—to catch some slight flaw in his otherwise perfect performance as a pilot and officer. For example, Sandy Vandenberg knew that Jim prided himself on his professional and personal appearance, so he was pleased to spot his chance when he saw Jim's picture in the Las Vegas newspaper one Saturday morning. The Rotary Club had invited Jim to speak to their group the day before and had secured press coverage for the event. Sandy cut Jim's picture out of the newspaper and was ready for him when he came into the coffee bar on Monday morning. Whenever Jim walked in, Sandy was never sure whether he would say, "Good morning" or completely ignore him, so he immediately sidled up to Jim and said, "I understand you gave a talk at the Rotary on Friday."

Jim said, "Yeah, how did you know about that?"

Sandy replied, "Well, I saw your picture in the paper. But I didn't know you were nonrated (not a pilot)."

Jim grabbed the news clipping out of Sandy's hand and cursed. In the news photo he wasn't wearing wings on his uniform. He hadn't noticed their absence, and Martha must have missed it, too—a rare "gotcha" that kept Jim's students smiling to themselves for a few days afterward.

Jim's meticulous, thorough training kept others smiling: the commanders of units that received his graduating students. For example, Vandenberg and his fellow gunnery-school graduates went from Nellis to the Eighty-sixth Fighter Bomber Wing at Landstuhl, Germany. The group commander, George Simler, was ecstatic. He said to Sandy and the others, "You mean you guys have dropped bombs and fired guns?" They were desirable commodities because they had fifty to sixty hours in the F-86 and had fired guns at moving targets, dropped bombs, done some skip-bombing, and practiced aerobatic maneuvers.

THE LIGHTWEIGHT FIGHTER PROGRAM

Late in 1952 the Pentagon called Kasler and a number of other aces to Washington, D.C., so they could discuss a proposed lightweight fighter. Included in that group of aces were Bob Latshaw, Iven Kincheloe, Hoot Gibson, Boots Blesse, Harrison Thyng, Francis Gabreski, and J. C. Meyer, the four-star commander of Strategic Air Command. Gabreski and Meyer between them had more than sixty confirmed kills in World War II and Korea.

Their discussion centered on what they would need in a future war. Obviously, they needed something better than the F-86 to go up against MiGs; only much better pilot performance had enabled them to maintain air superiority in Korea. Jimmy Doolittle was also there and took notes. He asked all the pilots what they thought the Air Force really needed, and there was some dissension in the ranks. The F-104 Starfighter came out as the supposed answer, but Jim considered it inadequate for air-to-air combat. It was fast, but needed a country mile to make a turn.

From a pilot's perspective, Jim doubted the meetings about a new lightweight fighter did any good. He didn't think the Pentagon's decision makers listened to the aces but rather produced what they wanted to see on the line. Jim's ideas about a new fighter plane were shaped by his experiences tangling with MiGs in Korea. Pilots needed an airplane that would fly high, turn well, and carry more than enough power for combat. Jim wanted a faster airplane with more altitude and maneuverability: an air-superiority aircraft that could intercept and shoot down other fighter planes. To him, that was the classic definition of a fighter.

On the other hand, the Pentagon apparently fixed on the need to intercept the Soviets' long-range nuclear bombers, so they fashioned the new lightweight fighter based on those preoccupations. The stubby wings of the F-104 were hopeless for turning in a dogfight with a fighter like a MiG-15, but short wings reduced drag and allowed the Mach 2 speed needed to intercept a long-range bomber (see fig. 10). In the original version, the F-104 carried no gun and only two Sidewinder heat-seeking missiles. Later designers doubled the Sidewinders to four and added a Vulcan cannon—typically called the Gatling gun. Eventually, it grew into a fighter-bomber for multiple roles. The Germans used it as their nuclear-strike aircraft in the 1960s, but Jim considered it a poor choice for that role as well.

An unfortunate quirk in the design of the early F-104 was an ejection seat that propelled the pilot down instead of up. Perhaps the downward ejection seat was inspired by concerns about clearing the T-tail in a high-speed ejection. At any rate, downward ejection cost several pilots their lives, including Jim's friend and fellow ace from Korea, Iven Kincheloe, who lost an engine during takeoff. Apparently, he tried to roll the plane over before ejecting but didn't have enough altitude for the chute to work properly. A seat that ejected upward probably would have saved him.

The Pentagon's fixation with intercepting Soviet bombers was apparent in the interceptor version of the F-101 Voodoo, which had a rotating door on its belly: one side for conventional missiles and the other for the nuclear-tipped Genie rocket. The plan was to fire an unguided Genie into a flight of Soviet bombers and detonate the nuclear warhead. Fortunately, the United States never had to use it for that purpose. In test firings, the rocket proved unstable and unreliable.

All new fighter aircraft of that time exhibited growing pains, and jet aviation in general experienced considerable trial and error. The United States was great at producing aircraft, but designers seemed ignorant about gravitational stresses and metal fatigue. For instance, the F-86 had to be grounded at one point because wings were coming off in flight. Inspectors discovered that after stressing a certain number of times, the main spars developed cracks and eventually failed. Every F-86 had to have its wing spars replaced. Engine failure was also common in those early years. With so many things likely to go wrong, the flying profession demanded tremendous skill, bravery, and calm in the face of peril.

F-100 PROJECT OFFICER

Kasler had instructed for about a year and a half at Nellis when he received an invitation he couldn't refuse from Bob Latshaw, a good friend and fellow ace from Korea. Latshaw was running the research and development (R&D) element of the Fighter Weapons School at Nellis. He wanted Jim in R&D, so he appointed him to be project officer on the new F-100 fighter-bomber. Edwards Air Force Base—the flight test base—received the first six F-100A models, whereas Nellis accepted the seventh through twelfth airplanes off the production line.

When the manufacturer brought the first F-100 to Nellis, a North American test pilot came to talk to the R&D fliers. He warned, "When you take off in this airplane, make sure you keep pulling back on the stick. Do not relax pressure on the stick once you lift off or you'll get this thing in a porpoise." Being a hotshot fighter pilot, Jim assumed he could handle anything with wings, so the test pilot's warning didn't bother him. The pilot checked Jim out in the cockpit, showed him how to start the engine, told him a few things about the controls, and then said, "Okay. Go do it." There was no two-seat trainer at the time.

Jim took off in the F-100, relaxed pressure on the stick (as was his custom), and immediately went into a porpoise—pitching up and down just as the test pilot said he would. He was able to recover control, but the F-100A was the most difficult airplane he ever flew. While in formation he had to work the controls continually just to keep his position. The airplane was absolutely—ridiculously—unstable. Chuck Yeager and other test pilots at Edwards came to the same independent conclusion, although Jim didn't know that at the time.

Right after Nellis received the first F-100As, the commander told Kasler to take one out to Edwards. Jim was excited and let his thoughts run ahead of him. *Maybe they're going to have me join the test crew and participate in the official flight tests,* he mused. As it turned out, they just wanted his airplane at Edwards; they didn't intend to make him a member of the test team. Jim was temporarily disappointed, but he quickly became busy with other issues. Iven Kincheloe took him out to Edwards's gunnery range, where they were working on General Electric's M-61 Vulcan cannon. Everyone called it the Gatling gun because that is what it looked like with its six rotating barrels. The original Gatling gun, patented in 1862 and adopted by the U.S. Army in 1866, also had six barrels. It had a hand-cranked firing mechanism that its inventor, Richard

Gatling, claimed could emit more than one hundred rounds per minute.

An early magazine article called the Vulcan cannon a "machine that shoots" because it would fire as fast as it could be rotated. Spitting out 20mm shells at the rate of one hundred rounds per second made it much more potent than its Civil War–era ancestor. Testing at the time involved firing the cannon from fixed positions at metal plates. The testers would fire a burst and then go out to look at the damage, which always was extensive. Unlike the staccato of earlier machine guns, a burst from it produced a loud, continuous roar as it poured out a stream of projectiles that shredded targets. Its only problem was that it sucked up conventional-linked ammunition so fast that the links broke. Thus, additional changes in feeding mechanisms were necessary to take full advantage of its power.

The Gatling gun was a great innovation for aerial combat—one Jim would become intimately acquainted with later when he flew the F-105 Thunderchief. Yet, although he was unaware of it at the time, a debate was raging in the Pentagon's hallways about whether future fighter planes should have a gun at all. Many suggested that a gun in a fighter plane was an anachronism from World War II and Korea, not belonging in any future war. Fortunately, that thinking didn't entirely hold sway, so the M-61 Vulcan cannon found its way into aircraft as diverse as the AC-47 and AC-130 gunships in Vietnam (.308- and .223-caliber) and the A-10 Thunderbolt II or Warthog (upscaled to 30mm)—the most potent tank killer of the Desert Storm campaign in Kuwait and Iraq. Contemporary frontline fighters, such as the F-14, F-15, F-16, and F-18, still use it.

When Kasler returned to Nellis, he led tests on how the F-100's afterburner heat affected runways. Jim found he couldn't light the afterburner while sitting still on the runway because its heat and force would rip up the asphalt. Consequently, he and other pilots devised a rolling takeoff. After Jim started rolling, he would say, "Afterburner now!" and then light it. Fighter pilots still light the afterburner that way. At the same time, Jim continued flying and evaluating the aircraft, noting instabilities and potential problems with its construction.

After careful analysis, Jim wrote a report on the F-100, stating that it was worthless in the Air Force inventory and that it would be a disaster for ordinary pilots to try to fly it. When the report went out, Air Force generals and North American's company representatives and engineers came roaring into Nellis loaded for bear. The F-86 Sabre had been highly successful in Korea, but North American's future was riding on this new airplane, the F-100 Super Sabre. Because the generals wanted a better airplane to counter the Russian threat, they loved the F-100, which would easily fly higher and faster than an F-86 or a MiG-15. The F-100's four 20mm cannons certainly were a huge step up in firepower from the old .50-caliber machine guns. Together, the four cannons in an F-100 produced nearly the same rate of fire as the single Gatling gun in the later F-105—about one hundred rounds per second.

The brass called all project officers into the briefing room, as well as Kasler's commander, Major Latshaw. A brilliant mathematician and analyst, Latshaw began telling them—the generals, engineers, and technical representatives—what was wrong with the F-100. But the North American people refuted everything he said, and the generals were getting upset. They insisted they had seen no obvious problems with this airplane, so they couldn't believe the F-100A was as bad as Kasler and Latshaw said it was. They didn't recognize a clear sign of trouble that had occurred just the day before at Edwards. The leading test pilot for Britain's Royal Air Force had lost an F-100 during his checkout flight. He had moved into a classic porpoise on takeoff, couldn't recover, and crashed fatally five miles out. If a skilled test pilot was unable to control the airplane, that didn't augur well for other pilots once it entered the Air Force inventory.

They continued hashing out issues in the briefing, until a sergeant came in and handed Latshaw a note. He read it and then solemnly passed the note to a general. The latter read it, walked over to the North American people, and said, "Gentlemen, your chief test pilot, George Welch, has just been killed in an F-100 crash." He went on, "The aircraft is grounded until we determine what we are going to do. This meeting is over." Welch's death was a terrible loss for the United States. He was a national hero and a triple ace with sixteen credited kills in World War II—four of them over Pearl Harbor on December 7, 1941. He also had broken the sound barrier while flying level during the maiden flight of the YF-100, which was a first for a turbojet-powered airplane.

Welch was pulling 7.5 g's of pressure out of a Mach-speed dive when his F-100 simply broke up in flight. The tail folded up, one wing went down, and the nose of the airplane broke off ahead of the cockpit. Welch had an automatic parachute, but whether he ejected himself or was ejected by the breakup is unclear. Whichever way it occurred, he didn't live long after landing in his chute. Cameras mounted on his test model showed how the airplane came unglued: all the stabilizers and control surfaces collapsed.

North American had no choice but to ground all F-100s and call them back for major modifications. Jim and others from his squadron flew their example models back to the North American factory in Los Angeles. Six months and some 160 modifications later, they saw a much-improved F-100 roll back out. Besides major strengthening of the whole airframe, one obvious visual and structural change was an increase in the height of the vertical stabilizer to add much-needed stability at high speeds. Ironically, the original YF-100 test model had a taller tail section, but engineers had reduced the height to decrease drag in quest of more speed in the early production "A" models, which Jim called the "stub-tail A." Thus, the F-100 eventually came back as a very nice airplane, but the initial version had been a killer.

1954 GUNNERY MEET AT NELLIS

In 1954 the U.S. Air Force's worldwide gunnery meet took place at Nellis. Kasler was still in the Fighter Test Squadron when "Boots" Blesse and he were selected to try out for the team. But Jim didn't make the primary gunnery team because he had some shots in the tow target with excessive elongation, meaning he came into the target at too shallow an angle. In combat he typically came in behind the target, but on practice gunnery missions with a towed target that is too dangerous. A pilot is too likely to shoot the tow plane or fly into the target flag. The evaluators disqualified him for those elongated shots through the target flag and made him an alternate.

Jim's alternate status didn't last long, however. A day or two before the gunnery meet, Blesse's father died, so Jim took his place on the team. He and his squadron mates won the meet. He enjoyed the flying (and the victory), but he found especially interesting the program Nellis published for the meet. The brochure identified seven aces from the Korean War stationed at the base, as well as the number of MiGs each had shot down. It also stated statistics on the tonnage of bombs Nellis pilots dropped in Korea and other information on the group's successes. Reading these details in the brochure brought home to Jim what a privilege he had enjoyed at Nellis—flying and working with some of the finest pilots and officers in the United States Air Force.

CHAPTER 5

From Canada to Cuba

CHATHAM, NEW BRUNSWICK (1955–1957)

IN July 1955, Captain Kasler was reassigned from Nellis to Chatham, New Brunswick, for an exchange tour between the United States and Canada. By this time the Kasler family had grown to include Jimmy and Nanette, the twins who were born while they were at Nellis. They all moved up to Chatham, where the Canadians provided them a fine, well-maintained house.

Because of Jim's background, the Canadians put him in charge of their gunnery school. He was to supervise all gunners for two years—everyone who was flying their Sabres. The Canadians didn't call their aircraft F-86s, of course, but the planes differed in other, more important ways. Their Sabres had British Orenda engines of the same design that the Russians had copied for their MiGs. The Canadians' Sabre V could fly about four thousand to five thousand feet higher than the F-86E. The Sabre VI added five thousand feet to that advantage. Jim wished the Orenda engine had been in his F-86 in Korea: with so much more power, he could have climbed to meet the MiGs at their altitude. The Canadians increased their advantage by maintaining the Sabre's gun sights to absolute perfection—the same sight that experienced considerable problems in the United States. Considering the quality of these aircraft and their support equipment, Jim decided his two years flying in Canada were going to be fun.

55

Soon after Jim arrived, the resident pilots gave him a few rides in the Sabre V. The second day, they took him on familiarizing flights around the area—to Prince Edward Island, and so forth. The third day, Jim went down to the flight line, and it was raining hard, with about an eight-hundred-foot ceiling. Still, student pilots were taking off to go out over the ocean where it was clear and shoot at towed aerial targets. Jim was amazed. At Nellis the weather had always been perfect for flying. When he had flown in bad weather a few times in the Midwest, it had been scary because rain and lightning can destroy visibility and electronic systems. If that was going to be standard procedure in Canada, however, Jim knew he had better acquire some experience, so he asked the sergeant for an airplane. The latter said, without hesitation, "Sure, Captain, you can have an airplane."

The rain was pouring down as Jim took off and headed north. The day before, he had ridden with one of the pilots out over the coast, which was east of the base about thirty miles. He noticed the weather broke up somewhat out there. He was climbing in clouds to about twenty thousand feet when the airplane lurched suddenly. Jim asked himself, "What the hell was that?" The engine screeched and then flamed out. A little louder and with a touch of urgency, Jim growled, "Horseshit!" He turned the airplane around in the clouds and started gliding back toward Chatham. But he knew he couldn't get in there with the weather, so he eased the plane out toward the coast.

As a pilot of single-seat fighters, Jim habitually talked to himself as he flew, a habit he never broke over the years. As he was going through all the procedures to start the engine, he kept talking aloud to himself about "this lousy Canadian jet, this piece of shit" they had put him in. He didn't know his identify friend or foe (IFF) system was on—that he was transmitting everything he said. The Canadian commander, who was up in the tower listening to Jim cursing the airplane, knew he was in deep trouble.

Out over the coast, Jim broke out of the weather at four thousand feet. He had never lost an airplane or had to bail out, so he said, "Well, there's a fairly straight road running right through that little village there. I think I'll just set this thing down on that road." He wheeled around and lined up. Then, as he was ready to drop his landing gear, he took one last look at the landing area. Amazingly, this little village out in the middle of nowhere had telephone poles running along both sides of the road, so Jim didn't have enough clearance for the wingspan. Looking quickly for an alternate, he saw a big marshy area that was flat but contained hundreds of lakes. He lined up between the lakes.

By this time Jim had lost all electrical power, so he couldn't get the flaps to come down or work any of the auxiliary controls. He just glided down and bellied the airplane into a marsh full of blueberry patches. He didn't feel the airplane contact the ground, but he knew he was in the marsh, skipping along at a high speed. He could see one of the big lakes coming up, dead ahead, and he was trying to stop by standing on the brakes. Of course, because he didn't have the gear down, that was useless. Finally, he slid to a stop about ten feet from a drop-off into the lake, sat there, took a deep breath, and looked around. Everything appeared to be intact, so he rolled back the canopy, stepped out, and walked to the lake to see what he had avoided. The water's edge was thirty feet below a steep incline—Jim had just survived another close call and his second dead-stick landing with a jet airplane.

It was beginning to sprinkle, so Jim started back to climb into the airplane when he saw a Canadian helicopter coming to get him. They had a fix on him because he had been transmitting all this time, and they had heard every word he said about their lousy Canadian airplane. They picked him up and took him back to the base, where the commander gave him hell for sliding the airplane in on its belly. The civil engineers had to build a road into the edge of the marsh to get to it. Then they winched it in with cables, put it on a flatbed, and hauled it back to base.

But Kasler's decision to land the plane worked out for the best because the Canadians had lost five or six of their jets before he dead-sticked that one into the marsh and saved it. The only thing broken was the right navigation light on the wing tip—the globe over the bulb—with no damage to the airplane itself. They had it back flying within a month, having used most of that time to build the road for its recovery. More importantly, after an inspection, they found that their interlocking fuel system was bad. When one side failed, it threw debris to the other side, and the engine flamed out. They grounded all the airplanes and modified the systems. By getting that one plane down intact, Jim had saved a lot of expensive equipment and, probably, at least a few lives.

Another outcome of Jim's infamous incident in the blueberry patches was that the entire Royal Canadian Air Force immediately knew who the Kaslers were. As the only people on base from the United States, they received plenty of attention from the Canadians, who particularly liked Jim's sense of humor and willingness to join in. They were a hard-living bunch who enjoyed drinking, toasting, and thinking of strenuous physical games to play at the mess dinners. Jim contributed some ideas that brought them out at the end of the night bedraggled and ready for bed—in a sense, "out-Canadianing" the natives. Also, any time they had miserable weather that didn't allow them to fly, they went to the local hockey rink for curling or broom hockey. The latter used sawed-off broom handles and a volleyball, which the pilots tried to hit into a net after taking regular swigs of whiskey or beer. The game typically deteriorated into a broom-swinging fiasco.

Of course, Jim contributed far more to the mission than a mean "sweep shot." When he first arrived, he went to the individual maintenance squadrons and met all the officers and enlisted people. He usually remembered every name, which came in handy when he tried a small social experiment later on. Because Jim lived in a large house on base and bought liquor at bargain prices from the consulate at New Brunswick, he frequently hosted parties. But he broke Canadian protocol by inviting the maintenance troops and radar operators with the pilots and mixing them socially. Until then, the pilots thought all ground troops were shits, and the feelings were mutual. But thanks to Jim, they began associating with one another and developed a much more cooperative, cohesive organization.

The Canadians also considered Jim an excellent resource on flying and gunnery. He taught them how to use their radar and gave them some tactical instruction. They sent him on a speaking tour to their four air division wings in Europe—two in France and two in Germany. He talked about his experiences in the Korean War and taught pilots F-86 gunnery tactics in the Sabre V and VI. Jim also flew the Sabre VI in Europe, enjoying its power and ability to climb another five thousand feet above the Sabre V. It was a

magnificent airplane that wrapped naturally around an exceptional flyer.

The Kaslers enjoyed living in New Brunswick, despite its seem-
ing to be on the edge of the world (they were so far north that they
had to fly south to get to Nova Scotia). Jim, Martha, and the children could put on their ice skates in their house, walk out the back
door, and skate up and down the streets in the housing area where
they lived. Suzanne started kindergarten there, so she walked to
school (about a block away) through a tunnel of snow. Later she
asked Martha, "Mom, why did you let me walk?" Martha said,
"Because it was a lot easier for you to walk than to try driving
you there on icy pavement." That pragmatic attitude enabled the
Kaslers to adapt well to the north. They found it easy to remain in
New Brunswick for two years and still have very good friends from
that area.

TURNER AIR FORCE BASE AND AVIANO, ITALY
(1957–1958)

In July 1957, Kasler was reassigned to Turner Air Force Base in
Albany, Georgia, where they flew the F-100D. They also had two-
seater F-100Fs to use in training. During 1958, Jim attended Squadron Officers School at Maxwell Air Force Base, Alabama—the first
of three tiers of professional education for Air Force officers. After
completing this school, Jim returned to Turner, became the squadron's operations officer, and deployed on a temporary-duty tour
for six months to Aviano, Italy.

These frequent location changes illustrate why military flying
put so much stress on families (and continues to do so today). Long
absences were typical, such as Jim's months in Alabama immediately followed by a six-month rotation to Aviano. But even when
the pilots were at their home bases, they often went to Nellis a
month at a time for gunnery training. They also deployed a week
at a time to participate in firepower demonstrations, which were
vital to public support for the Air Force and its missions. These
absences were especially tough on spouses, who had to care deeply
for their husbands to put up with it.

As the operations officer for his squadron, Jim stayed extremely busy. Besides completing local training at Aviano, the squadron flew to Wheelus Air Base, Tripoli, Libya, in North Africa to use the El Uotia bombing and gunnery range. Training included navigating and meeting time on target, plus delivering practice and live ordnance. They refueled with KB-50s out of England. All of this training in Italy proved very valuable later in Vietnam, where precision flying and frequent refueling were the norm.

During that time at Aviano, Jim added nuclear-strike training to his practice with conventional weapons but didn't carry live nuclear weapons. Students of the cold war know about the nuclear-deterrent triad: heavy bombers, submarines, and land-based missiles. They formed America's side of the "balance of terror" intended to prevent nuclear war through a doctrine of mutual assured destruction: neither side could strike the other without being destroyed in a counterstrike. But few people today seem to be aware that single-seater fighter planes were assigned a nuclear deterrence role. Once airborne, one fighter pilot could have delivered the weapon anywhere within the aircraft's fuel range. Flying at high speed and under radar made stopping it unlikely.

Earlier, at Eglin, Jim had practiced delivering nuclear weapons only at high altitude. That was all a matter of computing time and altitude—no different from dropping the bomb on Hiroshima. But high altitude exposes a pilot to radar and missiles, as well as other fighter planes, so higher and faster Soviet missiles and interceptors had made that delivery mode obsolete. In the F-100, Kasler practiced low-level nuclear delivery with either a shape (a concrete-filled replica of the real thing) or the MN-1/A bomblet dispenser, which carried miniature practice bombs that accurately simulated a nuclear bomb's trajectory. A common method of delivering a nuclear weapon involved high speed at low altitude and pulling up to pitch the weapon at the target. But today's "look-down" radar makes such a delivery system obsolete, as well. No longer can anyone truly fly under radar.

The F-100 was slung too low to the ground to carry a fat nuclear weapon on the centerline weapons station. So Jim had to carry it on the inboard wing station and counterbalance the weapon with a full fuel tank on the other inboard station. That made for some tricky flying while releasing a bomb because he couldn't maintain balance with an off-center load. Nor could he drop the bomb and the fuel tank at the same time.

For obvious safety reasons, nuclear weapons also had a special jettison (unarmed) system in case of emergency. Jim couldn't just hit the "panic button" and jettison a nuclear bomb like regular ordnance to lighten the load if he got into trouble. In fact, one of the pilots in his squadron wrapped himself up on takeoff with a nuclear shape strapped to his wing. Jim often wondered if the inability to jettison that heavy dummy weapon quickly didn't contribute to the fellow's fatal crash.

One of the scariest things that happened to Kasler while flying occurred at Aviano. Italy's aerial acrobatic team, the Red Devils, came and put on a show. Afterward, the captain of the team asked Jim if he could go up in an F-100. Jim's squadron used their two F-100Fs for courtesy rides, so Jim put the Italian pilot in the backseat and gave him the stick. The Italian was a hotshot. He had that F-100 at six hundred knots and barely eighty feet off the ground, just screaming across the deck. Without warning, he suddenly did a snap roll, which normally should have pushed the airplane's nose downward and carried it into the ground. Jim started to reach for the stick but was too late and was sure they had bought it. But the airplane's nose never moved off level. Apparently, the Italian controlled the rudder to keep the aircraft from losing altitude during the roll. Although Jim took the stick away from him after that, he had nightmares about the experience afterward. He figured it had used up some of his luck—both men should have been dead.

SEYMOUR JOHNSON AIR FORCE BASE (1959–1960)

By the time Kasler returned to Turner Air Force Base from temporary deployment to Aviano, Italy, the Air Force was deactivating it as a fighter base. In January 1959 he was reassigned to Fourth Wing at Seymour Johnson Air Force Base in Goldsboro, North Carolina, where he continued to fly the F-100 and was soon introduced to the F-105 Thunderchief—nicknamed the "Thud." This Republic Aviation–built airplane was designed by Alexander Kartveli, the famous Russian-born designer of the P-47 Thunderbolt (when Republic was the Seversky Aircraft Corporation) and the F-84. Republic had asked Kartveli to design the F-105 as a nuclear-strike successor to the F-84F.

The Fourth Wing made Jim a test pilot on the F-105 and sent him down to Eglin Air Force Base in Pensacola, Florida, for flight training and weapons evaluation before his wing began receiving the first early "B" models from the production line. He was disappointed with the men at Eglin from another squadron who were supposed to be working on the manuals and procedures for the F-105. They hadn't done a thing when he arrived there—no manuals, no procedures, nothing. Jim and his team had to start from scratch. As the F-105 test pilot for his wing, he designed the pilot checklists for all systems, including gunnery and armament.

Variants of Republic Aviation's F-84 designs had proven less than spectacular, so they were looking for a way to stay in the game when they went out on a limb with no contract to build a radically modified, outsized aircraft based on a late-model, swept-wing F-84 with wing-root intakes. They stretched the fuselage to sixty-three feet to include an internal bomb bay built around the contours and dimensions of a low-drag Mk-43 nuclear weapon. A much more powerful engine, the Pratt & Whitney J-75, was to help it exceed Mach 1 in ground-hugging flight under radar. They intended the Thunderchief to be a single-purpose, nuclear-strike aircraft designed for low-level, high-speed delivery with very little conventional capability.

What evolved over time was a multirole fighter with full conventional capability, including the superb M-61 Vulcan cannon designed by General Electric. The Gatling gun, which Kasler had seen at Edwards while it was in development and testing, had found a home in the nose of the F-105. Republic's P-47 Thunderbolt had been the U.S. Army Air Corps's largest single-engine, single-seat fighter in World War II. Similarly, their F-105 Thunderchief became the U.S. Air Force's largest single-engine, single-seat fighter of the jet age, as well as the first operational Mach 2 fighter plane in the world.

The transition from the F-100 to the F-105 was an easy one for Jim. Even though the F-105 was a much larger, more complicated airplane, it was very stable to fly, quite in contrast to the F-100. At Eglin Jim flew two checkout rides in the very early "B" model, then went back to Seymour Johnson. In June 1959 the wing started sending him to the Republic Aviation plant in Farmingdale, New York, to ferry planes to Seymour. The 334th Squadron of Fourth Wing was the first nontesting Air Force unit to receive the F-105. As a morale booster at Seymour, names of pilots were painted on the left canopy rail (see fig. 11). The idea of painting a pilot's name on "his" airplane was a throwback to an earlier tradition and didn't last long.

Although most of the flying was routine, Jim experienced an embarrassing incident while ferrying an F-105B from the factory. He took off from Farmingdale with empty drop tanks on the airplane, and when he retracted his gear, both tanks blew off. The tanks landed in residents' yards, so they could have injured or killed someone: even empty 450-gallon fuel tanks are large enough to do considerable damage. Jim circled around to make sure they hadn't hit anything and then headed home to Seymour.

The next morning, an article in the Farmingdale *Observer* inaccurately stated that a third tank containing jet fuel had landed in a nearby state park. It also quoted an elderly resident as saying, "I thought a bomb had crashed. I ran to the door and when I saw that silver thing lying in my backyard I fainted." On that same morning, Jim reported for work to find someone had made up a newspaper with a dummy headline: "KESSLER [sic] BOMBS L.I. [Long Island]: C.A.B TO INVESTIGATE!" He had to chuckle at the prankster's ingenuity, even though it caused him to take a lot of extra needling.

After an intensive investigation, the hullabaloo subsided, and Jim continued flying without further incident. He always swore he didn't hit the emergency jettison switch, which sends jettison voltage to all external stores stations, but later he thought he might have done so accidentally. The switch was right next to the landing-gear handle. On later F-105s Republic moved it farther away from the handle and shielded it in a well. Jim's experience had something to do with that modification, which may have saved lives in combat.

MAXWELL AIR FORCE BASE (1960–1961)

In September of 1960 Jim went to Command and Staff College at Maxwell Air Force Base, Montgomery, Alabama. It was another square to fill in his military resume, but it was one not everyone received the chance to fill. The five hundred people selected that year had the best records of thousands in their Air Force year group. Despite their "star" status, however, the base had no housing for them, so everyone had to rent "roach palaces" in downtown Montgomery. Sandy Vandenberg had come into the class from the 413th Fighter Wing at George Air Force Base. Jim talked with him occasionally in the coffee bar. They also saw each other socially with their wives several times during the academic year. Other famous fliers, such as Robinson Risner and Chuck Yeager, were assigned to the Air War College (the Air Force's senior service school) at the same time, so Jim was in heady company.

Sandy Vandenberg and his wife Sue had a party one night for some of their friends and invited the Kaslers over. One of their classmates at Command and Staff College, Mike DeArmond, also attended the party. Mike had been a reconnaissance pilot in Korea, was shot down there, and became a POW. Vandenberg knew him from West Point, where Mike was one year ahead of him. Jim was standing in the hallway of the little cracker-box house Vandenberg had rented in Montgomery, and Mike was standing nearby. Sandy said, "Hey, you two guys don't know each other, do you?" They said no, so he introduced them.

After Kasler and DeArmond shook hands, Sandy said to Jim, "Mike got shot down in Korea and was a prisoner of the Chinese."

Jim snapped, "What's the matter, can't you fly?" Later he admitted that his question reflected a prejudice typical of "hot-stick" young fighter pilots who need to believe they are invincible to do their jobs. Being shot down must mean a deficiency in skill. A shoot-down from bad luck or inescapable firepower would be beyond the pilot's control, and most fighter pilots obsess about controlling their environment. DeArmond took no offense, but those words came back to haunt Jim after he was shot down in Vietnam.

Although Jim enjoyed his experience at the military school initially, an unexpected misfortune soon afterward soured his stay in Montgomery and hindered his military career. That October, the Fighter Aces were going to hold their first reunion in San Francisco. Jim was invited and planned to go. He phoned Casey Colman and asked Casey if he would fly out with him. But by then Casey was out of the Air Force, and he declined Jim's invitation.

So, on October 15, Jim selected a T-33 from Maxwell, intending to head for the West Coast alone.

Jim did what he thought was a proper preflight "walk around" and took off. Unfortunately, for some reason, the base's maintenance people thought they should leave the gas caps loose on the wing tanks but close the covers over the caps. Not long after take-off, Jim noticed fuel streaming from these tanks through the loosened caps. He called the tower to report it and said he would fly into Alexander to correct the problem. But Jim didn't know the siphoning action from the drop tanks also was sucking his internal tanks dry. About sixty miles from Alexander, he ran out of fuel and flamed out. He had plenty of altitude, so he began to let down but came in high, pitched out, and came around. Finally, he slid off to lose some altitude and touched down. He rolled up in front of the operations building and stopped, having landed a jet airplane with a dead stick for the third time.

Later Jim learned that all the siphoning pressure had ruptured the internal fuel cells, so he had to call Maxwell for another T-33 to pick him up and fly him back home. They gave Jim two rides and released him to fly again. But the inspector general came on the base for an inspection and asked what they were going to do with this guy who had flamed out. With the pressure on from the inspector general, the commander said, "Oh, we're giving him a flying evaluation board." Jim saw it was all nonsense—just people covering their tails. The base commander was getting ready to retire, so he didn't want any black marks against him. Still, an evaluation board was serious business—it could affect Jim's career or even result in his being grounded.

Skip Stanfield and some of Jim's other friends came down from Seymour Johnson to testify for him. A friend of Sandy Vandenberg's was among the members of the evaluation board. He told Vandenberg at a social event that evening, "Sandy, I just witnessed the future Chief of Staff of the Air Force talking."

Sandy said, "What? Who do you mean?"

He said, "I'm a member of the Kasler Flying Evaluation Board. I couldn't believe the horsepower that came in to testify on his behalf. After listening to them, I'm telling you, this Kasler is the future Chief of Staff of the Air Force!"

Despite these glowing comments, however, the board reached a "mixed" finding that stayed on Jim's record and probably delayed his next promotion: he wasn't promoted to major the first time he was eligible. Jim said he was a captain for so long that his son thought "Captain" was his first name. By this time, his lack of a college degree may have had some influence as well because the first class of officers from the Air Force Academy had graduated in 1959. The Air Force was pointing toward a four-year degree as a minimum requirement for officers. Jim could have gone to the Air Force's inspector general to get the board's decision overturned because the loose tank caps obviously weren't his fault. But he was a good soldier—and the delayed promotion didn't keep him from doing what he loved to do.

SEYMOUR JOHNSON AGAIN (1961–1962)

After Command and Staff College, Jim went back to Seymour Johnson and to flying the F-105. That meant a car trip from Alabama to North Carolina—an exciting time for Jim's children because they went to Jim's parents' house in Zanesville, Indiana, whenever they were traveling from base to base. As usual, this trip occurred near the Fourth of July, so they could go to the baseball diamond and set off fireworks. Later they ate watermelon in their grandparents' backyard and took advantage of some rare, relaxing hours with their father. Maintaining relationships with his children was difficult for Jim because he was gone so much on flying duty, but he did spend time with them whenever he could.

Once Jim began flying the F-105 regularly, he considered it one of the finest gun platforms ever built for stability and accuracy. It was fairly common to have 100 percent hits against a ground target, putting every fired round through the target cloth. The F-105D had replaced the "B" model and was to become the most common variant. This newer model had many refinements. The nose was more than a foot longer with a much larger radome. The Pitot tube had been moved from the left wing tip to the nose of the radome, making the airplane even longer. The Gatling gun now had the new linkless feed system. The cockpit instrumentation and layout were very different. But to Jim, the "D" felt much the same as the

"B" in flight. It was a good airplane that theoretically could fly in all weather.

Like most fighter aircraft, however, the F-105 had its problems early on, and Jim witnessed the results of one. From Seymour Johnson, members of Jim's wing flew down to Eglin Air Force Base in their F-105s for a firepower demonstration called *Silk Hat*, which President Kennedy was to review. On April 16, 1962, during the practice preparation for the demonstration, Jim and a wingman were following several miles behind another F-105 pilot, Capt. Charles Lamb Jr.—Jim's friend and fellow Hoosier from Indianapolis. Captain Lamb was simulating a nuclear-weapon drop using a high-speed, low-altitude, pitch-up, timed delivery. After his run, Jim and his wingman were going to strafe ground targets soaked with oil and flammables. They could ignite them with 20mm incendiary rounds in the Gatling guns.

Jim was watching Lamb's F-105 in front of him when he saw the tailpipe turn red and start glowing. Jim thought Lamb was in afterburner, but his tailpipe kept getting redder and redder. Suddenly, Lamb's airplane disintegrated—just exploded into little pieces—a horrifying sight for the men following him, who were helpless to do anything about it. Because this run was only for practice, President Kennedy wasn't around to see it happen. But the accident, combined with the President's intention to attend the demonstration, shook up the brass, so they cancelled it. No one ever found anything of Captain Lamb.

F-105s were involved in several similar midair explosions after fire-warning lights came on, and investigators couldn't figure out what had caused most of them until two and a half years later. On October 4, 1964, the pilot of an F-105 at Wheelus Air Base reported fire-warning lights on. His wingman, on seeing smoke coming from the tail section, suggested he bail out, figuring the airplane was ready to explode as others had with similar symptoms. "No," he replied, "I'm right here. I'm going to bring it in." Fortunately, he landed safely. Afterward, when the pilot was asked why he risked the landing, he said he figured he had more chance of getting hurt ejecting than he did by landing the airplane.

Maintenance found a crack in the hydraulic control system inside the aft fuselage. It was spraying hydraulic fluid onto the outside of the hot engine, which triggered a fire that had led to explosions in other aircraft. The pilot was fortunate to get the plane down in one piece. All the F-105s were temporarily grounded and modified after that, so he saved other pilots' lives by taking that calculated risk. The F-105 had several more groundings over the years, usually following the death of another young pilot.

THE CUBAN MISSILE CRISIS

While Kasler was still at Seymour Johnson, he took part in what became an extremely tense international incident: the Cuban Missile Crisis. It began for the United States on October 15, 1962, when reconnaissance photographs revealed Soviet intermediate-range missiles under construction in Cuba. The missile deployment came about because Nikita Khrushchev needed a forward base for the Soviet Union's less capable missiles in order to deter a potential attack by long-range missiles from the United States. At the same time, Fidel Castro was looking for a way to defend his nation from a second attack, which he thought inevitable because the United States had sponsored the failed Bay of Pigs invasion in 1961. But missiles in Cuba were unacceptable to the security of the United States.

On October 22, 1962, President Kennedy imposed a naval quarantine around Cuba and ordered flying wings to mobilize for possible air strikes on targets there. He further stated that a nuclear attack from the island would constitute an attack on the United States by the Soviet Union and demanded the Soviets remove all offensive weapons (including light bombers) from Cuba.

At this point, Kasler's wing headquarters called him at home and ordered him to come in that night. They said, "We've been assigned a Cuban MiG base as a target. We have reconnaissance photos of the base, its revetments, and so forth." They asked Jim to draw up the attack plan for the MiG base, and he spent half the night doing so. The next day, Jim went with his squadron to Orlando, Florida, where they stood alert with their F-105s. Twice they taxied out, thinking they were going to Cuba for an air strike, but each time the command called them back before they took off.

Some fifteen hundred fighters were ready to hit Cuba. Bombers were also poised to strike with conventional weapons. But on October 26, Khrushchev sent a letter to Kennedy in which he proposed removing Soviet missiles and military people if the United States would guarantee that it would not invade Cuba. On October 27, the crisis worsened briefly. A U-2 reconnaissance plane was shot down over Cuba, and Khrushchev sent a second letter demanding removal of U.S. missiles from Turkey in exchange for removing Soviet missiles from Cuba. Attorney General Robert Kennedy suggested ignoring Khrushchev's second letter and agreeing to the first. The Soviets then backed off, and the crisis wound down.

Jim always thought the United States was closer to a nuclear war during the missile crisis than at any other time before or since. At least twenty-four intermediate-range missile sites were ready for action, with the missiles in place. Although debate continues about whether nuclear warheads were mated to the missiles, some believe the Soviet commander in Cuba had ten to sixteen tactical nuclear missiles armed and aimed at Florida cities—or, possibly, at other cities in the southeastern states. Fortunately, the Soviet Union blinked first in the stare down, and effective diplomacy prevailed. Once the crisis passed, Jim's wing commander told him, "This thing is over. You can go home."

At that time, Jim had an appointment to go to the University of Nebraska in Omaha so he finally could finish his college degree. He needed the degree because it had become a must for all officers to achieve on-time promotions. He had taken a number of courses at Butler University and while stationed at various bases. The university also allowed some credit for military service, but he needed to finish a major and complete degree requirements. He had to pass an equivalency test to enter the university, so Sandy Vandenberg and another pilot, "Lash" LaGrue, gave him math lessons in the briefing room at Seymour Johnson. They went into the room, closed the door, and used the blackboard to tutor him in algebra.

Jim appreciated his friends' help and took full advantage of it. Although he had been an indifferent student in his early years at Butler, he excelled in flight schools, Air Force schools, and college courses once he discovered his chosen profession. He went to Omaha and took just six months to complete his bachelor of science degree, with a major in military science and a minor in business.

CHAPTER 6

Cold War Duty in Europe

BITBURG, GERMANY (1963–1965)

IN July 1963 Kasler transferred to the Thirty-sixth Tactical Fighter Wing (TFW) at Bitburg, Germany, for a standard three-year overseas tour. He was assigned to the Fifty-third Tactical Fighter Squadron. Like virtually every other tactical fighter base in Europe at that time, Bitburg had a "Victor Alert" area with nuclear-armed aircraft poised for launch at Russian targets. Jim had practiced delivering nuclear bombs with dummy loads at Eglin Air Force Base in Florida, but this was the first time he stood alert near live weapons. Bitburg also had a full array of conventional weaponry. Operational readiness inspections evaluated both nuclear and conventional roles.

The Fifty-third was a "Tiger" squadron, so their emblem was a tiger. They had a life-sized statue of a "tiger" mounted in front of their headquarters building, although it was actually a panther that had guarded the entrance to a German Panzer division's headquarters. Ever resourceful, they had repainted the panther yellow with black stripes to resemble a tiger. Most pilots in the squadron (including Kasler) wore a large, embroidered tiger head on the back of their flight jackets—above a stitched motto, "53rd uber alles" (over everything).

Just before Jim arrived at Bitburg, the former wing commander had made general and moved on. Col. Gordon Blood had just come out of a Pentagon assignment to this command position, which would earn him his first general's star in about a year. The Thirty-sixth TFW was a hot outfit, with other impressive names on the roster. For example, several ex-Thunderbird and ex–Sky Blazer pilots were onboard. Bobby Wayne was there. Credited with two early shoot-downs in Korea, Wayne also flew in and directed the flying sequences for the movie version of James Salter's *The Hunters*. Jim's old friend Skip Stanfield was the Fifty-third Squadron's commander briefly while he was there, but then moved on. Skip was the very image of a fighter pilot. He had been a Flying Tiger and reputedly was the model for the fighter pilot in the comic strip *Terry and the Pirates*.

As a side note, Stanfield's career after retirement from the Air Force also was colorful. He owned his own Boeing 707 commercial jet and flew with his daughter, Davy Kay, as his copilot. At one point he was transporting coffee for Idi Amin. He took his plane and flew out of Uganda just before the revolution there became nasty. Then he was in Indonesia until the government impounded his airplane. He had to go to the World Court to get reimbursed. He started an airline in Belize, but that didn't last long because of too many restrictions on his operations. Jim said the world had lost one of its great adventurers when Stanfield's daughter called him in December of 1998 to say that Skip had died in a skiing accident.

When Stanfield transferred from Bitburg, Robert M. White replaced him as the Fifty-third Squadron's commander. White, the former X-15 test pilot, was the United States's first "winged astronaut," as well as a test pilot for the F-105 in its fly-off with the F-107. He was the first person to reach Mach 6 (six times the speed of sound) in a rocket plane. Sandy Vandenberg was commander of the Twenty-third Squadron (and later became the Fifty-third Squadron's commander). Both White and Vandenberg would go on to fly in Southeast Asia and retire as two-star generals (see fig. 12).

Shortly after White became the Fifty-third Squadron's commander, Jim was transferred to headquarters as the wing's tactical evaluation officer. This position gave him the important responsibility of improving flying prowess and safety across the wing. Although the wing had many highly skilled pilots, it lost several F-

105s during Jim's tour at Bitburg, including one at the end of July, just after his arrival. In that case, the aircraft was carrying a nuclear shape in its bomb bay and never quite got off the ground on take-off. Eyewitnesses said they saw and heard the afterburner breaking up. Halfway down the runway, the pilot lifted off just enough to suck up his gear, settled back down onto his drop tanks (which exploded), and rode in afterburner until he hit the trees off the end of the runway. Apparently, he thought he could get the airplane into the air. Not much was left of him or the airplane once he plowed into the forest.

To Jim, this incident illustrated several points about safely flying fighter aircraft. The pilot was a hotshot who liked to preposition the landing gear handle to the "up" position, so the gear would retract smartly as soon as the weight came off its squat switches. It was a foolish risk that finally cost him his life. When he recognized he had afterburner problems, he should have chopped the power, deployed his drogue chute, and stood on the brakes. Once his landing gear retracted, he was in deep trouble. With catapult ejection seats, none of the Century-series fighters allowed a successful zero-altitude ejection. Had the pilot ejected, he likely would have died anyway from heavy contact with the ground. Also, the tail hook on the F-105 was fragile for its weight. Had he tried to grab the safety restraining wire, the hook would have torn off. He was still in full burner when he ripped through the backup arresting barrier. Lightening the load might have helped, but the drop tanks had already exploded in fireballs when he settled back onto the runway, and getting rid of the one-ton dummy nuclear weapon in his bomb bay wouldn't be likely. He was along for the ride with his tail dragging on the ground.

Because Bitburg's runway had a pronounced crown, or high spot, in the center, the pilot may have thought he could coax his plane into the air as the runway dropped away. But an airplane rotates about a lateral axis that runs through the wing tips. With his aft section dragging on the ground, there was no way to pitch his nose up. His fate was sealed. Off the end of the runway, his right wing dug into the earth and ripped off. The plane turned, slammed into a stand of trees, and disintegrated.

Another safety issue concerned the gully at one end of Bitburg's runway. It caused a wind shear problem that pilots should have been able to anticipate. They simply needed to punch up the power over the gully during the approach. Still, wind shear caught two pilots during Jim's time there—one flying an F-105 and another flying an F-102 for the tenant air-defense unit. Fortunately, although the wing had to write off both aircraft, the pilots survived.

As the wing's tactical evaluation officer, Jim was a stern taskmaster for young pilots. His nickname was "Stoneface" because he seldom showed his emotions and didn't talk much. His direct, nononsense approach to leadership and training struck some as overly blunt and critical, but it was his way of preparing them for the challenges ahead. After all, their lives depended on getting it right, with little room for error.

One typical experience involved Lt. John Brodak, then newly assigned to Bitburg (later to become Jim's cell mate in Hanoi). Brodak had flown the T-38 and then the F-100 at Luke Air Force Base, but he hadn't checked out in the F-105 before arriving at Bitburg. In fact, very few lieutenants were flying F-105s. The story went that shortly after the first F-105B models arrived at Seymour Johnson Air Force Base, a two-star general from Tactical Air Command headquarters was on the base for a visit and witnessed an F-105 make a landing approach with the gear up. When he learned a lieutenant was flying the airplane, he reportedly said, "We have too many captains in the Air Force to let a lieutenant fly this airplane." And that was the end of lieutenants being assigned to F-105s for some time.

When Brodak arrived at Bitburg, Jim decided he was going to learn more sitting in the backseat of a "T-bird" (T-33) than anywhere else. At that time, no two-seater F-105 "F" models were available to use for training and transition. Brodak wasn't pleased with Jim's idea, not having flown the T-33 and not wanting to sit in the backseat. But his resistance was brief because Jim said, "Lieutenant, that's the way it's going to be." Brodak logged several hours in the T-33's backseat before moving on to the F-105D. Later he admitted it was a good idea: the F-105 could bite an inexperienced pilot, and some accidents did occur as pilots were transitioning into it.

Brodak also discovered Jim was a demanding, meticulous teacher of F-105 tactics—just as he had been for the F-100 at Nellis a decade before. Brodak had taken minimum training in air-to-air gunnery at Luke Air Force Base because maintenance problems limited him to three missions. On one of those, he didn't get to fire: they couldn't get the dart (aerial gunnery target) to release from the tow plane. In the two opportunities he had to shoot at the dart, he scored no hits. When Jim asked how he had done, Brodak admitted he didn't have any techniques or good ideas about what he was doing wrong. Jim gave him a detailed briefing on what to do and what to look for, then took him up on a dart mission. Jim made a pass and hit the target. Then Brodak hit the dart on his first pass and was elated—but that elation didn't last long.

Back on the ground, as soon as they entered the debriefing room, Jim started chewing him out, telling him what he had done wrong. Jim said he camped right behind the dart, didn't have proper overtake speed, and had gotten too close to the dart with his airplane. Again, Jim was tough on the pilot—very blunt and critical—but Brodak got the point. It was possible to hit the dart or cable, or to ingest debris from hits on the dart into the intakes, which could kill an engine. Later on, an F-105 did run into a dart at Wheelus Air Base in North Africa. The cable cut into the wing and caused considerable damage.

Although Jim had demanding responsibilities, he and his family considered Bitburg a good assignment. They lived off base, at 9 Echternacher Strasse, right next to the church and graveyard that would become famous when President Reagan visited on May 5, 1985. Like President Reagan, Jim didn't know Nazi S.S. troops were buried in that churchyard. (Neither did most people, apparently.) Flying over such a peaceful-looking landscape, it was hard for Jim to imagine all the wars—ancient as well as modern—that had swept back and forth across that terrain.

The Kaslers always were comfortable living without collecting things of their own and were not materialistic. For example, they owned no furniture, so they used some from the air base supply. The living room suite was dreadful looking, with a horrid pattern in the material. Still, their living space was comfortable enough, with rooms on the second and third floors, plus a flat roof above the landlord's architectural studio for the children to play on. Jim did own one thing: an old Volkswagen Beetle—so old that a hole had rusted through the floor. That's what he drove Suzanne and the twins back and forth to town in. The age and appearance of the car didn't matter to Jim or Martha, even though some Air Force people were driving expensive European sports cars.

The Kaslers weren't the type of family in which Jim would take one of the children and go spend a couple of days somewhere. He was always too busy with military duties. But they did take some family trips to various places, such as Amsterdam in the Netherlands, and they learned to ski in Austria. Whenever they went to the officer's club as a family, Jim made sure they were all well dressed and neat. But once they went inside, the children could sometimes sneak away and race and tear around the club—despite Jim's stern response when he found them.

Of special interest to Jim was a nice golf course in nearby Luxembourg. He had always liked the game and had played a bit in Indianapolis—going out with his father to a little course near the latter's home. But contrary to a popular misconception about military officers, Jim had found time to play no more than four or five times a year. The fighter-pilot business left him little time for leisure.

Family life was pleasant enough, but flying out of Bitburg was serious business. They were at the height of the cold war, and everyone could feel the tension. Fighter planes routinely patrolled overhead. President Kennedy came to Germany while they were there to give his "Ich bin ein Berliner" speech, and the Kaslers also were at Bitburg when Kennedy was assassinated. The family was playing cards when a special report came over the television on the Armed Forces channel. It stunned them. Assassination of a United States President was unthinkable to Jim; it signaled the end of America's innocence and was the progenitor of the later assassinations of Martin Luther King Jr. and Robert Kennedy.

Knowing that the children were experiencing a lot of change, Jim teamed with another young F-105 pilot, Lew Shattuck, to make Christmas 1963 special for them. Shattuck was one of the squadron's few young, unmarried F-105 pilots, so the Kasler family "adopted" him while he was at Bitburg and made him part of their holiday activities. Jim and he put toys together and arranged memorable festivities for the kids. (Later Shattuck's career paralleled Jim's in a more unfortunate way: he was shot down and became a POW in Vietnam.)

Jimmy and Nanette were eleven to twelve years old during the

Bitburg tour, so their most vivid childhood memories of their father come from that period. Many of these memories focus on discipline because that traditional role often fell to Jim whenever he came home from a flight or a temporary-duty assignment. Before going to Vietnam, he could get upset with the children about relatively small peccadilloes because he wanted them to be as perfect as possible. Today, the younger Kaslers understand their father was trying to teach them that everyone has problems and obstacles to overcome, but the best people take responsibility for their actions and move forward.

Kasler's perfectionism and his intention to have his children grow up honorably and respect others made him a tough disciplinarian: he allowed little room for making the same mistake twice. Jimmy was a special trial to him at Bitburg. The boy wasn't a troublemaker, but he was curious and a touch too bold, which put him in trouble's way. The local German police arrested him and his buddies twice for going into a farmer's field, which was not allowed. On many occasions, the boys caused the explosive-ordnance disposal unit to be called because they had found bombs or other old war munitions in the fields and bunkers around the town. They went down into the bunkers—some several stories underground— and dug for days. They found old Mauser rifles, ammunition, and helmets, all of which they traded among themselves to build their personal collections.

Jimmy also continually got into fistfights at school during the fifth and sixth grade. He insisted he wasn't malicious and didn't look for fights; for some reason, the fights simply found him. But it didn't take much to set him off, perhaps because he had inherited the famous Kasler temper from his father. Every time Jimmy got into trouble, Jim took his belt to him without discussion—just as Jim's father and grandfather or grandmother had done to him when he was a boy. It impressed Jimmy temporarily, but in the long run, it did no good.

Eventually, the school told Jimmy that if he were in another fight, he would be expelled from school permanently. In other words, he wouldn't be able to go to school until the Kaslers returned to the United States. He stayed out of trouble for a little while after the expulsion threat, but then another tussle occurred, and the school kicked him out. That day, Jim was away on a flight.

A big school party was scheduled for the evening—one for which Jimmy had been waiting months. He was excited about going to the party in his new three-piece, red-breasted suit, which they had ordered from Sears for the occasion. Because his father hadn't come home yet—and because mothers sometimes harbor a soft spot concerning their children's dreams—Martha let him go.

Jimmy was caught up in the party, having a good time dancing in the school gymnasium, when a hush suddenly spread over the crowd. He turned around and saw the people begin to part. When he spotted his father coming toward him, still in a flight suit, he thought, *Oh my God, I am in for it now!* Kasler threw him in the car and took him home, with Jimmy thinking all the while, *He is going to kill me.* But instead, Jim sat him down and said, "Look. You know hitting you hasn't done any good. Disciplining you, spanking you—I'm not going to do that anymore." He continued talking with Jimmy for a long time, explaining why he wanted him to act responsibly.

The incident demonstrates how Jim could change even deeply ingrained behavior if experience demanded it—a characteristic he was later to identify as one of the key elements of good leadership. Whether the cause was his change in tactics, or just Jimmy's abject relief that he didn't get his bottom blistered, the young man avoided trouble for the rest of the time he was in Germany. Fortunately for him, the military dependents' schools were so much better than those in Indianapolis, missing a few months of school didn't hold him back when Jim's assignment to Vietnam caused the family to move at midyear.

Kasler greatly moderated his temper in family relationships, but it continued to lurk. Certain things especially upset him, although he might find them humorous in retrospect. Sandy Vandenberg recalls an incident when he and Jim were getting haircuts at a local barbershop. When it was Jim's turn, he gave the barber explicit instructions on how much to take off and where. He was very particular about his haircuts. Once the barber was finished and Jim pushed out of the chair and looked at himself in the mirror, he nearly had a stroke. He started poking the barber in the chest while using some unpleasant language, then threw his military payment money down and went boiling out of the shop.

When questioned about this trait, Jim says wryly, "I have a nice even temper—consistently bad. But I don't carry a grudge, and my anger doesn't last long. It just flares. Everybody knows it, and I get a lot of ribbing about it." In fact, his friends noticed Jim could manage his temper when he wanted to—switching it on and off to blow off steam without getting out of control.

Although the younger pilots knew Jim as a hard-ass, he also had a great sense of humor, especially when the joke was on him. Throughout his military years, the men who came to know him well were always setting him up for a joke. Vandenberg learned about Jim's self-deprecating sense of humor while he and Jim were at Bitburg. Sandy joined Jim there the first time when he flew an F-105 into Bitburg for an overnight visit. Jim had just arrived and had a room in the bachelor officers' quarters (BOQ) with an extra bed, so Sandy moved in with him for the night.

Sandy couldn't help but notice that Jim had remnants of a black eye, so he asked him how it happened. Jim said, "Just before I left the States for Germany, I left my car in a parking garage. When I came back, the garage had closed for the night, and the guard refused to open up so I could get my car out. I got steamed and started threatening the guy—using some nasty language. The guard didn't take it too kindly. . . . He came out and popped me in the eye." Jim started laughing. He thought the episode was funny because his temper had overcome him, and he probably got what he deserved.

Jim also enjoyed carrying on with the Canadians stationed near Solingen, Germany, although their hijinks could sometimes make him a bit testy. Not long before he left for Vietnam in early 1966, they invited him, Vandenberg, and others from Bitburg for some "fun and games." Kasler and Vandenberg roomed together at the BOQ on the Canadian base. Of course, Jim had spent time with the Canadians before and knew how raucous they were. Sandy learned quickly. About halfway through the first evening, they had had enough, so they went back to the BOQ and to bed. About two hours later, in the middle of the night, a group of Canadian pilots came in with two female Canadian schoolteachers. They sat on the beds saying, "Come on. Don't you want to play?" Jim and Sandy just yelled, "Get out of here," and then rolled over and went to sleep.

When they arose in the morning, Jim said, "My goddamn boots

are missing." Sandy's were, too, but that wasn't all. When they checked their flying suits, they found two large holes where the Canadians had cut their wing and squadron patches out of the material, instead of cutting the stitching. They were leaving that day but had to get to breakfast first—without boots to protect them from the winter cold. They sat there trying to figure out what to do, both steaming about what the Canadians had done. Then Sandy spied some big, thick, red woolen Canadian blankets, so he said, "Let's make mukluks out of them." Jim helped cut and tear the blankets, tied them on like shoes, and then went to breakfast wearing them. The Canadians threw a fit because the Americans had torn up their blankets, so Jim and Sandy had the last laugh. They eventually received their boots back but never knew what happened to their patches.

As Jim and the other Americans boarded a C-47 for the flight back to Bitburg, the Canadians gave them a boisterous send-off. The Americans were terribly hung over from the previous night's drinking, but that didn't keep some of the pilots from going to the rear of the C-47 and pulling on the cables. The poor pilot up in the cockpit was trying to fly the airplane while the plane went up, down, or sideways with each tug on the cables. For Jim, it was a typically memorable experience with what was known then as the Royal Canadian Air Force.

Jim was an operations officer at Bitburg, with considerable responsibility for flight scheduling and training. As a result, he spent more temporary duty time than the average pilot at Wheelus Air Base in Libya. Normally, pilots averaged two weeks a year at Wheelus to qualify with various weapons, but Jim was often there for a month at a time, several times a year. Wheelus was familiar territory because Jim had flown F-100s there while he was assigned on temporary duty to Aviano, Italy, in 1958. This time, he had to qualify in two types of simulated nuclear deliveries with the MN-1/A bomblet dispenser: one for "lay down" and one for "toss bomb." Occasionally, he dropped a shape—a concrete-filled, full-sized replica. The F-105's displacement gear forcefully ejected this one-ton dummy bomb from the internal bomb bay. The gear was actually a large, nitrogen-charged piston mounted at the plane's center of gravity, so it gave Jim a noisy kick in the pants when it operated.

Conventional weapons qualification included aerial gunnery, ground gunnery, rockets, conventional and skip-bombing, and sometimes napalm. Kasler's wing had in their weapons inventory AIM-9B Sidewinder heat-seeking missiles and AGM-12B Bull Pup command-guided, air-to-ground missiles. But pilots rarely live-fired them. The 2.75-inch unguided rockets with folding fins were very erratic in flight, which made them unreliable. They were designed to ripple-fire from pods of nineteen, but pilots fired only a pair for qualification. Often, one went above and one went under the target at the same time. Jim found gunnery easy against the towed dart and the ground targets, and he did well in dive-bombing, but he found skip-bombing difficult. It required precise, almost instinctive timing.

Although flights were usually routine, some offered unexpected danger. For example, Jim lived through an odd incident at the El Uotia gunnery range near Wheelus Air Base. A 20mm projectile from his Gatling gun ricocheted off the ground and shattered the quarter panel on his windscreen. The panel blew right out, even though it was supposed to be bulletproof. Another time, when Jim was flying back from Wheelus to Bitburg, he heard little popping noises—small explosions—in the aircraft's nose. He declared an emergency, landed, and discovered 20mm rounds had been cooking off in the gun's ammunition feed system. After maintenance, someone hadn't reconnected the return tube that feeds hot air to the windscreen, so hot turbine air was igniting the ammo. Fortunately, the brass shell cases were rupturing and relieving the pressure. If an incendiary tip of one of those 20mm rounds had ignited, it could have blasted Jim out of the sky.

Other incidents gave Jim some comic relief from the routine (and occasional perils) of flying. Once, his flight was coming back from Wheelus and nearing Rome, Italy, when one of his pilots began having trouble with his airplane. The pilot decided he should land and declared an emergency. Jim contacted the tower at a nearby Italian base, told them he had a pilot with an emergency, and requested permission to land. The operator of their ground-control approach (GCA) radar picked up the troubled pilot and began guiding him in. Jim thought the ensuing radio communications would have made a good comedy routine. The Italian GCA operator said, "Blue Two. You-a twenty-five feeta below the glida path.

Pick it up." Soon he came on again. "Blue Two. You-a fifty feeta below the glida path. Pick it up." A little later he said, "Blue Two. You-a hundred feeta below the glida path. You-a pick it up or you-a gonna busta your ass!" At that point, Jim chuckled and then chimed in, "Blue Two. You get back on the goddamn glide path."

Occasionally, Jim had to endure activities designed to keep him humble, such as the Norwegian Ski Survival School. He went on hikes through the snow and learned how to carve a cave out of a snowbank. He and another would-be survivor tunneled in, then built raised pallets in the snow on each side to sleep on. They even cut a block of snow to use as a door. Once inside, they lit two candles for light and heat.

The Norwegians used snow weasels (tracked vehicles) to bring the cave mates cold beer, which the Germans had ordered for them. To Jim, it seemed silly to be drinking cold beer in freezing temperatures. During the night, this silliness turned into inconvenience because he had to go out into the cold several times to relieve himself of the beer. Finally, tired of braving the cold, he bored a relief tube into the snow and used that. Near morning, he awoke to find the cave hazy with smoke. His sleeping bag had edged too near a candle and was smoldering, so Jim had to beat it against the snow to put it out. *Apparently*, he mused, *the key to survival in cold country will be to avoid beer and candles!*

NATO COMPETITION AT CHAUMONT, FRANCE (JUNE 1965)

The payoff for Kasler's diligent flying and training came in June 1965, when the F-105s from Bitburg's Thirty-sixth TFW and Spangdahlem's Forty-ninth TFW represented the United States Air Forces, Europe (USAFE), at NATO's AIRCENT tactical fighter competition at Chaumont, France. Jim's title for the meet was "national detachment commander," meaning he was the unit commander for all Americans at the meet. They took three planes from Bitburg and two from Spangdahlem—the only two F-105 bases in Europe. One of the pilots from Bitburg on Jim's team was Capt. Dave Duart, who later joined Jim as a POW in North Vietnam. They also had Larry Wiggins and Maurice Seaver, each of whom would go on to shoot down a MiG-17 in Vietnam. Maj. Ray Kingston joined them from Spangdahlem. He eventually went into the record books with the most hours flying in an F-105. He had logged twenty-four hundred hours of early F-105 test flying at Republic and had been the Air Force's worldwide champion in special-weapons delivery in 1956.

Besides the Americans, the Fourth ATAF team included representatives from France, Germany, and Canada. Second ATAF, their opponents, included another unit from Germany, as well as representatives from Belgium, the Netherlands, and the United Kingdom. The Germans and Canadians sent F-104s. The French had F-100s, but this proved to be the last tactical weapons competition France participated in before they withdrew from NATO. The Royal Air Force flew their twin-engined Canberra bombers. The Belgians and Netherlanders flew swept-winged F-84s, which were museum pieces even then. Although the countries varied widely in equipment and tactics, Jim was pleased to see how well they cooperated during the competition.

Jim noted an especially huge contrast between the Canadians' spit-and-polish F-104s and the Germans' airplanes, which were poorly kept. The difference was more than skin deep. On the meet's opening day, a German F-104 flamed out while the pilot was making a low-level pass to familiarize himself with the range at Suippes, France. The pilot barely got out, but walked away unhurt. During the meet's second week, another German pilot punched out of an F-104, this time during landing. The airplane had pitched up excessively, and the pilot ejected about the time his main gear touched the runway. Luckily, the wind popped his chute open, so he could land and walk away. The embarrassing part was that the F-104 landed itself after the pilot ejected. It ran quite a ways down the runway before drifting off into a drainage ditch and collapsing the nose gear and right main gear. It was still sitting nose down in that ditch with its T-tail sticking up in the air when Jim left for home after the meet. The Germans said it was the second time this pilot had ejected from an F-104.

The Germans had already lost more than forty of their F-104s by that time, and they lost many more over the next few years. Col. Eric Hartman, the highest-ranking German ace from World War II, had tried to warn the German Air Force that they weren't ready for such an airplane, but his superiors didn't listen to him. Jim was aghast at the Germans' lack of professionalism. Their maintenance people simply weren't trained well enough to maintain such a sophisticated airplane, and some of their pilots apparently were afraid of the F-104. Frankly, Jim couldn't blame them too much because he had a very low opinion of the F-104 from his own experience reviewing its design in the 1950s. With its stubby wings, the aircraft was particularly unforgiving.

Surprisingly, Jim's side won the overall meet, despite the British Canberra bombers on the Second ATAF team. As a crewed bomber, the Canberra should have had a clear advantage over a single-seater fighter plane in the bombing competition. Although the competition at Chaumont was intense, the pilots found ways to have fun. At the end of the meet, for example, an F-84 "bombed" the control tower at Chaumont with toilet paper. The pilot had closed his speed brakes on the paper rolls. He made a high-speed pass, pulled up in front of the tower, and popped open the speed brakes, releasing the rolls of toilet paper to stream ceremoniously to the ground. Jim got a kick out of the pilot's bombing escapade and wished he had thought of it himself.

CHAPTER 7

New War, New Rules

VOLUNTEERING FOR VIETNAM

HAD things been allowed to run their course, Kasler would have spent his full three-year tour at Bitburg, then gone to a stateside assignment with another F-105 unit. But the war was on in Vietnam and heating up by 1964–1965, so Jim believed he should be there. He started volunteering to go but was told regulations forbade consecutive overseas assignments.

At that point, Colonel Blood had made his general's star and moved on, with Col. James Hackler Jr. replacing him as wing commander. Colonel Hackler must have grown weary of Jim's requests for assignment directly to Southeast Asia—in all, he volunteered five times. Finally, the Air Force changed the regulation prohibiting consecutive overseas tours because they needed F-105 pilots. Many had completed their one hundred missions in Southeast Asia and had gone home from the war. Others had been shot down. The F-105 was used heavily in the war as the main strategic bomber against targets in North Vietnam.

Jim and two other volunteers from Bitburg (Norm Wells and Lew Shattuck) were the first three pilots to go directly from Europe to Southeast Asia. Jim's reporting date was in February 1966, which meant he had until January to wrap up the family's affairs at Bitburg. Martha was upset about Jim's decision, but supported

85

it and vowed to make the best of things. The children were even more troubled by the change. They worried about Jim's going to war, of course, but they also had to move right after Christmas in January—in the middle of the school year. When the day came for their departure, Jim took thirty days leave to relocate them to Indianapolis—an obvious choice because Martha, Suzanne, and the twins considered Indianapolis their hometown, and Martha's mother was living there alone. Jim settled everyone in a little town house and enrolled the children in local schools.

Suzanne Kasler was fifteen years old, a tough age to be separated from her father, especially because she had always felt close to him. Whenever Jim and Martha dressed to go out for the evening, she went into their room, sat on the bed, and talked to Jim about her day's activities. When Jim came home from a day of flying at Bitburg, Suzanne was the first to greet him at the door. She had always had that kind of relationship with him. So the day Jim was to leave, Martha let Suzanne stay home from school and go with him to a local restaurant for a hamburger—just the two of them. They went shopping and bought a blue sweater that matched Jim's eyes. Suzanne also went with Martha to take him to the airplane when he was leaving. When he boarded the plane, he came back and waved to his family. Suzanne thought to herself that it would be a long time before she would see him again. At that time she was thinking a year, which is certainly long for a young person. Little did she recognize how protracted his absence would be—more than seven years from that fateful day.

Kasler left for San Francisco, on the way to become operations officer of the 354th Tactical Fighter Squadron at Takhli Royal Thai Air Base, Thailand. It would be his third war. Immediately after Jim left, the war escalated—at least, that's how it seemed to the family back home. As a military family, they were very conscious of the war, but the civilian community in Indianapolis was almost totally unaware that anything was going on in Southeast Asia. Other than early rumbles of protest, few expressed interest in the conflict. Of those who did think about Vietnam, most still considered it an honorable action, but that attitude was to change drastically during the years Jim was gone.

Jim learned that the F-105 was to become a "conventional" strategic bomber against North Vietnam. If using a tactical fighter plane as a strategic bomber sounds odd, consider the B-52—a strategic bomber used in tactical strikes in South Vietnam through much of the war. The war in Vietnam led to many unusual adaptations. The one thing the F-105 was not intended to do in Vietnam was intercept MiGs, although 27.5 MiG-17 kills were officially credited to F-105s before the war was done—25 of them using the Gatling gun.

When Jim started flying in Vietnam, right near the demilitarized zone at the Yen Bai military complex, the North Vietnamese had a big ring of heavy antiaircraft guns—probably 100mm types—plus three other minor gun positions. Most Thud pilots were "old heads," but Jim had some young men in his flight, including Fred Flom and Steve Diamond, among others. They all intended to put those guns out of commission permanently.

Jim carried different kinds of bomb loads while flying the F-105 to North Vietnam. On this day in May, because he and his squadron were going after those big antiaircraft guns, they each carried a pair of three-thousand-pound M-118 bombs. They knew their task would not be easy because of massive antiaircraft fire. Oddly enough, Chinese soldiers manned the thousands of guns all over North Vietnam, even though the Chinese and Vietnamese hated each other. The Chinese gunners were brave: they didn't abandon their guns and flee when under attack.

Jim had Steve Diamond on his wing as they rolled in on the gun emplacements. The Chinese were firing like crazy at them. After Jim released his pair of bombs, he rolled up and looked back. Five of those big guns had disappeared and been replaced by a huge crater the three-thousand-pound bombs had made. Other guns were still blazing away as he watched Diamond's bombs hit. Suddenly, the entire gun complex just disappeared. Nothing was left but two huge craters. The other, lesser guns were still firing, however, so the F-105s flew to a higher altitude and then dived straight into them, firing their Gatling guns. When their mission ended, the guns by the demilitarized zone were gone. Kasler and Diamond had knocked them out completely. While returning from Yen Bai, Jim's F-105 was hit through the wing, but he made it back to base after lingering in the area to fly protective cover for other airmen.

The 20mm cannon shells in the Gatling gun may not sound very potent, but a combat load contained a mixture of high-explosive and armor-piercing incendiary projectiles spewing at a rate of one hundred per second. That would shred anything short of tank armor or reinforced concrete. Jim's flight destroyed trucks, barges, buildings, locomotives, and other equipment with the gun. Often, the targets went up in flames, and others simply exploded. Sometimes they would spot trucks turning off the trail to hide under trees, but they couldn't hide from the Gatling gun. Jim believed in expending ordnance on the enemy, so he fired the gun on every mission and never had a jam. In fact, during his ninety-one missions, ordnance malfunctioned only once when three seven-hundred-fifty-pound bombs wouldn't release.

Steve Diamond and Norm Wells were with Jim on July 19, 1966—the day MiG-17s jumped their flight as they were running down Thud Ridge to bomb a bridge north of Hanoi. Suddenly, Norm called "MiGs!" Jim looked back, saw them, and called "Punch 'em off," meaning hit the pickle button to get rid of the bombs so they could fight. Pilots always flew "hot" over North Vietnam. As soon as they left the refueling tanker, they armed their guns. Then they set up their switches to arm the bombs, so they only had to press the pickle button on the stick grip to drop them. That way they could take the bomb racks home with them rather than cleaning everything off the airplane with the "panic button" if they had to get rid of their ordnance in a hurry. It also meant they were set up when they arrived at the target—no last-minute fumbling.

After Jim punched off his bombs, he broke right and spotted the lead MiG as it slid by him. Jim reversed and started to fire, but the MiG got up on him and suddenly zipped away. The next thing Jim knew, the MiG was on his tail. With sixty-five feet of fuselage and less than thirty-five feet of wingspan, Jim's F-105 was no match for the MiG in a turn. He saw Steve Diamond also had a MiG on his tail. Jim rolled around with that MiG-17 for nearly twenty minutes—kicking in the burner, trying to keep up his speed, dropping his leading edge flaps for tighter turning. It was a long, drawn-out engagement. The MiG was shooting continually at him, but Jim managed to stay ahead.

At one point in that long tussle, Jim came around and recognized that he had nearly run into the ground. He jerked back on the stick, looked over his shoulder, and saw the MiG—still on his tail—shudder and then suddenly fly away. Jim wasn't sure if that close scrape unnerved the other pilot or not—he may have been out of ammunition or just low on fuel. At any rate, he seemed to be heading home. Jim called Diamond, his wingman, but received no reply, so he put his Thud in burner and headed for the MiG airfield, intending to intercept the enemy. He spotted the MiG, but the tower at the MiG base also saw Jim and alerted the other pilot. By that time, flak was lacing the sky, so Jim just headed for home.

That incident went into the record books as the longest aerial engagement to date in the war. Meanwhile, Steve Diamond had been shot down. Later, after Jim was shot down, he asked about Steve, but the North Vietnamese said he had a ruptured spleen and died. Whether they were telling the truth or not Jim had no idea, but that's all he ever learned about what happened to a fine young man and a good pilot. After Jim's release, Steve's mother and sister came to see him, but Jim had little to tell them.

Jim's engagement with the MiG illustrates one of the typical constraints pilots had to operate under in Vietnam. All through the war, they had to allow the MiGs to fly out of a base in their bombing lanes when they could have bounced right over Thud Ridge and destroyed the MiG base and everything on the ground. Jim found it incredible that U.S. policy allowed the enemy to shoot down their pilots while essentially protecting that enemy from counterattack. He couldn't imagine what Secretary McNamara and President Johnson were thinking about when they allowed things like that to happen. He observed President Johnson's micromanagement of the war as reflected in his proudly proclaiming, "Those boys can't hit an outhouse without my permission." And McNamara's misdirected actions routinely strapped military forces in Vietnam, a fact he admitted in his book, *In Retrospect: The Tragedy and Lessons of Vietnam*. Jim always wondered why McNamara didn't step down and save the lives of thousands of Americans by turning the job over to someone who would listen to the military experts.

THE HANOI POL STRIKE (JUNE 29, 1966)

Until mid-1966, the U.S. Air Force's aerial bombardment of North Vietnam was restricted to targets of comparatively little importance. These restrictions were the direct result of a notion Secretary of Defense McNamara revealed when he declared, "The targets that are influencing the operations in the South, I submit, are not the power, the oil, the harbor, or the dams. The targets are the roads and the war matériel being moved over the roads." Also, no-strike areas surrounding Hanoi and Haiphong made a virtual sanctuary of these areas. The North Vietnamese were well aware of this sanctuary and took the utmost advantage of it, especially when positioning strategic war matériels.

It became increasingly obvious that destroying targets such as vehicles, roads, small bridges, and river traffic was hardly affecting the Communists' ability to carry the war to the south. In June 1966, Washington decided not only to increase the tempo of air strikes against the North, but also to include targets of greater strategic significance. The first of these targets was the great POL (petroleum, oil, and lubricants) facility located just outside Hanoi.

On the afternoon of June 28, Kasler had just returned from a mission and, after his intelligence debriefing, stopped in at the wing command post. The deputy for operations motioned Jim into his office and told him that his squadron had drawn the lead for the strike against the Hanoi POL storage complex. He also said the wing commander, Col. William H. Holt, would lead the mission. Colonel Holt had asked that Jim finalize the navigation and attack plan and prepare the combat mission folders for the strike. On June 21, when they had first learned of the upcoming strike, they had been directed to identify to Wing Operations the pilots who were to participate, selecting them according to their skill and experience. It was one of the most difficult decisions Jim ever had to make because he considered every pilot in the squadron qualified and knew how disappointed those not selected would be. Two of his most experienced flight commanders, captains Shattuck and Wells, helped him plan the mission.

Planning for air-to-ground combat is the most exacting in the Air Force because this kind of combat is the most dangerous, as the casualty records of World War II, Korea, and Vietnam show. Moreover, low-level navigation at speeds above five hundred knots requires great skill because a one- or two-degree heading error can throw a plane miles wide of its route in just a few minutes. Timing is also essential because each attack element must mesh exactly for an effective mission. Three things are necessary to increase an air-to-ground combat pilot's chances of survival: planning, precisely executing the mission, and luck. Of course, experience and skill in planning and execution can decrease the need for luck.

Jim's team spent six hours planning, checking, and double-checking every facet of the mission. This was their first detailed study of defenses in the Hanoi area, and they found little in the aerial photographs to comfort them. The enemy's air defenses, formidable from the start, were becoming fiercer each day. By every estimate, Hanoi had the greatest concentration of antiaircraft weapons ever assembled. North Vietnam as a whole contained from seven to ten thousand fast-firing antiaircraft weapons of 37mm or larger caliber. In addition, the Russians had built the Vietnamese a sophisticated radar and communication network to detect and coordinate their SAMs and MiG fighters.

Surprise was impossible. For one thing, the Navy's attack fighters were to strike the Haiphong POL complex fifteen minutes before Jim's time over target. For another, the defenses would certainly be alerted in the Hanoi area because aircraft from the 388th Wing would precede their wing's twenty-four aircraft in the attack.

To an outsider, the intelligence planning room resembles a madhouse in a paper factory. Once the mission leader has laid out the route and attack plan, pilots must prepare their own charts. They cut, glue, and then fold the charts accordion-style. They draw routes down the center of the page and tick off time and distance. Each turn requires another chart because the route line must remain centered for ease of navigation.

By midnight, Jim and his team were satisfied with their work and headed for their quarters. Usually, a briefing for the day's first mission occurred between 1:00 and 9:00 A.M., but this one was special. Except for a few selected strikes, involving only a few aircraft, the Hanoi raid was the only one scheduled for Jim's wing on June 29. Their briefing was scheduled for 8:30 A.M., with time over target at 12:10 P.M.

On the morning of the strike, Jim walked into the wing intelligence building at 8:10. General Simler, the deputy for operations of Seventh Air Force, was standing by the door with Colonel Holt.

Simler looked at Jim and said, "Major Kasler, would you like to lead this mission?"

Startled, Jim said, "Yes, sir, I certainly would!"

Simler took from Holt the combat mission folder Jim had prepared for the colonel the previous day and handed it to Jim. Holt didn't look happy.

Jim said, "Sorry about that, Colonel." Apparently, he sounded a bit flippant because Holt muttered something and stalked into the briefing room. Jim hadn't meant for it to come out the way it sounded. He knew how eager Holt was to lead the mission and was sincerely sorry. Every fighter pilot dreams of leading a mission of this importance, but few get the chance.

As it turned out, all the wing commanders whose units were participating in the Hanoi raid—whether for the strike, top cover, or support—had scheduled themselves to lead their wings. But General Moore, commander of Seventh Air Force, issued orders to remove them from the mission. When everyone entered the briefing room, Jim took the mission commander's seat. The briefing officer nearly had a heart attack. He kept motioning that Jim was in the wrong chair until Colonel Holt finally gave him the word.

The general briefing preceding a mission is little more than a refresher of items the pilots have already learned and memorized about the route, tactics, and target defenses. Pilots are most interested in the weather and bombing winds in the target area. The weather for the Hanoi area that day was perfect for fighter-bomber operations. It was forecast as clear with light and variable winds to ten thousand feet. General Simler concluded the briefing with a short talk in which he emphasized the importance of the Hanoi POL complex to the Vietnamese supply lines. He pointed out that it contained 20 percent of North Vietnam's petroleum supplies. He also made it clear that under no circumstances, even if hit, was any pilot to jettison bombs into the city of Hanoi.

Kasler's sister wing, the 388th (based at Korat, Thailand), was to start the attack on the POL complex with eight aircraft. They planned to approach the Communist capital from the south, low behind the screen of high mountains southwest of the city. At the mountains, they would pop up and then dive in low over Hanoi and strike the target.

Jim's wing—the 355th—was to strike from the north. They

planned to cross the Red River one hundred miles northwest of Hanoi, turn east, and descend to low altitude to avoid the SAMs. They intended to run parallel to and north of Thud Ridge, the five-thousand-foot razorback mountain running west to east through the heart of North Vietnam. That ridge had earned its nickname because so many F-105 Thunderchiefs, or Thuds, had been shot down on or near it. The eastern tip of the mountain ends twenty-five miles due north of Hanoi. Jim's unit planned to screen themselves behind the mountain until they reached the eastern tip and then turn ninety degrees south toward Hanoi.

The operations order also directed that all attacks from the 388th and 355th wings had to be carried out on a south-to-north heading to keep from tossing a hung bomb into the city of Hanoi. Approaching from the north, Jim had to do a 180-degree pop-up maneuver in order to strike the target as ordered. The attack order meant that every aircraft would be rolling into the bomb run at nearly the same spot, heading in the same direction. This shooting-gallery approach was an antiaircraft gunner's dream and a fighter pilot's nightmare. To protect civilian populations, however, such orders were commonplace in Vietnam until the very end of the war. Of course, pilots want attacks on divergent headings to confuse the gunners and, thus, keep them from zeroing in on one predictable spot.

Each aircraft carried eight seven-hundred-fifty-pound bombs—six on the centerline multiple ejector rack and one on each outboard pylon. In Jim's final briefing, just before the pilots headed for their aircraft, he had directed split-second delayed fusing for each bomb on the outboard stations (see fig. 13). With an instantaneous setting, a near miss with those bombs would still set shrapnel flying among the fuel-storage tanks, thus increasing their chance of destroying the target.

The crew chief greeted Jim as he stepped from his pickup truck and walked around the aircraft with him on the preflight inspection. Jim told him, "If I give you the abort signal after I start the engine, get the ladder back up immediately because I'm heading for the ground spare."

The crew chief said, "Major Kasler, my assistant and I have spent the last nine hours checking every system on this airplane. You're not going to abort." The crew chief was right, and his confidence came from experience. In fact, most pilots say they have never found more dedicated or experienced airmen than those who worked on their aircraft during the Vietnam War. After Jim started to receive publicity, he always told newsmen his missions began and ended with the crew—he couldn't fly without them. For ninety-one missions in Vietnam, Jim had no aborts and only one minor armament problem—a fantastic achievement.

Jim's group started their engines and taxied to the marshaling area at the end of the runway, where the maintenance crews inspected the aircraft and pulled safety pins. They then lined up on the runway and were cleared for takeoff. Their takeoff weight pushed fifty-one thousand pounds—the maximum gross weight for the F-105 Thunderchief. In the hot Thailand summer, taking off this heavy meant a long ground roll and a lift-off speed of 235 knots. Jim breathed a sigh of relief when his landing gear was in the well, not because he was concerned about the heavy takeoff, but because 95 percent of aborts occurred on the ground. Now he was airborne with a perfectly functioning aircraft, leading the biggest mission of the Vietnam War to that date.

As the rest of the flight slid into position, Jim completed a slow turn to the north and contacted his radar site. They gave him a bearing to the refueling tankers, two hundred fifty nautical miles to the north. Approaching the tankers, he could see an ominous row of thunderstorms stretched across the horizon to the north. Obviously, the tankers weren't going to be able to maintain their refueling route as briefed. Although fighters can refuel and even join up in thin cirrus clouds, heavy cumulus clouds make refueling impossible because of turbulence and poor visibility. They began taking on fuel, but the tankers couldn't maintain their track because of the thunderstorms. Ten minutes before their drop-off time, the tanker lead said he had to turn back because he could not fly around the storms ahead. All the F-105s had refueled, but they weren't able to cycle through again to top off as planned.

Jim rejoined his flight in close formation, flicked on his radar, and picked his way between the thunderstorm cells. He was sixty miles southeast of his desired point of departure when he left the tankers. His timing had to be exact, so he had selected a prominent river junction in Laos as his starting checkpoint. As luck would have it, Jim's flight broke out at a small hole in the clouds, directly over the point of departure. He was three minutes ahead of schedule, so he made a 360-degree tight turn to use up time before setting course to the north.

Jim immediately reentered clouds, and when he next broke out after twenty minutes, he was directly over the Red River northwest of Yen Bai. His Doppler radar was working perfectly, and he was directly on course and on time. He turned right and began descending through several layers of clouds. Vietnam north of Thud Ridge was covered with ground fog. He dropped to three hundred feet, which was just above the fog bank. At higher altitudes, SAMs had a nasty way of suddenly popping up through clouds at an unsuspecting pilot, but at three hundred feet he was fairly safe.

Kasler's flight was skimming along the base of Thud Ridge, which towered above them to the right. As they approached its eastern tip, their external fuel tanks showed empty, so Jim ordered them jettisoned. He could hear Lt. Col. James Hopkins, leader of the 388th, departing the Hanoi target area, so he asked him about the weather. Hopkins said, "It's clear in the target area, but MiGs are airborne." Looking far to the east, Jim could see smoke rising from the POL tanks at Haiphong, which the Navy fighters had already struck.

When Jim passed the initial point at the end of Thud Ridge, he called the flight to push it up and started a turn south toward Hanoi. As he turned, the fog bank faded away beneath him and his flight broke into the clear. At that same instant, flak began bursting around them. Jim glanced to the right toward Phuc Yen airfield and could see the flak guns blinking at them. With Jim's flight running only three hundred feet above the ground, the Vietnamese had leveled their heavy 85mm and 100mm guns and were firing almost horizontally. This meant the shells were killing their own people as they struck the ground, reflecting how important the POL plant was to their war effort.

Jim's flight was running parallel to the northeast railroad that leads into the city of Hanoi. It was North Vietnam's most important supply link with the People's Republic of China, so flak guns of every caliber and description protected it. Ahead, Jim could see two gray smoke columns rising, one on each side of the Hanoi POL field that the 388th Wing had just struck. But they hadn't hit a major fuel tank. The sky was dotted with hundreds of white, gray, and black puffs—the remaining traces of flak shells that had been fired at the departing Korat aircraft. Thus, Jim had a good idea of what was awaiting him over the target.

Jim approached slightly left of target, called for afterburner, and began his pull-up. He climbed through eight thousand feet and started a slow turn to the right until he reached his roll-in point near eleven thousand feet. He cut his afterburner, dropped dive brakes, and rolled into the bomb run. As he was turning in, he could see three ten-gun, 85mm batteries on the Gia Lam airfield frantically firing at him and his flight. Ignoring them as much as he could, Jim continued his run. He could hardly believe his eyes— big, fat fuel tanks filled his view. He pushed his pickle button and made a rolling pullout to the right. When he cleared the smoke, he turned gently to the left around the target complex. The huge fuel tanks were erupting one after another, sending up immense billowing fireballs.

By the time Jim had circled to the target's southwest corner, each of his flight members had also made the bomb run and rejoined him. The smoke now merged into one huge, boiling, red-and-black pillar—an unbelievable sight. As Jim circled back, he could see flames leaping out of the smoke thousands of feet above him. He swung around to the north toward Phuc Yen airfield. He had seen two MiGs on the end of the runway when they began their dash toward Hanoi and had thought he might get a shot if either got into the air. (One of the many rules of engagement in Vietnam forbade attacking a MiG unless it was fully airborne.) But Jim changed his mind about looking for MiGs when he saw the intensity of the flak bursting around them. He banked his Thunderchief to the south and looked at the ground; so many guns were firing, the valley reminded Jim of a desert city viewed from the air at night. But it was daylight, and those winking "lights" were thousands of shots fired at them in anger.

After Jim crossed south of the Red River, the flak diminished as the gunners apparently switched their attention to the fighter-bombers behind his flight. He headed west, searching the roads for targets of opportunity. As he approached Hoa Binh on the Black River, he noticed a new road had been cut up the side of a high plateau that extended east back toward Hanoi. He popped over the rim of the plateau and dropped his nose to investigate. There, directly under his gun sight pipper, was a truck. He squeezed the trigger, and 20mm cannon projectiles tore into the truck, setting it on fire. Jim and his flight found twenty-five trucks on the plateau. They set twelve on fire and damaged at least six others. Apparently, the Vietnamese were floating supplies from China down the Black River on rafts to Hoa Binh, transferring them to trucks, and moving them across the plateau to Hanoi.

As Jim pulled out of one of his strafing passes, he looked back at Hanoi thirty-five miles to the east. It was a windless day, so the black smoke formed a perfect pillar reaching above thirty-five thousand feet. By now their fuel was running low, forcing them to return to base. Because they didn't have enough fuel to reach Takhli, Jim planned a recovery at Ubon if they couldn't get fuel from the airborne tankers. Looking back toward Hanoi again, Jim could still see the smoke column more than one hundred fifty miles away. When the ground control intercept (GCI) controller found a KC-135 tanker, the flight refueled over the Mekong Delta and headed for home (see fig. 14).

General Simler and Colonel Holt heartily congratulated Jim for planning and leading one of the most successful air-strike missions of the Vietnam War (see fig. 15). The F-105s destroyed more than 90 percent of the POL complex. In fact, it was one of the few targets in North Vietnam that never required a restrike because the Vietnamese abandoned the facility altogether. Amazingly, flak brought down only one of the strike's aircraft; the pilot, Neal Jones, was held in North Vietnam until February 1973. Three aircraft suffered battle damage, and one pilot had minor wounds.

The absence of North Vietnamese MiGs and SAMs puzzled Jim, although he was glad they didn't participate. MiGs engaged only one flight of SAM-suppression aircraft (Wild Weasels) and slightly damaged only one F-105. In a brief aerial battle, Fred Tracy was credited with the first MiG kill by an F-105 pilot. Compared to the first Ploesti oil raid during World War II, when German Me-109 pilots flew through their own flak to get at the B-24s, the North Vietnamese MiG pilots were far less adventurous.

A larger puzzle was why the Vietnamese had not fired any of the dozens of SAM missile batteries that rimmed Hanoi. On the day following the raid, they began firing SAMs in volleys at strike aircraft—a complete change in tactics. Jim wouldn't learn the answer to this question until two months later, after the North Vietnamese had shot him down and captured him. Considering the price he had to pay for this knowledge, he would gladly have remained ignorant forever.

Jim also learned later that the POL raid had a regrettable effect: it incited the Vietnamese to make some major changes in their camps for POWs. A few days after the raid came the famed "Hanoi march." The prisoners who could walk were marched through downtown Hanoi and subjected to brutal treatment by civilians. Following the march, many of the men were chained to trees in the camp. At this time, the systematic torture of POWs for propaganda began; it was to continue with little respite for three and a half years.

Although the F-105s had not faced MiGs or SAMs, the Hanoi POL strike was a supreme feat of courage, fortitude, and airmanship. The pilots who participated in the raid believed at the time that it was a major step toward shortening the war. Despite an almost perfectly conceived and executed mission, however, supplies of POL to the North Vietnamese slowed very little because Soviet tankers continued to discharge fuel supplies at Haiphong Harbor until 1972. Had the port been closed and had the fighter-bombers and B-52s been used together against strategic targets in 1966 (as they were later), the United States might very well have avoided the agonizing years of war that followed. Instead, the B-52s often participated in highly questionable missions in the south, such as carpet-bombing to clear the forest. These missions won no friends among the South Vietnamese, who were supposed to be allies, and they were ultimately ineffective.

TRUCKS, TRAINS, BRIDGES, AND SAMPANS

Kasler hoped the POL strike signaled a change in the U.S. policy of declaring military targets around Hanoi off limits. That's where all the North Vietnamese forces were concentrated and where the MiG base was. In fact, he made known his views about striking proper targets in a newspaper interview after the strike. Unfortunately, no one listened because Jim and his wing mates never seemed to get targets of much importance. Jim figured either the

United States's intelligence system in Vietnam was not very good or the White House had a stranglehold on the intelligence community and wouldn't let them do their jobs. His "frags"—orders for targets to be hit—usually said such things as "bomb road" or "bomb approach to bridge."

At the same time, Vietnam did have many small targets because the enemy moved war matériel by any means possible: trucks, trains, barges, sampans, and even bicycles. On every mission Jim flew north, he tried to hit any mode of transportation he saw. He dropped bombs on primary targets, such as roads and bridges, then used the Gatling gun during armed reconnaissance to hit anything important.

In Route Package 1 (Jim's bombing area) the Mu Gia Pass was one of those places Jim believed they should have closed and kept closed. It was a pinch point through which a tremendous amount of war supplies passed. They hit it whenever possible, but it never seemed to be their primary target. Near the Mu Gia Pass is a river called the Nguon Nay (which seems to have a different name on current maps). Jim popped out of the clouds one day and spotted typical-looking sampans being loaded to cross the river. He could see supplies stacked along the bank, so he shot up several of them. He often went after sampans because he knew they were moving war matériels.

The North Vietnamese complained about Jim's wing shooting at the boats, arguing that poor peasants used them to earn a living. Of course, it was propaganda. The North Vietnamese knew of the restrictions placed on F-105 missions and used that knowledge against them. They parked military trucks in towns and villages because they knew the F-105s wouldn't hit a village. They strung antiaircraft gun emplacements along dikes because the pilots weren't allowed to bomb the dikes. Hospital roofs often bristled with antiaircraft guns. They also claimed Americans bombed villages, churches, schools, hospitals, and dikes when they didn't.

Jim found a truck park next to the river where sampans were ferrying supplies. He could see the paths leading into the woods, so he dropped down to thirty feet and found a truck under the trees. When he strafed the truck, it blew up, indicating it was carrying a load of fuel. A couple of weeks later, he followed a set of railroad tracks in that same area running to a trestle bridge. Men were sitting on top of the bridge, rebuilding it, which made no sense to Jim because the rails seemed to end at the river. He thought, *With the ocean so close by, why would they send trains down there?* Still, he dutifully reported his sightings.

Every time Jim popped in there, he saw those sampans ferrying again. Right across the river truck tracks led into a forested area. Obviously, it was a truck park. They were coming up from the south into the truck park, then off-loading into the sampans to ferry supplies across the river. There was one big truck park just south of the river and another west of the Mu Gia Pass. This was a better route than the Ho Chi Minh Trail, especially in the rainy season when the roads turned to mud.

After Jim had hit the sampans a number of times, they changed their pattern. Radar showed a ship, probably their command center, tied up in the middle of the river with another boat tied up on the other side. A large building nearby probably housed their professionals. Jim reported these details but couldn't get the intelligence people to understand what the enemy was doing. He was deeply disappointed, convinced that they should have cleaned up the whole area with B-52s—the truck park and the Mu Gia Pass. They should have closed it and kept it closed. In the same way, Jim was certain the United States should have mined Haiphong Harbor and closed it years before they did. Most of North Vietnam's supplies were coming into port by ship and being off-loaded onto trucks and trains.

Later, when the Vietnamese moved twenty sampans and tied them up in the middle of the river, Jim looked at railroad tracks and saw the rails, which had been rusty, were now shiny—a sure sign of recent use. He followed the rails to a huge drop-off, where they circled around a mountain down into a valley. He found a train sitting in the valley and hit it. Evidently, they had dropped off supplies that night and were headed back to pick up more from the sampans. Of course, Jim thought, they wouldn't have anything to pick up if intelligence followed his advice because the F-105s would have gotten rid of every sampan in their coverage areas.

Up near Yen Bai, Jim found huge barges being used to float supplies down the Red River from China. He and other pilots saw four or five of them every time they went up there, all loaded with supplies. Also, two rail lines came down from China—one in the east and one in the western part of North Vietnam. Another hot spot that should have been a target was an old navy yard in their area that disguised gun emplacements. To see so many targets disregarded was tough on Jim and the others—especially the commanders who had to send pilots into danger. They were certain allowing sampans and trains to operate prolonged the war. At the same time, ignoring gun emplacements put them directly at risk. For example, Lew Shattuck, one of Jim's buddies from earlier duty stations, was shot down over the old navy yard. The gunner who got him seemed to have a 23mm gun like the ones old MiGs used, and he fired tracers. (Shattuck bailed out and was rescued, but later he was shot down again over North Vietnam and taken prisoner.)

The pilots reported these activities, but nobody paid attention. Many (Kasler included) believed they could have run the war better from the fighter base at Takhli by just letting pilots decide which targets to hit. Instead, Jim observed, three-piece suits in Washington were running the war without taking much advice from the military. He found it a shame—a tragic waste of lives. At first, the F-105 wings had experienced pilots who could overcome many of the dangerous restrictions through skill and experience. Toward the end of the war, however, they had to bring in pilots who didn't have enough training, sometimes even from cargo airplanes and bombers, to fill fighter seats. With limited knowledge of fighter airplanes and operations, they suffered much higher losses.

CHAPTER 8

Shoot-Down and Capture

ON August 8, 1966, forty-year-old James Kasler took off from Takhli Royal Thai Air Base on his ninety-first mission, including seventy-five over North Vietnam and sixteen over Laos. He was already the stuff of legends: an eighteen-year-old B-29 tail gunner over Japan in World War II, a Korean War jet ace with six MiGs to his official credit, and now—many believed—the premier F-105 attack pilot in Southeast Asia. One of his wingmen had dubbed him the "one-man air force" in a *Time* magazine interview published on that very day. Kasler's fellow fliers admired him especially for his phenomenal vision and his aggressiveness. He could roll over a target zone and see twenty things other pilots didn't see. His Hoosier voice would come in on the radio, saying, "Did you see the glint off that ack-ack barrel and the two trucks parked in the trees? There's a bunker down there, too." Then he would demolish with cannon fire or bombs everything he had seen.

Jim's squadron mates called him "the Destroyer" because he always expended all ordnance against the enemy on each mission, including 1,029 rounds of 20mm shells from the Gatling gun. It had accounted for many of his flight of four's 219 buildings, 66 barges, 53 railroad cars, 44 trucks, 36 fuel tanks, 28 bridges, and 16 flak sites damaged or destroyed—a record-setting performance in air-to-ground combat for the Vietnam War. For the strike he led against Hanoi's POL plant in June 1966, Jim had won the Air Force Cross, the Air Force's highest decoration for valor.

103

Jim's August 8 mission was against a cluster of warehouses in the Hoang Nhi barracks area. This warehouse target in Route Package 5, about fifty-five miles northwest of Hanoi, was heavily defended by an array of antiaircraft guns. He knew the dangers well: on four previous missions he had limped home with battle damage, including a shell-shattered canopy. Otherwise, the mission didn't seem unusually challenging. They were to evaluate the effectiveness of low-level delivery of ordnance on this strike. The flight of four included captains Wells and Ayers, Lieutenant Flom, and Jim as mission leader. Things were going well. They came in at two hundred feet off the deck and hit the target with cluster bombs. They could see their hits on the supply depot, which were good. So Jim decided to put the rest of the cluster bombs on another supply area down the river, just a little east of Binh Bay.

When Jim's flight arrived at the target, a little cumulus cloud was lying right over the target area, so he started to turn out. But for some reason the flight seemed to have closed too quickly on him, and as he banked up to abort his run, he saw a 37mm projectile go right into the belly of his wingman Fred Flom's aircraft. Flom was only about two hundred feet above the ground at the time because it was another intended low-level strike. The belly of his aircraft immediately began smoking, and yellow and red flames were flaring out of it. Jim told Flom to turn out 240 degrees and head for the Red River. Then he rolled up over Flom and fell in behind him to take a closer look.

They began climbing to gain a little altitude and had gone only a few miles when Jim knew Flom's airplane was going to blow up. He had seen these symptoms before in battle-damaged F-105s. Jim yelled for Flom to eject several times before he finally did. He was doing about five hundred fifty knots at one thousand feet above ground level when his canopy came off. The airplane started to roll to the right. When it reached about ninety degrees from vertical, Flom ejected. The seat had barely cleared the cockpit when his airplane exploded in a fireball. His chute opened immediately, and Jim saw a chunk of metal fly through the parachute canopy. Jim was only about fifteen hundred feet behind and could see Flom was unconscious, hanging in the chute harness. The blast had knocked him out. Unfortunately, he landed limp in his chute, right on a roadway near a village.

The flight circled until Flom landed. Jim called for a rescue combat air patrol (rescap) and made two passes to keep the heat off Flom and give him a chance to escape, but he was low on fuel. By this time he had already jettisoned his drop tanks. He collected his flight and headed south of the Red River to a refueling tanker. Frankly, Jim didn't think recovery was likely north of the Red River and so close to a village.

Jim's flight had refueled and expected to go home, but they received a call to support Flom's rescap. They flew back to the shoot-down site as quickly as possible. Jim located the spot on the road where Flom had landed, but he wasn't there. Apparently, he had already been captured. Flak began exploding near him, so Jim headed northwest to get out of it. He saw two guns firing at him—*fifty-seven millimeter*, he thought. He broke right to evade the cannon shells, but should have gone left because he took solid hits. Still, he had been hit hard before and was able to go on with the mission. He hadn't lost an F-105 in ninety missions, and he wasn't about to give up on this one, especially not deep in enemy territory.

Wells and Ayers were with Jim as he headed south across the Red River. But the cockpit immediately filled with thick smoke, and he knew he was in trouble. His first impulse was to blow the canopy to clear the smoke in the cockpit. He had to be able to see. But he couldn't locate the auxiliary canopy jettison handle on the left console, so he used the ejection-seat handle to jettison the canopy. When the canopy blew off, the smoke cleared, but he had other problems. He was fifteen miles south of the Red River and had regained some altitude when his controls started running away from him. The engine was losing power, and the stick was not responding well. He knew the hydraulic system had been hit. Thunderchiefs at that time had not been modified with a backup hydraulic system—nor did they have a system to stabilize flight if hydraulic fluid gushed out. Jim was losing control.

Despite his best efforts, the F-105 rolled uncontrollably toward the ground. It was time to get out while he had a little altitude left. The stick was walking around as he reached for the ejection handles, and it migrated over onto his right thigh and locked there. Jim knew what that would mean when he fired the ejection seat, but he had no choice. When it fired, the stick deflected his right knee into the canopy rail, snapping his right femur just above the knee and splintering it near the hip. The thighbone jammed up through the groin area into his abdomen like a splintered spear and stayed there.

As soon as Jim came out of the airplane, the pain was horrendous. When his chute opened, he looked down and could see a lump on his abdomen, waist-high above his g-suit. That was the upper end of his femur. His right leg was hanging with no thighbone to support it. He reached into his survival vest and pulled out his emergency radio to call the other members of his flight, but he was so woozy from pain that he just put the radio back in his vest next to his chest.

Jim had punched out near seven thousand feet; when he had descended to one thousand feet, his vision started to clear. He could see he was coming down in an area of large rice fields—in open country. But as bad luck would have it, he drifted and fell in a little wooded area. Had he come down in the open, Ayers and Wells might have kept the Vietnamese off him with their Gatling guns until a rescue helicopter arrived. The A-1 Sandies were already en route because of the rescap called for Fred Flom.

When Jim landed, his right leg collapsed under him. He wasn't feeling much by then, until he struck the ground. In his foggy condition he hadn't released his survival pack, so it remained on his back. He lay on top of his right leg, which was twisted underneath him. Still, he managed to pull back away from the survival kit, unhook all his equipment, and get his leg straightened out in front of him. Then he pulled out his radio and called Ayers and Wells, the remaining two members of his flight. "Right leg badly broken," he said. "Alert the rescue team. I'll come back on the air on the hour."

It was then 9:40 A.M. His flight mates were orbiting two thousand to three thousand feet above Jim when he called, and no flak was in the area to bother them. "Rescue team inbound," they said, adding that the Jolly Greens and A-1s were on their way because of Flom's shoot-down.

Jim thought he would have a better chance of being rescued if he could drag himself out onto a dike in the rice paddies—into the open. But when he tried, he couldn't crawl because of the dense underbrush and his shattered right leg, which kept getting tangled up. It was a hindrance—worse than useless. He finally gave up on crawling into the open, deciding instead to stay put and wait for help. He took the .38-caliber revolver out of his survival vest, cocked it, and put it underneath a little bush next to him. *If the Vietnamese are going to start whacking on me,* he thought, *I'll take some of them with me.*

About twenty minutes passed. It was a few minutes before 10:00 A.M., so Jim decided to call Wells again. As he picked up his radio, he heard clicking all around him, and he knew the Vietnamese were nearby in the forest. The clicking sounded like bamboo sticks knocked together—signals, apparently. Suddenly, a Vietnamese with a big machete jumped out in front of Jim, right at his feet, with a blood-curdling scream. He was wearing only a loincloth, and he had the machete raised as though he were going to hack Jim to pieces. Jim grabbed for his revolver, but fifteen or so other Vietnamese—men and women—jumped out all around him, grabbed him, and started tearing off his clothes. *Apparently*, Jim thought, *they've never seen a zipper and don't know how to use one.* Instead of untying his boots, they broke the laces to get them off. They ripped off his g-suit, flying suit, and boots. Then they tore the watch off of his arm. He was down to his undershorts, wondering if they were going to strip him naked.

With his clothes off, Jim could look at his right thigh. The area from his knee to his groin was nearly flat because it lacked bone to support the muscles. Later he learned the top end of his broken femur was splayed out like fingers on a hand where it jammed into his intestines. Why that didn't sever an artery or some major blood vessel Jim didn't know. If those sharp, splintered bone ends had punctured his intestines, he would have died of peritonitis because the Vietnamese never opened his abdomen to check for punctures. He was extremely lucky on that score—if one can consider it lucky to be captured, nearly crippled for life, and suffering tremendous pain.

The Vietnamese who captured Jim were all civilians. *Only one seemed to have a rifle—an old Enfield,* Jim thought. Most of them carried machetes or knives as weapons. They were poorly dressed in ragged, heavily worn clothing, obviously living in poverty. When they saw the condition of Jim's leg, they sent for a medic. The technician appeared suddenly, wearing trousers and a white jacket, and he carried a medical kit in a little wooden box. He looked at

Jim's right leg and gave him a shot in the left one—probably a painkiller. Then he yelled directions in Vietnamese. Some of the others went to cut a small bamboo palm trunk to use as a splint for Jim's leg. They split the bamboo palm down the middle, padded his leg with moss, and then wrapped the splint with vines.

The Vietnamese brought what looked like a fishnet, put Jim in it, and ran a bamboo pole through it. They picked him up and started running one hundred feet or so across a little dike through the rice paddies to a road. Woods lined both sides of the road, and as they started up it, the A-1 rescue planes flew in at one to two hundred feet, circling, looking for Jim. But his captors threw him in a ditch and placed a large banana palm leaf over him to keep him hidden. It was blisteringly hot, so he was thirsty and miserable. Although the A-1s circled for about forty-five minutes, he knew there was no hope of a rescue. He just wanted the planes to go away so the Vietnamese would remove the palm leaf. When the planes finally left, the Vietnamese lifted the leaf, gave Jim a drink of tea, and began carrying him toward their compound. He wanted to pass out because of the excruciating pain, but he remained conscious throughout the journey.

By this time, Wells and Ayres had run low on fuel again and departed to refuel. When they returned, the Vietnamese had already carried Jim away. Nearly fifty aircraft were involved in the attempted rescue, which went on for hours. Wells and Ayres each flew nearly nine hours that day trying to find him and Fred Flom. Both received the Distinguished Flying Cross for their efforts, which, regrettably, were unsuccessful.

When the Vietnamese arrived at their village compound, they took Jim to a large pavilion-type building made of bamboo. It was thirty by sixty feet, with a dirt floor and without electricity or other modern conveniences. They carried their water from a stream and, apparently, cooked in a corner of the one-room hut, which housed thirty or more of them.

The people seemed friendly before the militia arrived. They laid Jim out on a wide board, elevated above the ground. When he asked for a drink, they brought him water they had boiled in a little teapot. A couple of the young men came up and pretended to wrestle with him. They were smoking bamboo pipes by sucking on one end of the bamboo. Everyone went for a siesta about noon in an upstairs shaded area of the building, formed by planks that lay across half the roof. Later in the afternoon, though, four armed militiamen arrived in an old one-and-a-half-ton flatbed truck. The people who had been friendly suddenly cooled off and wouldn't come near Jim anymore. Meanwhile, a medic came to give him another shot. Jim assumed it was pain medicine, but he wasn't feeling well.

The militiamen tied Jim tight to the board and put him on their flatbed truck, then covered him with branches to hide him. When they started off down a bumpy road, his head was banging hard against the board. He couldn't hold it up. The guards seemed to recognize the problem because they stopped after two hundred yards and cut him loose from the board. For some reason Jim couldn't understand, they also cut the splint off of his leg and threw it off of the truck. They grabbed him by the shoulders, pulled him up against the back of the cab of the truck, tied his elbows together, and placed more leaves over him.

Two of the guards were in the cab and two were on the flatbed with Jim. One of them tickled his face from time to time with a leafy branch. Now and then he'd reach down and slap Jim in the face with his hand. The guard seemed to enjoy harassing him, but Jim was in so much pain from his leg that it didn't matter. Two or three times they had to pull up under trees and hide him because planes were flying overhead.

By the time they reached the Red River, it was dark, so they stopped at a town. They had Jim blindfolded with gauze wrapped around his face. He could hear a crowd coming and speakers going. One of the guards on the truck began yelling, and Jim could hear people running. They jumped up on the truck and started beating him—throwing rocks and mud at him—for about fifteen minutes. Then he heard a police whistle blow. Everybody cleared away, but the guard who had been tormenting Jim in the truck slapped him in the mouth twice.

Finally, they boarded a ferry to cross a river. The water was smooth, so Jim had a few minutes of relief. He knew they were getting near Binh Bay because he could hear the switch engines working in the rail yard. They departed the ferry on the other side of the river and drove through four more villages. In each village, they put Jim through the same routine, allowing the people to vent their anger by beating and stoning him. Besides his serious injuries from the shoot-down, he was collecting a lot of bruises.

At 1:00 or 2:00 A.M., they pulled up into the mountains. They ran the truck into a little culvert with water in it and couldn't get across, so they had to get out and push the truck backward up the road. At that point, they stopped and pulled Jim off of the flatbed. His leg simply fell, having nothing to support it. Remarkably, the sharp ends of broken bone that protruded into his abdomen didn't puncture an artery.

The Vietnamese pulled Jim into a six-foot-square bamboo shack and laid him on something that looked like an old door. It was about 2.5 feet wide by 5.5 feet long. The shack had a bamboo front door built similarly to the portable blackboard stands used in schools. It covered the shack's entire front side, but Jim was there only a few minutes when they moved it away. They brought a table, set it in front of the shack, and put a Coleman lantern on the table. Ten of them set chairs around the table, and fifteen others gathered around Jim or nearby. Then they started interrogating him to get his name, rank, and serial number. They kept asking, "Who are you flying with? What squadron?"

Jim gave them his name, rank, and serial number twice, but refused to answer any other questions. They motioned to a fellow who ran around the side of the table and beat Jim in the face with his fist. They wanted to know his unit's name. Because all his patches were on his flying suit, he thought he could tell them that if he had to. They also had his wallet. He had forgotten to remove his post exchange ration card with Takhli Air Base on it, so they had that information as well. They asked who his commander was, but he refused to answer. They beat him again, so he gave them the name of his previous squadron commander, who had already gone home to the United States. Jim was determined from the first not to give them anything useful.

The interrogators asked Jim what kind of mission he was on. "Just bombing a supply area," he said. But they pounced on him and said he was dropping bombs on civilians.

Jim said, "No, I wasn't."

They kept asking, "What kind of mission were you on? What is tomorrow's mission?"

He told the truth: "I have no idea. We don't have that information." They continued for an hour or so, but Jim wasn't pleasing them much. They stunned him once with a punch that probably cracked his nose—a bone chip worked out of it four or five weeks later.

After they'd beaten Jim four or five times, one man suddenly came up the road and handed a note across to the main interrogator. The interrogator said, "Hanoi says you are a brigade commander."

Jim said, "No, I am an operations officer for my squadron."

So the interrogator read the note and told him again, "No, Hanoi says you are a brigade commander."

Jim said, "You can see my rank: I am a major in the Air Force. There is no such rank as brigade commander in the U.S. Air Force." That ended the conversation because Hanoi apparently had found out who he was from the *Time* magazine article that had come out the day before with his interview in it. They stopped the interrogation and went away, leaving two guards in front of the shack.

During the night the guards were talking, and Jim must have been delirious or suffering hallucinations, for he thought they were talking about beheading him. He doubted the Vietnamese guards spoke English, and he certainly couldn't understand Vietnamese. Only the chief interrogator had spoken English to him. The next morning, as Jim was lying in the shack, he could hear a grinding wheel right outside. They were sharpening machetes. Jim thought, *Well, you are about to lose your head. Just like those bomber crew members the Japanese captured in World War II.* Through a crack in the door, he could see them spreading leaves they had cut on the dirt road in front of him.

A few minutes later, Jim saw twenty-five or so Vietnamese coming up the road, carrying cameras—old box cameras of designs he had never seen before. He figured this was going to be the best-recorded beheading in history. Someone pulled the portable door away. The commander, another English speaker, came up to Jim.

"How old are you?" he asked.

Jim said, "Forty." The commander handed him a cigarette and lit it.

"Are you going to kill me right now?" Jim asked. But the commander just looked at him, turned around, and walked away.

Four men picked up the door with Jim on it and carried it out onto the road. While he lay there, the Vietnamese were edging around behind him. Everyone seemed to have a hand behind his back. Jim looked around, trying to determine which person had the machete—which one was going to kill him. He kept glancing around until the commander finally figured out what he was doing, chased some of the people off, and made them all come out in front of him.

They put a pith helmet on a girl in uniform who was eighteen or nineteen years old and all of four feet tall. Then they gave her a rifle with a bayonet on it. She held the bayonet down by Jim's ear, and they all took pictures (see fig. 16). They were obviously staging a picture-taking session. Jim was to become very familiar with this propaganda method during his years in captivity. They dragged him over and put the top half of his flying suit on him, though it was badly torn from the way they had ripped it off. Then they put his survival vest on, but the vest was empty because they had stripped everything from it.

Right behind the shack was the wreck of an old airplane, probably French. They put Jim on the leaves in front of this wreckage, then brought out two chairs. Two men sat down with pads and pencils, pretending they were interrogating him while everyone took pictures. Once the picture taking was over, they put Jim back in the shack until 10:00 P.M. A man showed up with a little bowl of rice, a similar bowl of coarse sugar, and a cup of hot water that was brownish-colored from the tea they put in it. Jim took them but couldn't eat anything. He drank a little water.

"You eat," the man said.

Jim replied, "I don't want any."

So the man took the sugar, dumped it into the hot water, stirred the mixture, and made him drink it. He seemed to understand that Jim needed some kind of sustenance to survive.

The simplest bodily functions became a challenge for the seriously wounded flyer. Later that night, he was lying on his back and had to urinate. Of course, he couldn't move anything, and he was trying to figure out what to do. Finally, he called the guard and told him he had to go. The guard understood no English, so he just held up his hands as if to say, what am I supposed to do? Jim pointed to the bamboo and said the word. Somehow the guard got the message and cut him a chunk of bamboo to serve as a relief tube. Jim filled it and tossed it over the side of the shack.

Late the following afternoon, a medic showed up. He looked at Jim and gave him a shot for pain. He sent the guards into the woods for bamboo to make another splint for Jim's leg. Again they used moss to pad it and vines to tie it together. He had a notepad and wrote out the word "Hanoi" and the figure "5" beside it. Then he motioned as though driving a vehicle. Jim assumed the medic was telling him he was headed for Hanoi and that the trip would take five hours. It actually took eight.

That night they put Jim in a jeep-style vehicle with a bed that wasn't big enough to stretch out in. They dragged him up against the back of the cab, tied his elbows together, and blindfolded him. They had thrown shrapnel in the bottom of the truck bed, so he had a miserable ride to Hanoi, lying on the metal shards. Again hate rallies occurred during stops at four or five villages. Jim was smacked by people in the villages and punched by the guard who had hit him earlier. He was in misery, hoping he would pass out, but that never happened.

They approached Hanoi about 3:00 A.M. and drove up to what sounded like a cabaret because a lot of music and noise came from the building. The guards stopped and went in. Soon, one came out and untied Jim's hands, although he didn't take off the blindfold. Then he shoved a bowl up to Jim's mouth. Jim took it and started drinking, surprised to discover it was beer. Although most of his treatment was physically and mentally punishing, occasional "kindnesses" occurred without apparent motivation.

HOA LO PRISON: THE HANOI HILTON

Shortly after Kasler had his bowl of beer, they took off for Hanoi again. About an hour later, they arrived at what Jim later recognized as the Hoa Lo prison in downtown Hanoi, a place ironically known to POWs as the "Hanoi Hilton," but the name translated more accurately into English as the "fiery furnace." The entrance had an arch-shaped double door with a double iron gate on the outside, just wide enough for a small truck to drive through, but not a one-and-a-half-ton truck or anything of similar size. This gate was the beginning of a series of heavy iron gates that sealed shut as one proceeded to the inner prison. Thick concrete walls, fifteen to twenty feet high, surrounded the prison compound, which took up a trapezoidal block at the city's center. The Vietnamese had divided it into four areas that the POWs would name "Heartbreak Hotel," "New Guy Village," "Little Vegas," and "Camp Unity" (opened late in 1970). It was a formidable, heavily guarded fortress from which escape was virtually impossible—especially for wounded, beaten POWs on near-starvation diets.

The guards took Jim into room eighteen, an area about twenty-five by thirty feet that was in a corner of the Heartbreak section just outside New Guy Village. The POWs called it the "Green Room" because of the green paint on its interior walls. The Vietnamese dumped Jim on the floor on a collapsible stretcher. After a while, two men walked in. Jim dubbed one "the Commander" and the other "the Wheel." (About a month later they both disappeared from the prison system.) One spoke English fairly well. Both marched past him and sat down at a table nearly twenty feet away from him. They addressed Jim as "Kasler" and asked him a few basic questions. Then they told him he was going to have to confess his crimes against the Vietnamese people. Jim said, "Negative. I'm not doing that. I have committed no crimes, and I'm not doing anything."

They came over and threatened Jim: "If you know what's good for you, you'll cooperate. You're in our hands now. Do what we tell you, or else." They also said, menacingly, "You're very sick. If you want to live, you'd better cooperate."

Jim said, "I'd rather die first. I'm not going to do anything for you." They both walked out.

A bit later, the Commander came back and threw a big stack of papers on Jim's lap—twenty or more letters they had forced other prisoners to write. Jim recognized some names on the writings, but he couldn't make heads or tails of what they said. He knew if he could read the letters he might learn what the Vietnamese were trying to get out of the POWs and better parry their attempts. But he was in too much pain. When the Commander returned, he asked, "Have you read the letters?"

Jim said, "No. I couldn't read them."

The Commander kept coming back every two hours. Finally,

someone brought Jim a bowl of dry rice, which he didn't touch. They gave him no water all day.

That same afternoon Jim recognized Fred Flom's voice in the next room. He was obviously in a lot of pain. Jim heard him ask, "Can't I even sit down?" Later Jim would learn that Flom couldn't recollect his own shoot-down. In fact, he couldn't remember the two weeks before his shoot-down and capture. He knew only that he woke up in pain in prison with one arm in a cast and the other splinted.

That evening, two Vietnamese reporters came into the room to interview Jim. He had never seen two scruffier-looking men in his life. Later he learned all journalists in North Vietnam dressed that way—it was a kind of costume for the role they played. They sat down and asked a guard to interpret for them. Jim gave them only his name, rank, and serial number, but he did tell them he had been shot down near Yen Bai. They asked if he had led the attack on the Hanoi POL facility. Jim said yes because the media had covered the attack prominently and named him in the stories. Their interview concluded, the journalists left him alone.

A medic came, took Jim's pulse, looked at his leg, and said something to the two Vietnamese. He thought the medic was telling the guards he should be taken to a hospital soon, and they nodded. About 1:00 A.M., they picked him up, put him in an ambulance, and told him to keep his mouth shut. Flom was lying next to Jim in the ambulance, obviously in pain, groaning and completely out of it.

At a hospital they took Jim out of the truck, carried him into an X-ray room, and removed the splint, which was in tatters anyway. They took two X-rays and, oddly enough, the doctor showed Jim one of them. He could see the broken-off section of his thighbone jammed up into his abdomen, with jagged edges splayed out at the top. He knew he needed an operation but wasn't sure the Vietnamese could operate properly. They carried him out of the room into another one that was twelve feet square. There they placed him on a large, square, reddish-beige mat fixed to the floor all around with red tape. Otherwise, the room was bare. Jim thought, *This must be the amputation room where they lop off my leg.*

After they laid Jim on this mat in the middle of the floor, they brought a mask with ether. They cupped the mask on his face, started giving him the ether, and told him to count. He could feel them grab his right leg and start pulling. At the same time, they were shoving needles into his leg to inject painkillers. When Jim reached forty-two and was still counting, they took the mask away. He was lying with his eyes clenched shut because he didn't want to watch them cut off his leg. Suddenly, he felt a cold line across his thigh. He remembered feeling the same thing during a knee operation in 1960, so he thought they were amputating. He started yelling, "You rotten sons-of-bitches! Any quack in the States could fix my leg!" Jim gave them hell, calling them every name he could conjure.

The doctor picked up the back of Jim's head, held it up, and told him to look. So he opened one eye and saw they were wrapping a very thin plaster of paris cast—really just gauze—around his leg. They hadn't cut it off! He had felt the cold, wet gauze going on. Further, they had relieved a tremendous amount of pressure by somehow working the bone down out of his abdomen into his thigh. That was Jim's first relief from pain, so he was very grateful for their efforts. When orderlies picked up the stretcher to carry him out, he threw the doctors a highball salute. Three or four of them returned his salute, and two smiled. He could see the North Vietnamese weren't all bad, although they usually were stern-faced and emotionless.

The Commander and the Wheel then took Jim to a large Army hospital near the Red River and put him in a room by himself. They started talking to him about the war and South Vietnam, trying to get him into a political discussion. Jim said nothing. He just lay there because he hadn't slept for days. They weren't asking him questions. They just told him how long they had fought and how just their cause was, which Jim viewed as propaganda intended to soften him. Finally, he fell asleep as they were talking to him.

The next morning the Commander came in with a man Jim called "the Professor." Jim would see the man again in the prison system. He was from the political bureau, a liaison between "downtown" and the prison camps. The Professor weighed only about eighty pounds—a little guy with dark gums who spoke fairly good English and often acted as an interpreter. Jim saw him in some Vietnamese propaganda films. He tried to get Jim to write a letter condemning the war and the U.S. government—that sort of thing. Jim wrote, but nothing of that type. They took his letter and tried to make him change it, but he simply wrote the same thing again.

Jim asked them, "What kind of people are you, trying to get me to say things against my government? You wouldn't want to say anything against yours." The Professor said he wouldn't be saying anything against the U.S. government, just the present administration. But Jim refused. He did write that he had received humane care, medical treatment, and a third splint on his broken leg. In each case, though, he tried to show something was phony about what he wrote. Eventually, they became disgusted with him and abandoned the letter writing.

After a few days, the interrogators started coming in, trying to get information out of Jim. One day they asked, "Do you speak French?" Of course, he didn't. They said, "Okay. Tonight you will meet a woman from Radio Luxembourg. She will interview you and allow you to send a message to your family." That afternoon they took Jim into the cast room and put an enormous cast on him. They built it up to his waist and down to his foot, making it thick and reinforcing it with several stays. It weighed so much he couldn't move. Of course, it did nothing for his broken leg because they hadn't set the bones (see fig. 17).

They put Jim in another room, where later that night he would see Madeleine Riffaud, the woman who owned Radio Luxembourg. *Small world*, Jim thought. He had driven by Radio Luxembourg's broadcasting station on his way to the golf course when he was stationed at Bitburg, Germany. He also had listened often to this woman's voice over the radio, and the station's English-language broadcasts were popular with many American servicemen in Europe. This time, though, Jim found no pleasure in hearing her speak.

Riffaud started telling Jim—through the interpreter—about the horrors of war. *Right! All that jazz*, Jim thought, and paid no attention to her. She said she had talked to Robbie Risner—an ace from Korea and the first living recipient of the Air Force Cross. She considered him a serious and intelligent man, unlike Kasler. She told Jim she had visited a Catholic community that the Americans had bombed intentionally and refused to admit responsibility for. Jim knew that, if such an incident existed, it surely was an accident. He never knew of a single intentional American attack against a civilian target—certainly not against a school or hospital or church, as was often claimed. On the contrary, Jim and his flying mates went out of their way to avoid such incidents, even when it meant more peril for them.

Martha Kasler later read Riffaud's commentary, which stated that of all the prisoners she talked to in Vietnam, Major Kasler was the most callous and obnoxious. Jim took a certain satisfaction from that. He saw such interviews as playing into the enemy's hands and undermining the brave work of U.S. and South Vietnamese forces.

The next night, the Commander came in and said, "You will not open your mouth." They carted Jim into the X-ray room and placed him on a table. More than fifty photographers were there—Caucasians, Vietnamese, and Chinese. The Vietnamese pretended to take X-rays of Jim while the photographers took pictures. Then they took him across to the cast room for more pictures. They had a fancy cast machine but never used it. It had chrome poles, with little holders for feet and ankles, knees, and on up. They spread-eagled Jim on it and took more photographs. He already had a cast from his waist to his foot, but they built it up from his waist to his neck—a full body cast. It was so tight he could hardly breathe—and served no purpose other than propaganda.

After the photo session, they took Jim back to his room. He was immobile. He lay there for a couple of days before the Commander finally came in. Jim told him, "If you're through with your goddamn propaganda, how about cutting this thing off so I can eat." A few hours later, they came in and cut off the top part of the cast but left the bottom part intact.

THE KASLER FAMILY COPES WITH UNCERTAINTY

At home in Indianapolis, Martha and the children had been reading the newspapers every day, playing a kind of Russian roulette. They looked to see how many F-105s had been shot down, who the pilots were, and whether they knew any of them. With the F-105 community being so close, they knew many. The day Jim was shot down—August 8, 1966—was the day before his daughter Suzanne's sixteenth birthday. That night, the twins, Jimmy and Nanette, were staying at their grandparents' house in Zanesville, Indiana. It was 11:00 P.M., and everybody was in bed except Jimmy, who answered a knock at the front door.

There stood a chaplain and a lieutenant from nearby Bunker Hill Air Force Base to tell Jim's father and mother that their son had been shot down. Jimmy knew the men had bad news before they said a word, but he thought the news was going to be that his father was dead. Everyone gathered to hear them say Jim was missing in action. Jimmy went into a separate room with Nanette and prayed, which was not a common response for them.

Oddly enough, Jim's father and mother said they were terribly upset but not surprised to hear the news of his shoot-down because Rex Kasler had dreamed of it the night before. In his dream two military men came to the door and wanted to read "a message about Jim." Rex said he didn't want to hear it, backed away, and woke up. He feared it was a premonition and felt heartsick all day.

Jim's mother marveled at how calmly Martha took the news. She said, "Air Force wives seem to be trained to take news like this a lot better than parents. She . . . never did get hysterical, although of course she is as concerned as we are." The news was shocking to Martha at first, but she and the children adjusted to it and insisted they were confident Jim would make it okay. She told the press, "I believe that what he was fighting for is right and worthwhile. This is his job, and I understand completely why he volunteered for Vietnam duty, even though I don't necessarily like the outcome."

Despite Martha's calm public demeanor, she was deeply concerned about Jim's condition. She refused to accept the possibility of his death in captivity, but she did expect him to come home with only one leg and other disabilities because she knew he had been badly injured when he bailed out. She had seen Jim twice on North Vietnamese television—once when they put him in the huge body cast. On that occasion, Jim could barely lift his head, look at the camera, and lay his head back down. But his appearance before the cameras assured Martha and the children that he was alive and that the North Vietnamese would have to account for him.

Initially, the family didn't talk to others about Jim's fate and kept all subsequent information to themselves. Soon afterward, though, Suzanne had a movie date one night at a downtown theater. As they walked out after the movie, she saw her father's picture on the front page of a newspaper at a nearby newsstand. The paper carried a huge headline about Jim's being shot down, as well as the picture a French correspondent took afterward. The French had released the story and photograph to United Press International. Then a full segment about Jim appeared on the *Huntley-Brinkley News Hour* on television, so many more people learned about the shoot-down.

The principal at the children's school made an announcement on the public address system, but Suzanne, Jimmy, and Nanette let other students know they would rather not talk about it. They didn't want to receive sympathy from others or to deal with discussing what their father was doing in Vietnam. They were also concerned people would want to meet them or be their friends because of Jim's being a POW. In those fragile teen years, they were fighting to establish their own identities and wanted to be thought of only for themselves.

Occasionally, however, Kasler's notoriety as a POW worked in the children's favor, as Jimmy was to discover just two weeks after Jim's capture. Jimmy was a newspaper delivery boy in Indianapolis and was good enough at it to receive the "Newspaper Boy of the Year" award for 1966. But he dearly needed a bicycle after having had one stolen at the public pool in June of that year. He had been working at various jobs and had saved $70 so he could buy a gold-colored, twenty-inch Stingray with a fancy five-speed gearshift. For security, he bought the best lock he could find. On August 23, 1966, he rode his new bicycle to a store in an Indianapolis shopping center but didn't lock it because he expected to be gone only a few minutes. When he returned, it was gone.

Jimmy was devastated until the newspapers discovered his loss and published an account of the theft under the front-page headline, "Kasler's Boy's Bicycle Stolen." Almost immediately, money began to roll in from donors across Indianapolis and the surrounding area. In all, people sent Jimmy thousands of dollars for a new bicycle. Martha made him send every dime back, of course. She allowed him to keep only one item from Jim's cousin, Bill Kasler: a bicycle exactly like the one that was stolen. Jimmy was a bit disappointed about having to return all the money. Still, he never forgot the experience, especially because one of the letters he received (with money enclosed) was a touching, well-written missive from E. Howard Hunt, an assistant to the President!

Although the Kasler family knew where Jim was, his shoot-down and capture were particularly difficult for them—partly because they were anxious about his safety and partly because the government continued to insist that they say nothing about his imprisonment. The Johnson administration's policy was to let the public assume the pilots would be repatriated immediately and to quell speculation about them. The gag order did make some sense. Air Force officials had received heavy criticism because they had revealed so much about Kasler, which made the North Vietnamese single him out for mistreatment. The officials knew Jim's captors would exploit any public information about him.

Another major difficulty for families was the lack of communication with their POWs, especially after early 1967. The Kasler family received only about three-dozen notes from Jim over his six years and seven months of imprisonment. Nearly all were limited to six short lines on an official North Vietnamese government form (see fig. 18). Fortunately, Jim was able to write two longer letters at the beginning of his internment, before the Vietnamese hardened their policy. His first letter was four pages long and dated November 10, 1966, but Martha didn't receive it until January 1967—five months after his shoot-down.

Jim's first letter contained news of his broken leg and operations, advice about finances, and encouragement to the children regarding school and activities. But Martha drew special comfort over the years from two parts of it. In one section, Jim wrote,

> What I do or what I am would mean nothing without you to share it with me. I have relived our life step by step in my day dreams and found it a wonderful experience to look back on our years together. I know we are going to have just as many more.

Also, he entreated her to keep active and "try not to worry too much. Above all, try to keep a happy home. I know you will."

The more Martha reread the letter and thought about the words "keep a happy home," the more they stood out. She recognized Jim must have had some foresight about his situation and known that his imprisonment might last longer than Martha would want to believe. Keeping a happy home made it possible for the children to thrive and for her to go on, so she decided to find routines and interests that would give pattern and meaning to their lives.

Martha understood the government's rationale about remaining silent to some extent, but she didn't believe they recognized how the gag order affected many parts of the family's routine. For example, one day in late 1967, she went to the Department of Motor Vehicles to get a license for their car.

"Your husband also has to sign," the clerk said.

"He can't," Martha said. "He's in Southeast Asia."

"Easy enough," said the clerk. "Just send it to him and have him sign and return it."

Martha could see she wasn't going to get a license if she kept silent about Jim's incarceration, so she said, "Jim can't sign the paper because he's a prisoner of war."

The licensing people were incredulous. A year after Jim's capture, they still had no idea the Vietnamese were holding Americans as POWs in North Vietnam. Nearly every day, Martha had to consider the government's admonitions while talking with friends, associates, and the public, weighing the potential effect on her husband's well-being.

CHAPTER 9

Tempering in Hanoi's Fiery Furnace

ALTHOUGH knowing Kasler was alive consoled his family, not knowing how the North Vietnamese treated him at that time probably was a blessing. The North Vietnamese had almost immediately advertised that he was a prisoner. They wanted to show the world they had captured the "one-man air force"—the big Korean War ace and hot F-105 pilot. Jim's notoriety may have saved his life, but it also led to more suffering and more torture because they wanted something from him that they could use for propaganda.

One day, an interrogator asked, "What did you think of our air defenses when you led the Hanoi POL strike?"

Jim said, "I figure you probably got a new air defense chief the day after."

The Vietnamese became agitated and rushed from the room. The next day, three or four of them came in and asked, "Where do you get your information?" They obviously thought U.S. intelligence had learned about the defense chief's firing, but Jim told them it was just a good guess. In fact, their policy of holding SAMs in reserve changed after the POL strike, when they weren't firing them much. The F-105s hit the POL plant without facing that threat, although Chinese gunners had filled the sky with flak, as they did throughout North Vietnam.

Jim was determined not to give the interrogators anything useful, but he learned quickly they already had a lot of military information. From the shoot-downs they had maps, bombing tables, and other notes the pilots carried with them. Although Jim lied to them about everything he could, they seemed to understand that military information goes cold in a hurry. In fact, they knew they were unlikely to win the war on the battlefield. Their strategy was to wring statements from the POWs to use for propaganda that would win the war politically. That strategy turned out to be correct: they lost every major military battle but won in the political arena.

After Jim had been in the hospital about three weeks, the North Vietnamese told him they were going to operate in order to put a steel pin in his leg. The doctor came into his room beforehand and showed him what he was going to do. They cut the heavy cast off, but he still had the thin cast underneath. Jim knew he needed the operation and just wanted to get it over with.

The day before the operation, they took Jim into a bathroom next door where all the washbasins were cleaned—a filthy place. They laid him out on the floor, threw cold water on him, and took the thin cast off. A toothless old man who washed the bedpans tried to dry-shave his leg, but all the skin was dead from being in the cast so long and covered with big, filthy boils. The man ripped big chunks of skin off of Jim's leg, creating a bloody mess. Then he handed Jim the safety razor to shave his face. He hadn't shaved in three weeks. Jim put the razor on his beard and pulled a few times, but he couldn't make much progress. So the old man grabbed the razor out of his hand and raced across his face with it. The next morning, the doctor came in and looked at Jim while the old fellow stood outside the room. The doctor was none too pleased with the old man's work. He stepped outside and screamed at him, but that was a classic case of closing the barn door after the horse was out—the damage was done.

Two hours later, they picked Jim up, carried him back into the washroom, and placed him on the floor. This time they had a bar of soap and some rags, so they washed him with soap. Early the following morning, they came in and gave him a shot, then carried him into the operating room about 8:00 A.M. The operating room had rudimentary lighting and equipment but no heat. They laid

Jim out on the table and gave him sodium pentothal, which knocked him out.

The next thing Jim knew, he was back in his room at 1:00 A.M., lying in about two inches of bloody water that had collected in a trough on the bed. He felt horrible. Blood was spurting out of his thigh, and the wound from the operation was open. A nurse was watching him, but she just shrugged her shoulders when he asked for help. *Perhaps the wound was supposed to stay open,* Jim thought, but that didn't seem right.

When Jim woke again in the morning, they had a blood transfusion going. He remained in critical condition for five days with a high temperature. Slowly his temperature went down, and he came out of the fever. The doctor had run a steel rod down through his hip into his thigh, then strapped the shattered bone pieces to it. Jim was fairly pleased with the operation because it promised at least to allow him to save the leg and walk again. But the incision wasn't clean, so he would have infection problems for a long time.

About mid-September 1966, boils started popping out all over Jim's body because the infection was spreading through him. The boils were large, and great gobs of green stuff came out of them. They appeared on his thigh near his crotch and on the back of his ears and neck. The Vietnamese had to lance one on his head to relieve the pressure.

They took Jim to the cast room again so they could place a very thin cast on his leg and up around his chest. But this time they used no stays, so it was breaking down across his thigh by morning. The doctor came in and ordered him back to the cast room. That night they built another cast, using two one-inch-square boards to reinforce it. One board cut sharply into his knee. Jim knew he would be crippled if they left it there, but he endured twelve hours of agony before he finally talked the doctor into cutting the board away. They wrapped more plaster in its place, which eventually caused an odd-looking knot on his knee.

The next night, the Commander came into the room with a tape recorder. "You must write a letter confessing your crimes," he said.

"Negative," Jim said, "I'm not doing anything."

The Commander said, "If you do not write this letter, I'll report you to the Hanoi Central Committee, and they will take action against you."

Jim just laughed. The Commander then ordered everybody in the hospital who had anything to do with Jim—doctors, nurses, and people from the cast room—to come into his room and scream at him for two hours. They swore, cursed, jumped up and down, and beat on his bed. It was quite a performance. Although no one touched him, they were very menacing. Jim lay there and looked at them, but he thought, *Oh boy, I'm in for it now.*

They all left, but soon the Commander came back and said, "You're going to regret your decision." Then he left again. Jim figured he went to make a phone call because four Army guards came into the room later that night and told him to get up.

"I need crutches," Jim said, "and clothes." He wore only a little piece of cheesecloth he had stolen from the cast room to cover himself. Fortunately, the weather was warm. To Jim's surprise, they brought him clothes—white, red, and gray-striped prison garb—and crutches that were about four inches too short and, therefore, useless. They put a pair of striped prison shorts on him, loaded him onto a cart to roll him out of the hospital, and put him in a truck.

The guards drove Jim to a prison camp the POWs called the "Zoo" and placed him in a room at the end of a building they called the "Stable." Someone was at the opposite end of the building, but the adjoining room was empty, so he had no contact with anyone. The room was fairly large by prison standards—about fifteen by eighteen feet—but it was filthy, with lots of junk lying around on the beds. The guards strung a mosquito net over one of the two beds (the other one had rotted out) and stuck Jim under it for the first night. The beds were simple wooden pallets made by laying planks on top of concrete stanchions. The guards gave Jim an old blanket that was lying on the floor, then left him alone for a couple days. He was a bit punchy from his operation. He had started running a fever before he left the hospital, and boils still covered his body. He had tried to get a doctor to do something about them, but they wouldn't pay any attention to him.

At one point, Dum-Dum (variously called "J. C.," "Marian the Librarian," "Goat," or "Colt 45" by different POWs) came into Jim's room. He was a "one-bar" interrogator at the Zoo—a low-ranking officer. He wanted to know how many airplanes the Americans had lost on the Hanoi POL strike. Jim said, "One."

That angered him because the Vietnamese always claimed seven. He screamed, "Your attitude at the hospital was very poor, and now you are going to confess your crimes against the Vietnamese people."

Jim said, "I have committed no crimes. I've done nothing to confess." Dum-Dum started calling him a son of a bitch, and so forth, but then simply left.

A few days later, Jim's fever was intense, but the guards still started harassing him about getting up and bowing. A guard would open the peephole flap on the door and say, "Bow." It was all Jim could do to even maneuver out of bed in the heavy body cast. He had to use the crutches to crank himself up because the bed was too low for him to step out. Of course, he couldn't have bowed in the cast even if he had wanted to. Nodding his head was the most he could do. It made them mad, so they came into his cell and smacked him around. Sometimes they did it every twenty or thirty minutes all night long, just as harassment to deny him sleep.

Eventually, Jim began to wear down from beatings, lack of sleep, and poor health. They often stood him up against a wall and pounded away at him, saying it was punishment for not cooperating with them in the hospital. Periodically, they beat him to get a written statement. Now and then, Jim wrote something, but he misspelled every word and made it as silly as he could. Anyone who read it must have thought he had an intelligence quotient of about twelve. They tried to get him to condemn the U.S. government and its policy in Vietnam, which Jim refused to do. They also continued trying to extract a confession for war crimes.

In one case, they interrupted demands for a confession and told him to write a letter to pilots flying over North Vietnam. Jim was supposed to tell them about the flak, the dangerous antiaircraft guns, and so on. He wrote a bland letter, but they took it away, changed it to suit their purposes, and came back a little later to make him sign the altered version. At one point, they were still trying to get Jim to condemn the bombing, but he refused. He was lying there on the bed, which was the only way he could write. The guard standing over him started slamming him in the back of the head with his fist while Jim was writing. When Jim looked up, the guard punched him in the mouth. His ring cut Jim's lip. The cut became infected, leaving him with a scar that took years to go away. He alternated between punching Jim on the back of the head and smacking him on the ear.

Jim could have taken the beating if he had been in better health, but he was still suffering from the leg injury and operation, plus the fever, infection, and lack of sleep. Because he wouldn't write what they wanted, they forced him to make a tape recording. Jim didn't believe he recorded anything they could use, but giving them anything distressed him. He thought the worst thing he said was that the Vietnamese and Americans should stop killing each other and seek peace at the negotiating table. That was more psychology than substance—and it was true. They tried to get Jim to write a letter to Senator Fulbright, but he refused.

After Jim completed the recording, the Vietnamese relented somewhat. A medic came in and gave him some pills—probably sulfanilamide and penicillin. He took them for seven or eight days during the middle of October. Around that same time, he received the first toilet paper or soap he'd had in North Vietnam. As often happened with the POWs, Jim had diarrhea at the time and had been using a little washrag they gave him to wipe himself. He was on the bucket, or "bo," seven or eight times a day. When he was very sick, he just pulled the bucket up beside the bed and did the best he could to hit it. Jim was nearly helpless in the cast—sick and beaten up besides. Until almost Christmas of 1966, he was in that room continuously, never once let out for air or light.

JOHN BRODAK, CELL MATE AND CARETAKER

The Vietnamese finally took Kasler out of his room at the Stable for interrogation. Standing in front of the interrogation room was John Brodak, with whom Jim had been stationed at Bitburg, Germany, and Takhli, Thailand. In the flurry of F-105 losses during August of 1966, Brodak was among three shot down on August 14. He led a flight of four against a fabrication plant near Thai Nguyen, dropped his bombs, and then started to climb out. But the aircraft lost altitude twice more before Brodak ran out of fuel and had to eject.

When Brodak bailed out, he was flying at glide speed—250 knots. He received minor scrapes and a sore back from falling

Fig. 1. Jim's parents, Rex and Inez Kasler, at their fiftieth wedding anniversary. Their strong Midwestern values prepared Jim for a life of service to his country and community. Courtesy of James H. Kasler.

Fig. 2. Jim bought this first car for $25 and drove it all over Indianapolis during three years of high school. It wasn't much for dates, but it was economical and easy to maintain at the gas station next to his home. Courtesy of James H. Kasler.

Fig. 3. Jim began his combat career in a B-29 bomber during World War II. As an eighteen-year-old tail gunner, he flew combat missions over Japan and took photos of ground zero after the atomic bombs fell on Hiroshima and Nagasaki. Courtesy of James H. Kasler.

Fig. 4. James and Martha Kasler at their wedding reception on April 9, 1949. Their union and love would survive everything combat, captivity, and life could throw at them. Courtesy of James H. Kasler.

Fig. 5. Jim (center foreground) was the first man to solo, and he became cadet commander of his F-80 jet training class at Williams Field, Mesa, Arizona (1951). He is shown here with his subordinate commanders (l-r): E. F. Tabaczynski, H. M. Rountree, and R. E. Fiebig. Courtesy of James H. Kasler.

Fig. 6. North American F-86A. This aircraft was renovated, painted with Kasler's name, and inscribed "Martha Lee" to commemorate his service in Korea. It is on the grounds of what was Fort Benjamin Harrison, Indiana. Jim flew in it, but he became an ace with six MiG kills in a different F-86A. Courtesy of James H. Kasler.

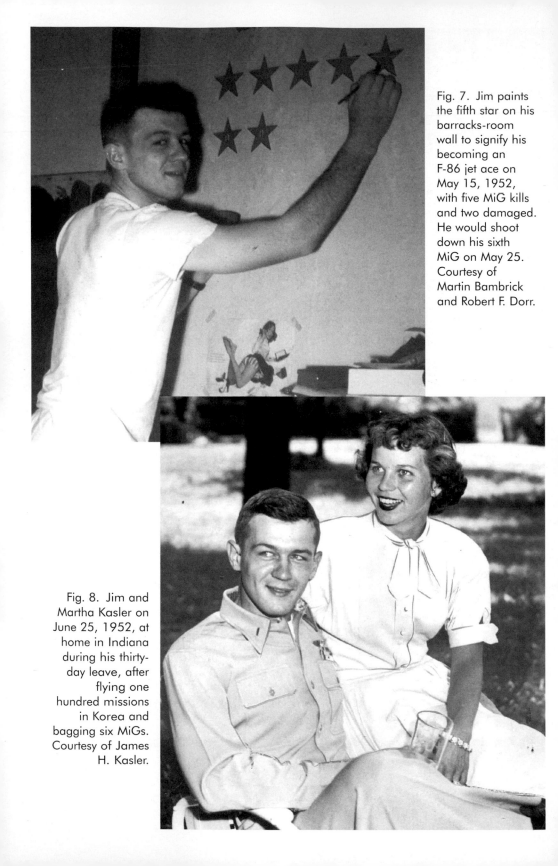

Fig. 7. Jim paints the fifth star on his barracks-room wall to signify his becoming an F-86 jet ace on May 15, 1952, with five MiG kills and two damaged. He would shoot down his sixth MiG on May 25. Courtesy of Martin Bambrick and Robert F. Dorr.

Fig. 8. Jim and Martha Kasler on June 25, 1952, at home in Indiana during his thirty-day leave, after flying one hundred missions in Korea and bagging six MiGs. Courtesy of James H. Kasler.

Fig. 9. Six jet aces at Nellis Air Force Base in 1953. Left to right: Bill Wescott, "Boots" Blesse, Jim Kasler, Bob Latshaw, Clay Tice (not an ace), Iven Kincheloe, Bill Whisner. Courtesy of James H. Kasler.

Fig. 10. Lockheed F-104C Starfighter, shown here in Royal Canadian Air Force markings. It was the darling of the U.S. Air Force's brass, who focused on intercepting the Soviets' long-range bombers during the 1950s. But Kasler considered it hopeless in a dogfight because it took "a country mile" to turn. Courtesy of Charles L. Byler.

Fig. 11. Then-captain Jim Kasler in his F-105B. His name appears just below the canopy. Jim flew the F-105 on alert during the Cuban Missile Crisis (1962), in a nuclear-readiness role at Bitburg, Germany (1963–1965), and in ninety-one combat missions during the Vietnam War (1966). Courtesy of Theo W. van Geffen.

Fig. 12. Major Kasler (center back) at the 53d Tactical Fighter Squadron's formal dining out in Bitburg, Germany, 1965. Left to right: Mike Reynolds, not known, Kasler, former X-15 "winged astronaut" and squadron commander Bob White, and Ian McInerny. Sandy Vandenberg and his wife, Sue, are behind McInerny. Courtesy of James H. Kasler.

Fig. 13. Kasler (center) goes over last details with pilots of the 355th Tactical Fighter Wing before leading a daring attack on Hanoi's POL complex on June 29, 1966. AP/Wide World Photos.

Fig. 14. Jim descends from his F-105 after leading the strike that permanently closed Hanoi's POL facility. This mission cemented his reputation as the premier F-105 attack pilot in the Vietnam War and got his picture on the cover of *Time* magazine. Courtesy of James H. Kasler.

Fig. 15. Jim receives congratulations from Brig. Gen. George Simler (left) and wing commander Col. William Holt (right) for planning and leading the wing's devastating strike on the POL complex near Hanoi. Courtesy of James H. Kasler.

Fig. 16. A Vietnamese girl poses with an old rifle trained on Kasler shortly after his shoot-down and capture. His shoot-down occurred while he was flying cover for his downed wingman, Fred Flom. Jim's courage and valor on this mission earned him his second Air Force Cross. Courtesy of Communist News Agency of North Vietnam.

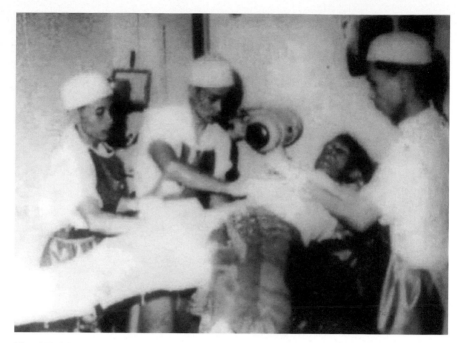

Fig. 17. Vietnamese medical staff apply a large cast to prepare Jim for a publicized interview with Madeleine Riffaud, owner of Radio Luxembourg. The cast was a fake, applied solely for publicity and without care for Jim's severely broken bones. Courtesy of Communist News Agency of North Vietnam.

Dear Martha, Suzanne, James & Nanette
I am well and think constantly
of you all. I hope and pray
that you all all in good health
Give my love to our parents and
my love to you all. — Love Jim

NGÀY VIẾT (Dated) 19 July 1968

Fig. 18. The North Vietnamese government required all letters from prisoners of war to fit on this six-line form, which further limited the infrequent communication allowed for POWs. The Kasler family received only about three dozen notes from Jim over his six years and seven months of imprisonment. Courtesy of Martha Kasler.

GHI CHÚ (N.B.):

1. Phải viết rõ và chỉ được viết trên những dòng kẻ sẵn (Write legibly and only on the lines).

2. Trong thư chỉ được nói về tình hình sức khỏe và tình hình gia đình (Write only about health and family).

3. Gia đình gửi đến cũng phải theo đúng mẫu, khuôn khổ và quy định này (Letters from families should also conform to this proforma).

Fig. 19. Mike McGrath's drawing shows a common torture technique in North Vietnamese prisons—one he experienced often as a POW. For Kasler, the guards added "hell cuffs" on his arms and wrists. They cut off circulation and lacerated his skin to the bone. Courtesy of Naval Institute Press and John M. McGrath.

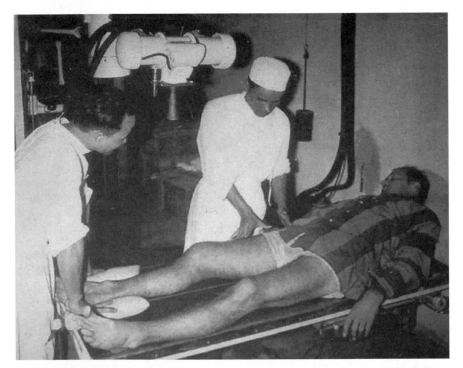

Fig. 20. Vietnamese medical staff explain an operating procedure to Kasler before a 1969 operation on his leg. Although procedures and conditions were primitive, this medical attention likely helped keep him alive. Courtesy of Communist News Agency of North Vietnam.

Fig. 21. After years of illness and brutal torture, Jim's face was haggard and gaunt, but his defiance of the Vietnamese captors still shines through. Courtesy of Communist News Agency of North Vietnam.

Fig. 22. A joyous reunion and homecoming at Wright-Patterson Air Force Base, Ohio, on March 8, 1973. Colonel Kasler rushes to greet (from left) his daughter Suzanne, wife Martha, son James, and daughter Nanette. United Press International.

Fig. 23. Some of the hundreds of POW bracelets that well-wishers returned and piled on the Kaslers' porch in Indianapolis immediately after Jim was released from Hanoi in March 1973. The button near the center was one of two commonly worn to support the POWs; the other said, "P.O.W.'s Never Have a Nice Day." Courtesy of Irene H. Luckett.

Fig. 24. Colonel Kasler flew a similar F-111 Aardvark as vice commander of the 366th Tactical Fighter Wing, Mountain Home Air Force Base, Idaho, after his release from North Vietnam and graduation from the Air War College. That he could return to flying a sophisticated jet aircraft after years of captivity, injury, and abuse is testimony to his fabled skill and determination. Courtesy of USAF Museum, Wright-Patterson AFB, Ohio, and Mark Houpt, F-111.net.

Fig. 25. Jim signs and sends this photograph to people who request his autograph. He is happy to respond to these requests, which continue regularly more than thirty years after his retirement from the Air Force. Courtesy of James H. Kasler.

Fig. 26. Poster commemorating the 1993 Gathering of Eagles at Maxwell Air Force Base, Alabama. Kasler's picture, squadron symbol (335th Fighter Squadron, Korea), and signature are fourth from the bottom in the left panel. His F-86 from the Korean War is in the middle column of the center panel. Courtesy of Perry D. Luckett.

Fig. 27. Left to right: Russian general Vitali Popkov, Charles "Chuck" Yeager, Russian general Konstantin Treschchov, and Kasler—shown here at the 1993 Gathering of Eagles. Jim was honored as "one of the sky's greatest" and the only person in history to receive three Air Force Crosses for valor in combat. Courtesy of James H. Kasler.

Fig. 28. One of Jim's unframed paintings from his home in Momence, Illinois. He is a self-taught artist whose work shows command of light, perspective, and detail. Courtesy of Perry D. Luckett.

Fig. 29. This stark Civil War scene, painted by Kasler before his POW years, hangs in his home in Momence, Illinois. It incorporates the fine strokes no longer possible for him because of damage to his wrists caused by repeated torture in North Vietnam. Courtesy of Perry D. Luckett.

Fig. 30. Maxine McCaffrey's portrait/collage of Jim and his experiences in and after the Vietnam War reflects the characteristics that enabled him to prevail during thirty years of dangerous flying, combat, and captivity. When he retired from the U.S. Air Force in 1975, he had served under seven presidents. Courtesy of Perry D. Luckett.

Fig. 31. Colonel Kasler's medals and decorations include three Air Force Crosses (top center)— a distinction unequaled in U.S. history. His seventy-six military awards for valor and service make him one of America's one hundred most decorated soldiers of all time. Courtesy of Perry D. Luckett.

through trees but didn't suffer any broken bones, as so many did, from ejection or a hard landing in the chute. Unfortunately, after one night in the woods, a militia girl discovered him. She yelled for help, and the militia captured him, stripped him, and took him back to the closest village. They began the journey to Hanoi— carting him around at night and placing him in a village during the day. Each night, the villagers hurled stones at him and beat him with bamboo sticks. After a time, the militia pulled him into the back of a truck and drove through the night to the next village.

After Brodak arrived at the prison he went through initial interrogation for nine days. The Vietnamese tied him up and left him without food or water in what the POWs called the "knobby room." They tied him to a rusty, two-meter-long iron bar, with manacles on both ankles and wrists, strapped over and doubled back onto the bar. At that time he was weak from lack of food and water but still didn't have major injuries. After they took him to the Zoo, however, he developed severe infections on his ankles and minor ones on his wrists from the rusty manacles. He lost about fifty pounds during the next month or two and weighed less than one hundred pounds when he became Jim's roommate in December. Still, on a diet of rice and sulfa pills to work on the infections, he had regained enough strength, so the Vietnamese decided he could take care of Jim.

Dum-Dum told Kasler and Brodak they would be roommates, admonishing them to obey all camp regulations, and so forth. He called them "sons of bitches," "criminals," and "motherfuckers"— his favorite English expression. They occupied room one of the "Pigsty," just across the alley from where Jim had been. Although in relatively good health, Brodak continued to have terrible infections on his legs from the irons used to make him write a confession. The Vietnamese came in and lanced his legs a few times while he was rooming with Jim. He still carries scars around his ankles and all over his legs from this mistreatment. Despite the torture, however, Brodak had given them no information, and Jim always admired him for his courage.

About January 8, 1967, Brodak came down with dysentery—the uncontrollable type with which one couldn't even make it to the bucket. He and Jim substituted a little can. Then Jim also contracted dysentery. Burdened by his cast, he had no hope of making it to the bucket. Between them, they had excrement everywhere: the floor, the blankets, the beds, their clothes, themselves. They couldn't do anything about it because this kind of diarrhea gave no bodily pressure as a warning. It just cut loose. Jim had the runs until about the latter half of January, when it finally subsided.

Eventually, the Vietnamese hauled Jim off to the hospital and removed the cast. It had been on four months, and Jim has scars from it today. At the time, his knee wouldn't bend at all. When he came back to the cell, huge overlapping scabs covered his leg. They were as big as silver dollars, one on top of the other. Amazingly, though, his leg had few open wounds. It continued to blister, but he simply scraped off the scabs and let them stack up on the floor.

The day after the cast came off, the Vietnamese took Jim back in for interrogation. Reverend A. J. Muste was in Hanoi to visit Ho Chi Minh, so they wanted Jim to write a welcome letter to him on behalf of the POWs. Muste was eighty-two years old at the time, having capped a lifetime of leadership in antiwar and nonviolent protest by forming a coalition against the Vietnam War. In 1965, more than fifty thousand people had paraded down Fifth Avenue in New York to support his suggestion that the United States withdraw its forces and disarm. To young men facing conscription, he always recommended "holy disobedience." However sincere Muste may have been in his beliefs, Jim was in no mood to welcome a person whose visit would become just another plank in Hanoi's propaganda campaign, so he said, "Shove it up your ass. I'm not writing anything."

As punishment, the Vietnamese put him "on the wall" for a couple of hours. Standing up against a wall while holding your hands above your head may not sound so hard, but anyone's arms will become remarkably heavy after only a few minutes. Furthermore, Jim had to stand on one leg and keep his crutches anchored under his arms at the same time. Ironically, Muste died just seventeen days after meeting with Ho Chi Minh, but his speeches became part of the prison system's radio broadcasts. Jim always grew angry whenever he heard Muste on the radio because the reverend had caused him considerable personal pain.

After Jim came back from the interrogation for Muste's visit, dysentery seized him again for two weeks. He was losing a lot of weight. Because he couldn't eat the usual prison food, the Vietnamese brought him some special brown noodle soup that they thought might spark his appetite. Brodak had to eat most of it, but it seemed to help—Jim's dysentery gradually subsided. That gave him little relief, however. His leg developed osteomyelitis and started to puff up to about twice its normal size with infection. By that time, he weighed only about 125 pounds. His leg continued to swell for a week—a large, very painful inflammation. Then it burst open, and green gobby junk started pouring out. Finally, he and Brodak persuaded the guards to call a doctor. The doctor probed around in the hole in Jim's leg with his scalpel. The green stuff shot out like a geyser, which helped relieve the pressure. The doctor gave Jim penicillin shots for a week, and the infection started to clear.

About a week after that, the guard came and told Brodak and Kasler they could go wash. Jim began to get up but felt so bad he told John to go ahead without him. Although he wasn't sure what was wrong, he knew he was sick. That afternoon, his leg started swelling again. Eleven days passed before they could get the medics to look at it. By then, it had puffed out to half-again its normal size. The suture line stuck out like the casing on a spoiled sausage.

Finally, the guards took Jim to the hospital. But the doctor looked at his leg, instructed the camp medic on using needles to give him shots, and sent him back to camp. The medic gave him a shot a day for three or four days, then stopped. The leg kept swelling for thirty days, looking like it was ready to burst. Jim was in agony. He couldn't sleep or eat and was losing weight so rapidly he thought he was going to die. In fact, he probably would have died if not for Brodak, who cared for Jim and put his own blanket on him when Jim was shivering from the cold and fever. Each POW had only one thin blanket, so Brodak had nothing to keep himself warm at night.

During this very difficult period, Kasler and Brodak had contact with their fellow POWs through the tap code, which enabled them to communicate throughout the building despite attempts by the Vietnamese to stop them. Although Jim had only a working knowledge of tapping techniques, Brodak became very adept at it. Again, Brodak proved his special value as a roommate to Jim because communicating was vital to Jim's resistance and survival while racked with illness and fever.

Air Force captain Carlyle Harris had introduced the tap code to the POWs in New Guy Village during late June of 1965, so it was well developed by 1967. An instructor of survival training at Stead Air Force Base, Nevada, had shown Harris the code during a coffee break. The tap code required a five-by-five matrix that would correspond to twenty-five letters of the English alphabet. By dropping the letter K and arranging the remaining twenty-five letters into a five-by-five box, the POWs produced the following basic design:

	1	2	3	4	5
1	A	B	C	D	E
2	F	G	H	I	J
3	L	M	N	O	P
4	Q	R	S	T	U
5	V	W	X	Y	Z

To designate the letter "A," prisoners tapped once for the first row, then once for the first letter of that row (tap—pause—tap). For the letter "B," they tapped once to signify the first row, then twice to signify the second letter of that row (tap—pause—tap, tap). For the letter "J," they tapped twice for the second row, then five times for the fifth letter of that row (tap, tap—pause—tap, tap, tap, tap, tap). The least-used letter of the alphabet, "Z," required the most taps: five to designate the bottom row, followed by five to designate the fifth letter in that row.

The POWs abbreviated ingeniously to cut these taps to a minimum, thereby reducing the physical demands on tappers and receivers. A common abbreviation, for example, was GBU for "God bless you," which became the universal sign-off signal at Hoa Lo. They also used "X," tapped alone, to signify a sentence break, similar to "stop" in a telegram. Coding the system was as simple as reordering the rows or columns, but tapping and scrambling techniques matured as the POW population grew and the Vietnamese grew more skilled at breaking the code.

Kasler knew many people in the Pigsty's ten other rooms, so

communicating became a way of renewing old friendships as well. The F-105 pilots were a particularly close group, all having served together at one time or another. Murphy "Neal" Jones, for instance, was the one pilot shot down during the Hanoi POL strike Jim led. Jones still had a broken arm from the shoot-down. In fact, it remained broken more than three years later and is shorter than the other today because of that neglect. Beyond the F-105 community, Jim also knew F-4 pilot Richard "Pop" Keirn, who was shot down by a SAM near Hanoi. He had been a prisoner of the Nazis for seven months near the end of World War II. Fifteen of the Vietnam POWs had served in World War II, with eleven seeing hostile action. Many had served in Korea, too.

One night in early April 1967, the Vietnamese packed Jim off to the hospital. The Commander, who spoke English, was there. Jim asked, "What's wrong with my leg?"

He said, "You have a bone infection."

"What would cause that?" Jim asked.

"Shut mouth," he said. The conclusion was obvious: the surgery had caused Jim's infections, but they didn't want to admit it. A sterile operating room could have saved him a lot of misery.

They took Jim into the operating room and tried to knock him out by putting needles in his hands. An attendant asked, "How you feel?"

Jim said, "I'm a little woozy, but I'm still conscious." Suddenly, a knife went into his leg. Jim yelled, "Hey! Wait a minute!" They put a mask on him then to try to knock him out but started opening his leg before he went under. Jim didn't care. Opening the leg relieved a tremendous amount of pressure. They made a thirteen-inch-long incision right down to the bone. Sutures weren't part of this medical procedure, though; they let the wound close by itself. After the pus exploded out of his leg, they stuffed the incision full of gauze with yellow salve on it and took him back to his hospital room. By that time, Jim was finally unconscious.

When Jim awoke, he was still in the hospital. He stayed there two nights before the Vietnamese moved him back to his cell with Brodak. He and Brodak tracked how often the Vietnamese changed the bandage after that. It was every six to eleven days, no fewer than six, no more than eleven. Meanwhile, the horrid-smelling putrescence that oozed out of Jim's incision was making both men sick to their stomachs. Apparently, Jim was decaying from the inside out. The first time the medic came in to change the bandage, he pulled the gauze out of the gaping hole in Jim's thigh. Brodak was fanning the flies and gnats off Jim's leg, so he got a good look into the wound. He could see the bar and steel rings holding the bone together. Jim talked the medic into giving them a piece of oilcloth they could wrap and tie around his leg to hold down the stench.

They gave Jim special food while he recovered: meat and potato soup, as well as bread, which he hadn't seen before—two loaves of French bread a day. In the morning, for about the first two weeks of his recovery period, they gave him a cup of hot milk—canned, of course. The pressure in Jim's thigh had caused so much pain, he couldn't even think about food. With the pressure gone and the pain reduced, he could eat again. The Vietnamese also moved Art Black, an enlisted paramedic, in with Brodak and Kasler during the latter part of May. Presumably, they thought Black's medical skills would further help Jim to recover.

But Jim's respite didn't last long. His captors caught the men communicating and, to punish them, put them against the wall with arms raised. Of course, Jim's leg began swelling again, so they eventually let him sit down. Just three days later, however, they said he and Brodak had bad attitudes and moved both men to the Pool Hall.

THE POOL HALL

The Pool Hall was a penalty building containing ten rooms. The Vietnamese allowed Brodak and Kasler only one bath per week and kept them confined to their room. This room was smaller than the one they had left—only about eight feet square—and rats played with dishes the guards left stacked after the prisoners ate. The back rooms had no windows—just two four-inch apertures at the top of the walls. Two people occupied each room, so the building housed twenty prisoners. Ventilation became even worse about two days after the POWs moved in when guards bricked up the windows to the top. The cells stayed hot in the summer and cold in the winter.

Because Jim was senior ranking officer (SRO) in the Pool Hall and because of his notoriety, the Vietnamese were still trying to get information from him. Brodak, as his roommate, often was punished, too. The Vietnamese also considered other people in the Pool Hall badasses or troublemakers. For example, Bob Purcell always gave them a hard time, sometimes risking punishment to climb through the access panel in the ceiling of his cell, from which he carried scraps of food and water to other prisoners through a crawl space. He ran this service during siesta, returning to his bunk just before the guards made their rounds. Bunny Talley, Mike Brazelton, Tom McNish, Marty Neuens, Burt Campbell, and others caused the Vietnamese some problems.

One of the guards at the Pool Hall was Mongolian, apparently, and a brutal son of a bitch. Most POWs called him "Magoo" for his squinty-eyed resemblance to the cartoon character. Others knew him as "Billy the Kid" or "Eliot Ness." He beat them all the time—occasionally concocting an excuse, but often for no reason at all. He also played tricks to create occasions for punishment. For instance, he always filled the soup dishes to the brim, boiling hot. If someone spilled a bit, he used that as an excuse to punish him. He worked with an interrogator the POWs called "Elf"—a tiny, repugnant man with a similarly sadistic nature. He and Magoo regularly smoked pipes of pot or opium, and the glazy-eyed Magoo came by afterward to knock them around.

By this time, the Vietnamese had pretty much given up on getting confessions from the prisoners. Instead, they wanted to interfere with their communications, so they often caught people tapping. Or they might simply accuse people of tapping or use a slight noise or talking in a room as an excuse for torture. In August 1967, the Vietnamese started pulling people out of Jim's building and torturing them to write an autobiography, which most of them had already done. Most would give some brief biographical tidbit because they didn't feel it was military information—anything to cut some of the torture. But the Vietnamese typically extracted a small or innocent detail and then pressed for more.

Marty Neuens and Burt Campbell were the first ones pulled out for a few days of torture with ropes and irons. Then they took Tom McNish and Mike Brazelton, forcing them to write an autobiography and to reveal Jim's orders for the building, their communication code, and how they were using it. (McNish had developed a high-speed flash code that greatly helped communication between buildings.) Eventually, the Vietnamese broke people to learn what they wanted. Although resistance was heroic, the POWs found their captors could get anything out of them when the torture continued long enough.

Up to this point Kasler had endured other punishments, but not ropes and irons. Then their peephole opened, and the guard called "Ka" (Kah), Jim's single-syllable name in Vietnamese. Similarly, Red McDaniel was "Moc" (for "Mac"), and they called Larry Guarino either "Ga" or "Ga-ree-no." English sounds were often impossible for them, but they didn't need perfect English to inflict pain. Elf did the interrogation. He was a tiny man with narrow shoulders who looked like he weighed about forty pounds, but he was mean. Elf told Jim he had committed crimes against the Vietnamese people by giving orders to other prisoners. Elf said he was busy at the moment but would see Jim later, then dismissed him to his room.

Back at the Pool Hall, Magoo put Jim in hand irons by placing the backs of his wrists together behind him, pulling his shoulders back, and then ratcheting the irons right down to the bone. Magoo had trouble getting the irons on because Jim has large wrists, and that was enough excuse to smash him on the side of the face or the ear with his hand. He left Jim like that for twelve hours. Jim asked Brodak to hold his elbows together to see if that would relieve some of the pressure, but it didn't help the pain. When they finally removed the cuffs, he couldn't use his hands or arms. He was completely numb, yet the pain never stopped. Brodak had to feed him. Magoo came back and slapped the irons on again, but this time normally—with the insides of the wrists together. Jim stayed in those irons for thirty-two days; he was let out only twice a day for fifteen minutes to eat. His hands were purple and grotesquely swollen as a result.

After fifteen days of this treatment, Kasler had lost his appetite and wasn't eating much. So Brodak took some leftover rice and dumped it into their "bo"—the waste bucket. He was taking a chance because prisoners weren't supposed to throw away food; the Vietnamese saved it for their hogs. As though he had radar, Magoo opened the door, pulled the lid off the bucket, saw the rice, and stormed out. Soon the guards came and took Jim out of his irons for a quiz—with Elf again.

"You have committed another crime against the Vietnamese people by throwing away food," Elf said. "Now you are going to be punished."

The guards took Jim back to the room, where he saw Brodak standing outside with four or five guards and their bucket. They marched him over to the end of the Pigsty where the Vietnamese had an old toilet but no water supply. The toilet just went down by pressure. The place was filthy because they emptied waste buckets from all the rooms there. They threw the two men into a room and gave them a bamboo wicker screen to sift the feces and retrieve the rice out of their bucket.

One guard they called "Slug," who was very strong for a Vietnamese, came and beat them with his fists. Repeated blows to the face and chest bloodied them both. To recover the rice, they had to push diarrheic waste through the wicker screen by hand. Jim tried not to put his hands in any deeper than necessary because he didn't want his wrists to get infected where the skin was broken from being in irons. But his attempts were futile.

John said, "I think they are going to make us eat it."

Jim replied, "We're going to die first."

When they finished separating out the rice, however, the guards merely threw it in the toilet and took them back to their room. They allowed the men to wash their hands with soap but then put them directly back into the irons.

Jim saw only one good thing about being in irons: he couldn't reach his nose. Touching his nose would have caused a terrible sinus infection because of the bacteria that remained on his hands. As it was, he had a horrendous summer head cold. His nose was stopped up, and his head felt near an explosion. With his hands strapped behind his back, he couldn't blow his nose, so he asked Brodak to help him—not a very satisfactory arrangement. Finally, he became skilled using his feet. Because he couldn't bend his right leg, he had to work one of his shirts up to his knees, then bury his nose in the shirt and blow. These discomforts worsened what was already a tough time for him.

After thirty days, a burly Vietnamese guard they named "Lantern Jaw" (or "Death") put Jim through ropes and irons twice in

Elf's interrogation room. They kept him there about thirty-five minutes each time, but he never gave them the satisfaction of making any noise. Jim took it the first time, when they put the cuffs on straight, though his wrists were still swollen and his hands were tender. The second time, they crossed the cuffs diagonally over Jim's wrist bone, which tore the skin right off the bone. About fifteen minutes into the second session, Jim said, "I surrender."

Unfortunately, it did no good to surrender; they continued for the same amount of time whether one surrendered or not. He had been through survival school, but it didn't prepare him for this treatment. It couldn't, of course, because no one could imagine such torture, then devise a method to survive it. Continuing the torture after Jim surrendered was a mistake, however. He saw no reason to surrender in subsequent sessions.

They left Jim in irons and started asking him questions, such as "What orders did you give the building?"

He said, "To refuse to work downtown, to refuse to do any productive labor, to refuse to give anything without torture."

They asked him what the tap code was and tried to trip him up by giving him a different code or a different way of carrying it out. Because the prisoners used different methods for the code, Jim didn't see any danger in the Vietnamese having their tap code, so he recited the code others had already given them. Even when someone explained the tap code to them, they often couldn't follow it, probably resulting from the significant differences between the languages and alphabets.

They put Jim in a building the prisoners called the "Garage" for a couple of days. They also put him in leg irons, the kind they called "traveling irons," which was an ironic misnomer because they were too cumbersome for travel. Now Jim was in hand and leg irons. Before that, Brodak had been helping him go to the toilet; without help, he had no recourse but to soil his clothes and remain in them.

During that time, the Vietnamese applied torture once for communication and then again to make the prisoners write something they could use for propaganda. They tried to make Jim write a response to the question, Why is the United States in South Vietnam? So, to see if it would placate them, he simply wrote, "The United States is in South Vietnam to stop the spread of militant

Communism in Southeast Asia." Surprisingly, they bought it. They also asked about the morale of the men in Jim's building. He told them the morale was bad because of poor food, their poor treatment and torture at the hands of the guards, and their having received no packages or letters—conditions the Geneva Convention was supposed to preclude. Again, they accepted Jim's answer, although one would have expected them to consider such remarks unacceptable. After two days they took him out of irons and moved him back into the room with Brodak.

The Vietnamese intentionally weakened prisoners with insufficient food as another way to wear them down. By this time, Jim had recovered enough to get some of his appetite back, but they fed him (and the others) only twice a day: a little rice, plus a very thin green soup with a side dish, such as boiled pumpkin or some other squash or boiled greens—four or five little slices on a plate. Everyone was starving for calories of any sort, but especially for protein. The POWs were glad to get animal fat. Once in a while they received four or five little pieces of pig fat—pigskin with hair still attached and a little chunk of fat hanging on it. At first, they wouldn't touch it, but eventually they ate it eagerly.

The POWs were eating near 10:00 A.M. and again about 3:00 P.M. When they finished the second meal, they were still hungry, so the room hero was the guy who heard the plates rattling around the camp somewhere when the guards started serving food again. Also, up to that time, the Vietnamese had given them no sugar or anything sweet. So Kasler and Brodak sometimes sat talking about food, naming all the different types of candy bars they could remember: Clark Bar, Baby Ruth, Three Musketeers, and so on. They tried to think of how many different kinds of pies, cakes, and other desserts they knew. But their hunger often intruded on the reverie, especially when someone reminded them of the time before the next morning meal. Once, Brodak said cruelly, "Jim, do you realize it's going to be nineteen hours before we eat again?" Jim could have killed him.

THE TORTURER CALLED FIDEL: A FIRST LOOK

Right after Jim left the interrogation room, they took Brodak and tortured him. They forced the same kinds of responses out of him and made him write a few things. Brodak was in the writing room near the end of September 1967—the same time that Jim was in the Carriage House. A crack in the door of the Carriage House allowed Jim to look down Main Street, where he saw a Caucasian torturer the POWs called "Fidel" because they surmised he was Cuban. Unfortunately, Jim's first view was not to be his last. Two other men who had accompanied Fidel to the camp received the monikers "Chico" and "Sancho" (or "Pancho") from the POWs.

Theories abound regarding Fidel's true identity and various names have been suggested over the years. No definitive proof of his identity exists, however, and even the artists' sketches of him vary substantially. Whoever Fidel was, Jim devoutly wishes that he had been caught and made to pay for his war crimes.

Fidel was very husky and handsome. He had relatively dark skin, black hair combed back in a pompadour, but with a part, prominent ears, and good teeth. He always wore a shirt with two close-set buttons near the neck. The other buttons were normally spaced. He had several sports shirts, but always with those two distinctive, closely spaced buttons at the neck. He wore combat boots and blue cotton trousers with no crease.

Jim saw Fidel talking to Lump, the political interrogator in the camp. He thought Fidel looked a bit like his own good friend Larry Guarino, but on closer inspection believed the torturer most resembled Jack Bomar. In fact, the day after Jim had come to know Fidel, Bomar flipped open the flap on Jim's cell door and looked in at him. Jim was startled because he thought it was Fidel.

Although the camp had a commander, Lump gave all the orders. He was tall for a Vietnamese (about five feet eight inches), but Fidel was taller—a good six feet or more. Fidel certainly looked like a Latin, and he spoke vernacular English with an accent, the way a Cuban would. Jim had glimpsed him before, but this was his first chance to study him. Lump and Fidel were standing in the street in front of the headquarters building, demonstrating how to use irons, ropes, and other torture devices. They were consulting with political agents from downtown Hanoi, probably talking about the prisoners and what they were going to do.

Fidel was running an experimental torture program. He had come into camp in July 1967 and started pulling people into the interrogation room. Larry Spencer, a Navy officer from Jim's building, went in first. The next day, they moved ten men out of the rooms and put Spencer in charge of them. Fidel started torturing them one at a time to break them down. Jim didn't know if the Vietnamese taught Fidel or vice versa, but he suspected the latter. The Cuban seemed to be trying innovations on selected prisoners. Months later, Jim and ten others were to join the program.

The thirteen-inch incision in Jim's leg had closed most of the way, but the remaining gap kept draining from a persistent infection. He felt very ill and went through a period of fainting spells. The captors had stopped giving him bandages and had taken away his crutches. Although he tried to wash out old bandages to use again, he didn't have enough soap. He tied socks around his leg, trying to contain some of the pus and blood, but the infection worsened. He had to wear his long, red pants—even in the summer—just to keep the mess off of his bed. When he did get out to the shower, he turned the pants inside out and scraped off the collected crud.

By mid-November of 1967 Jim's condition declined further, so the Vietnamese took him to the hospital. They said then that he needed an operation but didn't come to get him ready for one until after the Tet offensive in March 1968. Six or seven days before they were to take him to the hospital, they started a series of shots that made him horribly nauseous. He also had a burning sensation throughout his body, but thought it was just the penicillin working through his depleted veins and arteries.

While giving Jim the shots, the Vietnamese also interrogated him. The Professor and Lump tried to get him to fill in the blanks on a paper they had written about U.S. bases in Thailand. Jim knew little about those bases, other than Takhli where he served, except the number designator of a few flying wings. They had had those designators for years, so he could tell them nothing of consequence. Still, he refused to fill out or sign anything.

Lantern Jaw came in, threw the irons down on the floor, and threatened Jim, but he kept declining to do what they asked. The guard put him on his knees, slapped him around a bit, and started putting the irons on him. Jim didn't feel he could take the ropes and irons after what he had gone through, so he agreed to fill in the blanks. He wrote the number designators for Takhli and Korat, then told them he didn't know the others, which he didn't. They became angry again and started yelling at him. They bounced him around and put him on his knees. He simply repeated that he didn't know the answers to their questions. The Professor and Lump went outside to consult, then sent Jim back to his room.

That afternoon Magoo showed up with a handful of penicillin pills. He tried to instruct Jim on how to take them. Jim thought Magoo might have been saying to take three a day for seven days until the twenty-one pills were gone, but he was difficult to understand. Jim took seven a day for three days, concerned all the while that Magoo would come back to count the pills and use any miscount as an excuse to pound him. The penicillin cleared his wound for a while, so the Vietnamese postponed his operation. But Jim's reprieve from infection didn't last long; his leg started draining heavy pus and blood again. Whenever he pushed his hand down his leg, the evil mixture boiled out of his wound. It continued month after month.

Jim was further distressed when his teeth started flaking, probably because the bone infection and poor diet were sapping calcium from his body. The entire enamel fronts of many of his teeth just fell off, and fillings started coming out. He was sure cavities would set in and destroy all his teeth. The combination of ill health and physical torture was gradually wearing on his psyche and ability to resist.

TORTURE AT THE ZOO AND THE CUBAN PROGRAM

In April 1968 the Vietnamese moved some of the young men out of Jim's building to the Zoo annex outside the walls. Eventually, they moved Brodak in with them. Brodak had continued to catch abuse because he happened to be Jim's cell mate. Every time they beat Jim, they felt obligated to give John a few whacks, too. One day after Magoo had left, John said to him, "I don't mean anything derogatory, sir, but I'd sure like to move away from you." Jim understood.

At the time, Jim thought the Zoo was activated for this April move, but later he learned from Mike McGrath that it had been in use since October 1967. McGrath was with the first group moved there. Initially, each group had no way of knowing of the other because of the high wall between them. Later McGrath climbed up the wall on his side and communicated with Red McDaniel using mute code.

Near the end of April, the Vietnamese came in and told them to roll up their gear. The preceding week they had caught Bob Purcell and Bunny Talley talking through the wall in back of the building. They put Bob on his knees in the room and brutalized him— beating the hell out of him several times a day, every day, for seven days. Jim and the other POWs could hear it happening. They were like savages tearing him to pieces: four or five of them on him at a time. He was allowed off of his knees only to sleep at night.

They moved Jim to room seven of the Barn and kept him alone, although Ron Byrne was in the cell next to him. Once or twice he was in contact with Ron, but the guards watched them closely. When they suspected Jim was communicating, they moved him down to room two and left the rooms on either side of him empty. Room two had a steel door and no window—just a little aperture up high. A bomb shelter, consisting of a big black hole with water in the bottom, occupied its center.

Jim was alone for four or five days in room two before they moved Dewey Smith, someone he had known at Bitburg, Germany, into the room next to him. He had no way to clear himself—to make sure the guards weren't listening—but he still made contact. Dewey communicated that Jim's family was all right and that Jim had made lieutenant colonel in November 1966. Dewey was shot down in early June 1967. Shortly after he moved in, the Vietnamese moved Bud Day and Bob Sawhill from the Plantation into the cell on the other side of Kasler. Bud Day was an F-100F pilot who would earn the Medal of Honor for his resistance. The guards caught Jim communicating with them, beat him, and put him on his knees on the concrete with his hands in the air for twelve hours. He had to put himself into a kind of trance to do it; otherwise, he couldn't have taken the pain.

The next day they were going to wash out the prisoners' rooms. Jim was too sick to do anything, so they put him in the building the POWs called the "Gym." He was there only two days before they moved him back to a solitary room in the Pigsty, where his neighbors included Pop Keirn, John Pitchford, Dave Luna, and Charlie Stackhouse. One day in June 1968, the guards caught Jim communicating with Stackhouse. The prisoners thought they had clearance in the building, but somehow the guard had slipped past them.

The Vietnamese took Jim to the interrogator Spot, who slapped him with an open hand and fist. Then Spot said, "I know you are very sick, and I know about your leg. What punishment do you think we should give you?"

Jim said, "That's for you to decide."

Spot hesitated a moment and then said, "You'll go back to your room and remain on your knees."

After Jim spent an hour on his knees, Spot and another interrogator from downtown Hanoi called him back for another quiz. Then they sent him back to his cell and put him on his knees for the rest of the day and night. They gave him a five-minute break every hour—their version of "humane, lenient treatment" because of his condition.

A few days later, they gave Jim another series of shots, which cleared the drainage from his wound. After the shots stopped, however, the same milky, sweet-smelling drainage returned a few days later. He had a fever, began losing interest in food, and fought off-and-on bouts of dysentery. Late in June, Spot called Jim into his office. He acted friendly, chatted, gave Jim a cigarette, and asked about his family. Then Spot said, "I have noticed the food is getting better."

"That's not true," Jim said. "The food has gotten worse."

"You're getting sugar and fruit," Spot countered.

"Yeah, a couple bananas a year, maybe."

"Food production is up," Spot said. "Things are improving in this camp."

"I don't believe it," Jim said.

"We are celebrating," Spot insisted. "We have shot down our three thousandth enemy airplane."

"You're lucky if you've shot down seven hundred," Jim said.

"Our numbers are accurate. The district commanders must go out and place their hands on each wreck to verify it. Also, more prisoners are in camp than ever before. My commander wants a man to meet a delegation and appear on television to mark this occasion."

Many delegations came to Hanoi—East Germans, Poles, Russians, Americans—and all wanted to see the POWs. For each group, the Vietnamese tortured the American POWs so they would give correct answers to questions that the Vietnamese required the delegations to ask. The questions were controlled, no matter where the delegations came from. The Vietnamese took no chances and trusted no one, not even their own allies. From what Jim had heard, the American delegates who came to Hanoi didn't seem to need much coaching from the Vietnamese. They could hardly wait to get on the "Voice of Vietnam" and echo the latest Communist propaganda. Their broadcasts to American troops (and the POWs) typically called for desertion or refusal to fight.

After his return to the United States, Jim recalled in particular when the Vietnamese broadcast a recording of Dr. Benjamin Spock speaking at an antiwar rally. He could tell Spock was pleased with himself because of the way he was giggling. Spock had hit on a great idea. He wanted each family in the United States to adopt one of the boys who was serving time for desertion or draft dodging. They would provide him with money while he was in jail and help him get started when he got out. As Spock explained, this program would encourage other young men to go to jail rather than serve their country. *Now isn't that heartwarming?* Jim thought. *That's just what every loyal American family needs: its own little adopted coward.*

Also, the reports these groups brought back to the United States often distorted the truth about the bombing of civilian targets and dikes in North Vietnam, apparently (Jim believed) because they wanted the North Vietnamese to win and were willing to betray their own country to attain that goal. For these reasons, he was particularly adamant about not meeting delegations because he didn't want to do or say anything that might aid their cause. So, when Spot demanded that he appear on television, Jim said, "Bullshit. I'm not meeting any goddamn delegation."

"You have no choice," said Spot. "You are in our hands now. We have kept you alive, so you owe us this appearance."

"I owe you nothing," Jim said.

Spot kept badgering Jim to agree to his demands. When Jim wouldn't respond, the interrogator left him with a copy of the *Vietnam Courier* and went out of the room, probably to talk to Lump. That's how Jim found out about Robert Kennedy's assassination.

He wondered how much other important news he had missed since his shoot-down. When Spot came back, he tried again to talk Jim into meeting the delegation, but Jim refused. Spot put him on his knees for an hour, then asked again. Jim refused. "Go to your room and roll up your gear," Spot ordered. That wasn't a good sign.

The guards put Jim into the Ho Chi Minh room, a filthy little cell on the back left side of the Auditorium. They didn't do anything to him that day, but on June 29 Spot called him in for a quiz. He had three sets of hand irons in different sizes, leg irons, and a pile of ropes—all the torture paraphernalia. Spot told Jim to sit down, gave him a cigarette, and again tried to talk him into meeting the delegation. Jim refused, adding that Spot could torture him or even drag him in front of the delegation, but he wasn't going to say a goddamn word.

This time, Beanpole (also known as "Ichabod Crane") administered the torture. He was five feet nine inches or so in height and very thin—hence, his nicknames. After putting Jim on his knees, Beanpole got behind him and hit him four or five times on the side of the face before putting on the irons with the backs of Jim's wrists together and the irons clenched bone tight. Then he wrapped the ropes above Jim's elbows and started cinching them together. Many of the prisoners couldn't take the pain in their shoulders, but Jim felt pain—excruciating pain—in his wrists.

At first, Jim managed the ropes and irons, which lasted forty-five minutes. Then the torturers took them off, slapped him around, and asked if he were going to meet the delegation. He said no, so they put on a different set of irons. After thirty minutes, he passed out from the pain. When he came to, they were taking off the irons. They let him sit for fifteen minutes or so, then bashed him around some more and put the irons on again. The pain was even worse. After about fifteen more minutes, Jim couldn't take further punishment, so he said, "I surrender." Instead of stopping, however, they continued to torture him. They wrapped the rope around his throat and cut off his breathing until he passed out again. When he came to, they were slapping him to wake him up and asking if he still surrendered. Jim said yes, so they finally removed the irons.

They wanted Jim to write something, but he couldn't use his

hands. He sat on a stool for three or four hours before some feeling finally returned. The Vietnamese gave him a copy of questions the delegation was going to ask and the answers he was to give. The questions included where he had been captured and by whom. He was supposed to say unarmed women and children captured him. Of course, that wasn't true. He also was supposed to say that he had seen hundreds of prisoners in the camp and that the American bombing had been fruitless because the Vietnamese economy was continuing to grow, with production up on all fronts and fruit, sugar, beer, and lots of extras in the prisoners' diets. They demanded that Jim agree America had sabotaged the Geneva Agreements of 1954 by conducting an illegal, immoral, and unjust war. They even wanted him to say the American representative in Paris had shown bad faith and was not negotiating. The list went on and on.

Jim knew he couldn't say any of what they wanted him to, so he tried to modify his answers. Spot kept threatening to put him back in irons, but Jim finally finished in shaky handwriting. He knew it would never pass. They sent him back to his cell, let him stew there a day, then moved him to the Ho Chi Minh room and put him on short rations—less than an inch of soup, a little handful of rice, and sometimes a small piece of bread. The starvation diet had little effect: Jim wasn't interested in food anyway because he was so sick.

On July 2, 1968, Lump called him in for a final briefing. He gave Jim a cigarette and asked about his family. He asked if Jim had ever been to Japan and noted that the Japanese were exporting a million dollars' worth of equipment to South Vietnam each year. This general nonsense lasted about forty-five minutes before Lump got around to the real issue: meeting the delegation. He handed Jim the questions and answers with red-pencil corrections. He had changed many of the answers to be much less negative.

Then Lump said, "Now you know what you must do."

Jim said, "Like I told your commander, you can torture me and you can drag me in front of the delegation, but I'm not going to say a goddamn word."

That upset Lump, but he didn't lose his cool. He took a stack of eight-by-ten-inch glossy prints out of a desk drawer and started showing them to Jim. The pictures were of antiwar demonstrations in the United States, of people marching through San Francisco and Washington, carrying protest signs with slogans on them such as "Communist Party USA" and "End the War." About the fifth picture Jim looked at, however, showed two elderly gentlemen in American Legion caps standing in the background. Their sign said, "Drop the bomb." The Vietnamese hadn't picked up on that. It gave Jim the little nudge of courage he needed because it made him feel he was not alone. Lump finally gave up and sent him back to his room.

The next morning at six o'clock, the medic came in. Jim was still very ill at the time, but the medic wasn't there to help him. A medical technician always came in before a torture session to wrap his leg, so blood and pus wouldn't spatter around the interrogation room. Spot was in the interrogation room again with the torture paraphernalia laid out. He told Jim he had better change his mind, but Jim refused. Spot sat on a stool and said, "Now, I am going to enjoy this." Jim had no doubt that Spot did "enjoy" torturing people; he was a genuinely sick person.

To be sure of controlling a prisoner, ten or twelve guards always remained nearby. They put Jim on his knees. Beanpole slapped him repeatedly, then ran him through the ropes and irons for forty-five minutes. The second time, they changed the irons around to increase the pain. Jim was lying there on his left side with his eyes closed as they were putting on the second set of irons. Suddenly, someone said, "Kasler." Jim looked up, and there was Fidel. He grabbed Jim by the shirt, pulled him up, and started shaking him. "What kind of shit are you trying to pull?" he demanded. His English was good, idiomatic, and laced with obscenities. "Shit" and "motherfucker" were among his favorite expressions.

Fidel supervised the irons this time. About halfway through the session, Jim was lying on his left side, and Fidel was getting exasperated. In retrospect, Jim recognized that Fidel became upset if a prisoner didn't scream or yell out. Jim never gave them that satisfaction during any of the torture—he never uttered a sound. At any rate, Fidel slammed his boot heel into Jim's chest. Intense pain shot out of Jim's heart all the way down his right arm to his fingertips. Fidel apparently understood how badly he had hurt him with the boot kick because he never did that again. Meanwhile, he was cursing and yelling, "Who do you think you are, you son of a bitch.

What are you trying to do?" After about twenty minutes, they took the irons off and placed Jim on a stool by the desk. Fidel sat down behind the desk and started talking to him.

"How many children do you have?" Fidel asked.

"Three."

"Why are you doing this? Why are you refusing to talk to the delegation?"

"Because I have to."

"Who knows you're here in this camp?"

"Nobody."

"Well, what are you pulling this shit for? You don't have to go through this. Just go see the delegation. I have the paper here. I can change it around. We don't have to back you into a corner. We're not going to make you say anything bad. Just go up before the delegation and say a few things. There's nothing wrong with what you are going to say."

"No," said Jim.

"Do you want a glass of water?"

"Yes."

"Are you going to surrender?"

"No."

Fidel turned to one of the guards and said, "Nuoc" (the Vietnamese word for water). They brought Jim some in the first real glass he had seen in North Vietnam. Fidel pointed a little fan at Jim, then, to cool him off. It was a boiling hot summer, so Jim was soaked with sweat. Fidel gave him a cigarette and left the room while he drank the water.

After a while, he came back and started talking again—just shooting the bull. He said, "Okay. I'm gonna get that paper over there, and we're gonna change it around."

Jim said, "Forget it. I'm not doing it." So Fidel put him back on his knees. Beanpole repeatedly slapped him and then placed him in irons again.

The irons were always worst for Jim the third time. He would do anything just to try to throw his mind into concentrating on something else besides the torture. He recited the Lord's Prayer, thought about his mother's pies, or remembered something he had done with the kids while they were in Germany—picnics or anything—just to try to get through it. He was on his side in a kind of stupor, obviously getting pretty foggy, when Fidel hunkered down next to him.

"Would you like to take a bath?" Fidel asked.

"Yes."

"Are you going to surrender?"

"No."

"Take off the ropes and irons," Fidel said to the guards. Then he told Jim, "All right. Go over and get your shit, and go take a bath. Change those filthy clothes. You smell like a pig."

Jim was wringing wet with sweat from head to toe. When he started out of the door, one of the Vietnamese did, too. Fidel grabbed Jim, turned him around, slapped him two or three times, and told him to show respect—to let the Vietnamese go first. Jim retrieved his gear and found himself standing in front of his old room at the Pool Hall, where John Brodak and he had lived for about a year. He went to the bath area but didn't have enough strength to pull the water bucket up out of the well. The bandage had come off of his leg, so the pus and blood cascaded down. Fidel came over and pulled the water bucket up for him. He washed off, went to his room, and put on his other set of pajamas.

Again, Jim's reprieve ended quickly. The guards took him right back to the interrogation room, where Fidel sat him down and tried to convince him that he should change his answers for the delegation. Jim said he didn't even want to see the paper because he wasn't going to change the answers or go before a delegation.

Fidel ordered Jim back on his knees. This time, the guards wired his thumbs together behind his back and put on the irons with the backs of his wrists together. They used nylon webbing to tie his hands together and pulled them up behind his back. Then they put the ropes under his elbows and started cinching them up toward his head. One guard put his foot on Jim's head and hoisted his elbows above it (see fig. 19). This torture continued for forty-five minutes, after which they hauled Jim back to the table and tried to talk him into cooperating. He still said no.

The guards put him back on his knees. He was thoroughly dehydrated, with a big pool of sweat around him, but the brutality continued. After Beanpole slapped him numerous times, Fidel told the guards to apply very tight irons. They took fifteen minutes to put them on Jim's wrists while standing on his arm. Now and then, they became frustrated, so they reached up and smashed him in the face. After forty-five minutes of torture, they gave up. Because it was nearly 2:00 P.M., well into their siesta hour, they sent Jim back to his room.

Jim had just lurched into his room when Lump and a guard the prisoners called "Casper" arrived. Casper always wore a white jacket and a maroon windbreaker, and he didn't like to get his hands dirty. This time he was in his swimming trunks, so Jim knew he didn't want to soil his clothes while working him over. Lump told him to roll up all his gear and take it out of the room, which Jim did. When he stepped out and set his gear down, Casper started belting him with his fists. After ten minutes of continual punching, the guards put him in his room on his knees, hands over his head, stretching up as hard as he could. Fifteen minutes later, Jim passed out. When he came to, he tried to crawl to the water jug. They came in and took the water jug away, then put him back on his knees. He passed out again. When he regained consciousness, they put him on his knees a third time but didn't make him stretch toward the ceiling.

About 5:00 P.M., Fidel showed up at Jim's door and asked how long he had been like that. Jim said, "Since you left." Fidel told him to go over and lie down on his bed, so he crawled to it. Ten minutes later the door opened, and he struggled to get up, wearing just shorts. But Fidel ordered him to lie facedown on his bed. He started beating Jim across the buttocks with a huge truck fan belt, screaming as he lashed him: "Strike the enemy first, before they have a chance to hit you. Hit them hard." Jim hadn't seen these words in print, but he certainly recognized them. Fidel was throwing quotes at him from the magazine interview he had done just before he was shot down. Jim counted thirty-six whacks with the fan belt, which tore his buttocks and upper legs to shreds.

"Are you going to surrender?" Fidel demanded.

"No," said Jim.

Fidel said, "Stand up, you son of a bitch. Go get your clothes." After Jim went out and got his clothes, Fidel told him to put on his long, red pajama pants. Then Fidel left.

The guards came to escort Jim across the compound. He was carrying his gear but was barely able to walk. About halfway across, he had to sit down and rest. Finally, they dragged him to a room in the Pigsty where he saw Pete Schoeffel, a naval officer. When Jim saw Pete, he thought he had beaten the torturers and escaped having to meet the delegation because they were giving him a roommate. But he misread the situation. Fidel had already worked Pete over with the fan belt and convinced him to answer the delegation's questions. Pete was supposed to help persuade Jim to meet them, as well.

Fidel came into the room and said, "All right, Kasler. I'll talk to you tomorrow." Jim had received a cigarette from a guard, so he asked Fidel for a light. That set him off. Fidel smashed him in the face, knocked him down, and started beating him in the ribs. He screamed, "I'll take care of you, you smart-assed son of a bitch!" Fidel was so angry he ran over and started slapping Pete, too. Then he stomped out of the door.

Pete looked at the damage from Fidel's whipping. Jim's skin was hanging in shreds, and he was bleeding. Suddenly, Lump opened the peep and said, "Tomorrow, we are going to show you the determination of the Vietnamese people." Jim thought, *Oh shit. Now I've really had the stroke.*

The next day was July 4, 1968. The Vietnamese always made a big thing of America's Independence Day and gave the prisoners some little treat. It was good propaganda because the date represented the United States's overthrow of colonial power, which they considered parallel to their own situation. They passed out cigarettes. Although Jim didn't expect to get any, they gave him three. Then they came and told Pete and Jim to go take a bath. Nobody bathed on holidays, so the men figured they were going in for interrogation because Fidel didn't like to smell them.

The guards told Jim to roll up his belongings and moved him back into the Ho Chi Minh room. Jim was there about half an hour before Fidel called him in for a quiz. Fidel told him to take down his pants and turn around. He looked at Jim, then said, "How much of this shit can you take?" Jim felt like saying, "As much as you've got, buddy," but discretion prevailed. He kept his mouth shut. Fidel called him a stupid masochist and said he should think again about surrendering. But Fidel said, "I'm not going to punish you on a holiday. Go back to your room." Later the guards gave him a beer and a piece of peanut-brittle candy.

The next day, Fidel didn't show up, but at the crack of dawn,

Lump arrived. He opened the peep and asked, "Do you surrender?" Jim said no. About ten minutes later he was back in the interrogation room with thirty Vietnamese. They put him on his knees and started beating him, slapping him on the face a hundred times or more. They knew he wasn't going to see the delegation, so they didn't care if they marked him up. They put him through the standard ropes and irons again, then took out the small irons and worked thirty minutes to get them on, lacerating skin and injuring bones the entire time.

By the time the guards got the irons on, the pain was so bad Jim could hardly take it. But there was more. They put the ropes on him and pulled his arms up over his head, then down around his feet. The pain and pressure on his joints were horrible. Jim thought, *I might not make it. At my age, I could have a heart attack from the strain on my system.* He was in ropes and irons for a good forty-five minutes, after which the guards kept beating him for at least another half hour. They put him on his knees for the rest of the day, then took all his clothes and the mosquito net out of the room, leaving Jim lying on his bed wearing only his shorts.

That night, they put Jim in leg irons, made him sit up on his bed, and turned out the lights. The mosquitoes poured in, eager to pounce on his exposed flesh. Every fifteen minutes the guards flicked on the light to make sure he wasn't sleeping. When Jim looked down, he saw fifty or more mosquitoes on each foot. With no mosquito netting to stop them, they swarmed over his entire body. Although his hands were swollen and his wrists were torn to shreds, he tried to kill as many mosquitoes as possible as he lay awake all night.

The Vietnamese kept Jim awake the next day and throughout a second night. The following morning, Fidel was back in camp and called him in for a quiz. He insisted Jim was going before the delegation but offered to do a symbolic torture in front of ten prisoners so he could retain his honor. Jim said, "Bullshit. You bring ten POWs in here and I'll never surrender." Fidel cursed. He called Jim stupid and said Jim was going in front of the delegation even if he had to carry him in. Either that, or he was going to beat him to death. It was not an idle threat; Fidel probably was responsible for at least one prisoner's death.

That night, Jim was back in his room with the lights out, on short rations, with very little water, and being kept awake—all ways to wear him down. At 6:00 A.M., the door flew open. It was a whip-wielding guard, Cedric, who made Jim lie facedown and struck him about seven times with the fan belt. For five days, every hour from 6:00 A.M. to 10:00 or 11:00 P.M., someone beat him with that fan belt, trying to get him to meet a delegation. Because the Ho Chi Minh room was elevated and had a crack under the door, he could see the guards gathering just before the hour, getting ready to whip him. Cedric was there for each pounding. A different guard whacked him three or four times, after which Cedric finished the job. He did it slowly and seemed pleased, typically screaming like Fidel and even using the same phrases.

After four days of continual flaying, Jim couldn't control his mind anymore. He began to hallucinate, so he knew his body wouldn't take it much longer. On the fifth day, as they were beating him, he said, "Okay. I surrender." He didn't want to say it, but his vocal chords seemed to form the words involuntarily, as a reflex against further harm. Yet, they kept on beating him. Once, someone hit him across the small of his back. When his head popped up, the guard slammed it down with his foot, opening a gash above Jim's left eye. They continued the hourly beatings for six or seven more hours.

The guards said the Commander didn't believe Jim when he said he surrendered, so they made him write and sign a letter saying he was willing to do everything to the best of his ability. After that, they kept him in irons but threw the mosquito net back to him. As soon as he had gotten a good night's sleep, his surrender began to gnaw on him. For several days, what the POWs called "kiddie officer" trainees came around to ask if Jim still surrendered, and he said yes. But about the fourth day he answered no. Immediately, Cedric and Casper came in with thirty guards, put him on his knees with his hands behind his back, and started slapping his face. After a while, about half the guards left, perhaps because they didn't enjoy watching or because they simply had duties elsewhere. Casper and another man took turns slapping him. When they knocked him down, Cedric beat him all over his body with the fan belt.

The beating continued for three hours. Huge welts rose up everywhere on Jim's skin. His face was a hard chunk of leather, hanging down below his chin from the swelling. His eyes had nearly swollen shut. They had ruptured his eardrum, and blood was running down the side of his head. Once, he fell against the bed, and Casper kicked him in the ribs. He felt a sharp, vicious pain as a rib broke. He rolled on the floor holding his chest, as they tried to kick him in the same spot. Blood and pus were all over the floor. Then they jumped on Jim's injured leg, breaking the pin loose and jamming it up into his hip. They had gone berserk, like a pack of mad dogs, but Jim was nearly comatose and could no longer feel the beating.

Suddenly, Jim heard wrestling in the room—a fight that lasted for some time. Then the door closed and everyone was gone. Apparently, other guards had come in and pulled the tormentors away. Jim lay there on the floor for an hour or so, but guards came back and put him on his knees again with his hands in the air until 9:00 P.M. The broken rib and chest bruises hurt dreadfully. Finally, he just collapsed and, despite the guards' threats, could not make his arms respond. Jim told them, "Go ahead and beat me. I don't give a shit."

They ordered him to go over to his bed, so he crawled there. He had been without water all day long. They put down a piece of paper and told him to write to the camp commander and apologize for surrendering five times and taking it back the sixth. He wrote the note, and they hauled it off. As they were leaving, he asked for water, so someone finally brought him a cup.

Jim decided then that he wouldn't retract his surrender and get beaten for it again. Instead, he would wait until they made him do something and then fight them as well as he could. Several days later, Fidel came back to camp and hauled him into interrogation. He hadn't eaten for five days because he couldn't get his mouth open after the beating. Fidel asked if Jim would surrender, and he said yes. He asked what they had been doing to him, so Jim told him. Fidel seemed to disapprove of their treatment, even though he was a brutal devil himself. He probably was worried they would kill Jim, depriving him of a potential asset.

About the middle of July, the guards took Jim out and told him to bathe. They gave him a razor. He hadn't shaved for a long time. His reflection in the water stunned him; he was a sorry sight and figured he had lost nearly every vestige of his humanity. He managed to shave and bathe, noting while there that a case of beer and other bottles rested in the water tank. That night the Vietnamese had a big going-away party at the Coop (administration building) for the Cubans—Fidel and his buddy Chico. Casper sang throughout the day in a falsetto voice, like a girl. Jim heard speeches and caught a few words in English. Four cars came into the camp, signifying that senior officials were attending.

Jim didn't see Fidel again until a few days later, when the Cuban came into the camp and sent him to get a bath. Jim had been on short rations all that time. In one case, a guard handed him soup with a big lump floating in it. He lifted the lump to find it was a small dog's head, with ears, eyes, teeth, hair, and everything intact. He put the head aside and ate the soup. The Vietnamese seemed to enjoy putting things in the prisoners' food that they knew nobody would (or could) eat, such as the pup's head or a horse's hoof. They were also fond of chopping up various whole animals with a machete and dumping the pieces in the soup. The prisoners called it "fragged" chicken, dog, or whatever the animal had been because it looked like a fragmentation grenade had blown it to pieces.

Periodically, a bunch of puppies would run loose in the camp, eating in the dishes and the garbage until they were half grown. The guards entertained themselves by chasing the pups around camp. Eventually, they stoned the pups, broke their back legs, and tortured them to death. Later Jim learned they had some strange notion that torturing an animal before killing it would improve the flavor of the cooked meat. He supposed it was only a small step to the idea that torturing POWs was equally acceptable.

In the interrogation room Fidel said they were moving Jim to a larger space where he would be more comfortable. He also promised Jim would get out into the sun more and would receive a regular diet, with no more short rations. Jim told him he still surrendered. Fidel talked to Lump and sent Jim back to his room. The next day, Fidel called Jim back for interrogation but seemed in a mellower mood.

"Do you still surrender?" Fidel asked.

"Yes," said Jim.

"What kind of cigarettes did you smoke before you were shot down?"

"Viceroys," Jim replied. Fidel pulled out a fresh pack of Viceroys.

"Take one," Fidel said. "What type of chewing gum do you like?"

"Beeman's Juicy Fruit." Again, Fidel pulled out a pack and threw it on the table.

"We're going to take care of your leg," Fidel said reassuringly.

"Bullshit," Jim said. "You haven't done anything for two years and you're not going to now." Fidel insisted they would. When Kasler got up to leave, Fidel told him to take the cigarettes and gum with him.

Jim said, "I don't want them."

Fidel grabbed him by the shirt, shook him, and said, "Take them, or I'm gonna beat the shit out of you right now." So Jim took them. Fidel ordered him back to his room and told him to roll up his gear because he was moving to room eleven of the Pigsty.

The next morning, in August 1968, Fidel opened the peephole to Jim's room. When Jim started to get up, Fidel motioned for him to stay down. He stared at him for a minute, then left. It was the last time Jim saw him. Although he would still experience plenty of punishment and deprivation, his personal hell—the Cuban program—was over.

SIX MONTHS IN SOLITARY
(AUGUST 1968–FEBRUARY 1969)

When Jim tried to contact the men in the cell behind him at the Pigsty, they wouldn't answer at first, so he just tapped his name on the wall. They told him to stand by a minute while they got clearance all the way around the building. Then Jim talked to his old buddy, Norm Wells, who was in that room. Norm had been in Jim's flight the day he was shot down. Jim knew he had been shot down later because his picture was on the front page of the *Vietnam Courier* in December 1966. He appreciated Norm's words of encouragement.

Jim stayed in solitary for the next six months, all the while in agony. They took him out into the sunshine just four times over the next month for a half hour or an hour at a time. But, as he had predicted to Fidel, they did nothing for his leg. Some days he could walk; some days, he couldn't. Just walking to interrogation made him sick. He couldn't even think about food. They started giving him homemade dough cookies, whose smell alone turned his stomach. The guards put the cookies on the flap of his door. When he didn't take them, they slammed the flap shut and scattered them all over the floor. Finally, he ate a few because he had to eat something, but he risked more punishment by breaking up the rest and discarding them in his waste bucket.

A few days later, the Vietnamese gave Jim another series of shots. They weren't effective, though; his leg kept swelling to half-again its normal size, then started oozing thick blood all over the bed and floor. His body was trying to bleed out some of the infection, which eventually spread into his hip and created a knot about the size of a softball. The knot kept him from lying on his back. His only relief came when the leg would burst open and drain on the floor.

Jim also was fighting the mental anguish typical of solitary confinement, which led to hallucinatory delusions at one extreme and complete shutdown of brain activity and depression at the other. To fend off these self-destructive reactions, other POWs—such as George Coker—designed houses in their heads, putting in all the wiring, lighting switches, and trim. Some, like Admiral Stockdale, reconstructed works of art or literature. Jim worked hard to keep his brain active, at first by mining his memory. He often visualized himself in the middle of his old neighborhood and began thinking of all the people he knew, including their complete names and everything he could remember about them. He went to all his old classrooms and relived seeing his classmates. Sometimes, he recollected a particular building and tried to imagine each element of its construction. Generating memory activity in his brain helped him defeat the loneliness and stupor of continual solitude.

Meanwhile, other prisoners were going through "kiddie interrogations" by new-guy Vietnamese, who were rehearsing and learning English. They called a prisoner into the room and required everyone to listen to propaganda about how the Americans had sabotaged the Geneva Agreements. They took Jim over for one session, but he became so sick he had to lie down on the floor. After that, they didn't bother him.

Early in November 1968, they dressed Jim up and took him with other blindfolded POWs downtown to their war museum. The prisoners weren't supposed to see anybody, but Jim peeked and recognized the person next to him. They took him through ten exhibits by himself until he became so ill he just dropped to the floor, unable to see any more. He did go to an auditorium for a show about the fall of Dien Bien Phu. All the POWs who saw it thought it was terrible—a cheap political trick to further the Vietnamese propaganda campaign.

Jim's visit to the war museum occurred just before the U.S. presidential election. The POWs knew President Johnson didn't intend to run again. The bombing had stopped. While Jim was in the Ho Chi Minh room, the Vietnamese released three prisoners, but not before having them tape statements for propaganda. Jim heard two of the tapes. The prisoners said they were going home to work for peace and thanked the Vietnamese people, the Vietnamese army, and the Solidarity Committee. One of the released prisoners was James Low, the jet ace who had been in Jim's flight in Korea. Jim was disappointed, but not surprised, to see Low's self-serving capitulation, remembering that Low had similar inclinations in Korea. Though a capable flyer, he was focused on his own accomplishments and was not a team player.

Also in November, the Vietnamese took Jim to a hospital in an ambulance with Neal Jones, Paul Kari, and John Pitchford. As noted before, Jones had been the lone shoot-down on the Hanoi POL strike Jim led. The Vietnamese were being lenient for a change, so Jim talked to the other prisoners for a few minutes. They all received cigarettes to smoke, and the blindfolds were loose enough to peek around a little. At the hospital, they x-rayed Jim and then sent him back to camp. About two weeks later, the guards took him for interrogation. A doctor was examining several of his X-rays, and Jim could see the gaping black holes in his thighbone from the infection. The doctor didn't say anything to him that day, but Jim knew this deterioration could not be good.

Two days later, Rat called Kasler into an interrogation room but only to tell him the doctor said the leg had worsened. Rat asked if Jim would authorize an operation. Jim said yes, not much caring at this point if they cut it off because it caused so much agony. He just wanted them to do something that would allow him to enjoy food again—even what passed for food at the prison—and to get some relief from pain.

On December 15, 1968, the guards caught Jim talking on the wall to Norm Wells. This time, they took him in for a quiz and tried to force him to make a Christmas tape. Back in September, the prisoners' senior ranking officer in that compound area, Larry Guarino, had passed the word to Jim that he should give the Vietnamese something to appease them. "Don't give them anything of value," he said, "but write something." Larry thought Jim couldn't go through any more punishment just then and was giving him an out. So he took that approach: if he had to, he would write something to appease them. But he never gave them anything of value.

On December 20, Elf looked in at Jim and said, "The doctor said cannot stop infection, so let's cut off leg." After demonstrating his sick sense of humor, he snickered and left the room. Three days later, however, Rat told Jim to roll up his gear and get ready to board an ambulance for the hospital. The next morning, the hospital staff started him on intravenous vitamins, gave him fresh fruit, and put him on meat-and-potato soup, plus bread. A thin sponge mattress was on the bed. Jim had no appetite, so they began force-feeding him and kept it up for more than a week. Then the Bug told him they were taking him back to camp because they could take better care of him there. But after only eight days in camp, he went back to the hospital again.

In January 1969 Jim was still in the hospital when he received the first package that came through from Martha. Rat brought it in, and Jim signed for it. It contained pictures of his family, cookies, M&M candies, and other wonderful items, such as chewing gum and two or three plastic containers of his mother's homemade cookies. Jim found he could eat them better than hospital food. The bar of Dial soap and tube of Crest toothpaste were marvelous. Cigarettes were on the receipt, but they were missing. During the two and a half years of his imprisonment, Jim had received only two letters. By the beginning of 1969, families of POWs had received fewer than six hundred letters from only one hundred prisoners during the entire period of the war to that date.

ANOTHER OPERATION AND MORE PUNISHMENT

On January 26, 1969, a Vietnamese medical staffer took Jim across the hall and allowed him to take the first hot shower he had in

North Vietnam. They gave him a razor and had him shave his leg for the operation. A nurse wrapped the leg. Another nurse, who had a small child, befriended Jim. She was about thirty years old, Jim thought, and she was always nice to him. Jim showed her the pictures of his family, and she ooh'd and aah'd over them. Little things, such as scented soap, impressed the nurses, but American wealth astounded them. Jim showed them photographs of his house and family to let them know how things looked in the United States. The plastic refrigerator containers that held his mother's cookies especially fascinated them, so Jim gave them the containers when he left the hospital. But when he tried to give them candy and chewing gum, they refused.

That night they gave Jim a preparatory shot for the operation and then took him to the operating room and laid him out on the table (see fig. 20). Jim was there early, so he could watch the nurses and the anesthesiologist set up. The operating room was cold and dim. He must have looked worried because one of the nurses came over and reassuringly patted him on the leg. A camp medic the POWs called Doctor Zorba had told Jim earlier in his broken English that they were going to remove the steel pin from his leg during this operation.

Once more, they had trouble anesthetizing Jim: they poked the needle in several times and kept missing his veins. Finally, he went out. During the operation, they made another thirteen-inch incision in his leg, removed the steel pin, scraped the dead spots out of the bone, and took cultures of the material that kept oozing out. Osteomyelitis was eating away the bone. When he woke up, he was in a room with a nurse attending him. They had blood going into his arm and were keeping him warm with a blanket and electric heaters. Afterward, they started massive doses of antibiotics. They put just four stitches in the long incision but left two hoses running out of his leg after the operation to act as drains. Later the doctor removed one but had trouble getting the other one out, so he just cut it off. It must have been soluble because it caused no additional infections and didn't bother him.

Sanitation and medical practices were very different from U.S. standards, of course. The guard who bandaged Jim's leg was filthy, and the nurses didn't wear the typical whites. Their smocks were of various colors, well worn, patched, and changed infrequently.

Early in February, the guards moved Jim back to camp and told him he would be on crutches for a long time. They said he couldn't put any weight on his leg until the bone filled in, and they finally gave him a decent pair of crutches. The first night back, he stayed in the Outhouse. In the morning, Pete Schoeffel was standing outside his room; he carried Jim's gear to room seven of the Pigsty and nursed him while Jim was immobile.

Kasler received special food for a month, but after two weeks, the guard started stealing his allotment of canned meat. Because the infection began to flare up again by the end of the first week, they gave him massive injections for twelve days with very large syringes. The injections made a mess of his left leg, but they stopped the infection, so the doctors didn't have to amputate the injured one. Later Jim learned that none of the 566 POWs who came home was an amputee. That they were able to survive imprisonment with limbs intact, despite massive injuries and physical punishment, is testimony to their remarkable constitutions and iron wills.

When Jim came back to his cell, he started using Morse code instead of the tap code to communicate. Norm Wells had moved out of the room behind Jim after the guards caught them communicating back in December, and Charlie Stackhouse moved in for a few days. Just before Jim left for the hospital, they brought in George McSwain, Bob Wideman, and Charlie Plumb. While Jim was in the hospital, Pete Schoeffel was there as well.

Things appeared to be cooling off a bit in the camp, with fewer beatings, interrogations, and petty harassments. Then George McSwain decided to stop bowing to the guards and started acting as though he were crazy. He wouldn't stand when the guards came in, go to the showers, bathe, or pick up his food. Jim supposed it was George's way of harassing them back, but it was to cause both men harm later on. Of course, if they had thought George really was crazy, they would have isolated him and eventually made him disappear. None of the prisoners who went insane, such as Earl Cobeil, returned home.

At the end of April 1969, the guards caught Bob Wideman communicating, pulled him from his cell, and worked him over for a while. When Bob came back, he said he had told the Vietnamese that Jim was the ranking officer in the building, which wasn't true.

Pete Schoeffel outranked him, for example. But that didn't keep the Vietnamese from holding him responsible for their infractions.

A few days later, they called Jim in for a quiz with Horse, the camp commander. Eel was the interpreter. Horse started telling him how well the war was going for them, how many victories they had won in South Vietnam, and how the antiwar movement was growing in the United States.

Jim said, "Well, if it's growing, why did Senators Wayne Morse and Ernest Gruening lose their seats in Congress?"

Horse glared at Jim for a couple of minutes and then said, "The antiwar group may be small, but it has a big voice." *Ironically,* thought Jim, *that was true.*

Then Eel said, "You are the senior ranking officer in your building." Jim didn't deny it because he recognized they were looking for any way to get to him.

Eel went on, "You are responsible for everybody in your building—that they behave properly."

Eel's comment ended Jim's quiz. Apparently, they just wanted to make sure he knew the consequences if George McSwain didn't straighten out.

A few days passed before they took George McSwain for interrogation. They ordered him on his knees, but he refused. When they tried to force him, he just rolled up in a ball on the floor and stayed there. Unfortunately, the backlash for George's actions fell on Jim when Rat called him back in for interrogation. Rat ordered Jim to take off his shorts and lie down on the floor. One of the guards lashed him three or four times with the fan belt, which by now was actually a strip cut out of an old tire because the original fan belt had broken. They told him that a man in his building was not showing proper respect for camp authority and that he would be punished for it.

About a week later, George was still giving the Vietnamese a hard time, so Jim tapped on the wall that he needed to start acting normal. George assured him he would, but he kept up the petty refusals and odd behavior for some time.

ESCAPE ATTEMPT AND ITS AFTERMATH

On May 10, 1969, John Dramesi and Ed Atterberry escaped from the Zoo. Kasler learned about the escape from Bud Flesher, who was living next to him. They knew reprisals were coming, even though nobody had passed information about the escape plan beforehand. Unfortunately, the escape failed: the two escapees were caught the next morning, and the Vietnamese began an incredible round of torture—brutalizing forty-five to fifty men and beating Atterberry to death. The guards broke enough prisoners to learn everything they wanted to know. Although trying to escape was part of the Code of Conduct, this attempt became a disaster for the entire group.

Guards took Jim to room one of the Auditorium for interrogation with Gold Toothed Officer, better known as "GTO," a truly psychotic tormentor. GTO made him take off his clothes and lie on the floor, then had a little guard the prisoners called "Groomsey" (or the "Weasel") whack him about eight times with the fan belt. Of course, the failed escape was just an excuse to keep the pressure on him and others. Jim had nothing to do with the attempt because he had been way off in a corner of the camp, not in the line of communication with other buildings.

After the beating, when Jim stood up and told GTO he was insane, the latter truly flew off the handle. Jim thought he might have pushed too far. GTO screamed and ran around the room, hollering about McSwain and showing proper respect, except he called him "McSwim." Rat came in then and told Jim to go back to his room and communicate with "McSwim" that he must show proper respect for camp authority.

Right after Jim returned to his room, a herd of guards came in with writing pads and sat down on his bed. They told him to get on the wall and communicate with "McSwim" about proper respect, so they could copy the tap code. Jim gave a call-up signal, but the other POWs knew the Vietnamese were in the building and didn't answer. He tried twice, then said aloud, "Is anyone in that room?" Rat ran around and opened the peep and told the men in the room to listen to the message. By this time the POWs had gone to Morse code, so they weren't using the tap code anymore. Jim used the old call-up message, "Shave and a haircut" (tap, tap-tap-tap-tap) and sent the message Rat had ordered. The response should have been "two bits" (tap-tap). Several guards ran around to the other room, then came back and said the prisoners hadn't gotten the message. So the guards gave the other POWs a pencil and paper to copy it down. Jim sent the message again, and the prisoners botched it as though they couldn't read it very well.

The Vietnamese couldn't make heads or tails of what the prisoners were doing, so they dropped the effort. Instead, they went around to get McSwain for a quiz, but George was curled up on the floor. The guards came back into Jim's room and told him to tell McSwain to put on his clothes. He tapped, "Put on clothes," but George refused to go. The whole thing would have been comical in a different setting.

A day or two later, the guards took Jim to room two of the Auditorium. GTO was there again with the same routine: take off clothes, lie down on floor, and take about eight lashes. This time Beanpole wielded the fan belt. Rat told Jim to communicate to McSwain that if George refused to go to interrogation, he would take heavy punishment. On the way back to his room, he heard a commotion outside the washroom, so he got back on the wall to ask what it was. Charlie Plumb told him McSwain had gotten down in the corner of the shower when they came for him and braced himself there. They finally pried him loose and hauled him off for interrogation. After that, the Vietnamese didn't bother Jim about McSwain.

Two weeks after the escape in early June, Rat called Kasler in for an interrogation. Rat played verbal games with him to make him guess what he had in mind, but Jim didn't respond. The interrogator was very smug, suggesting Jim would get several new roommates, who would "teach him a lesson for his life." Later that day, Jim's door opened, and in staggered Ken Fleenor, looking like hell. He was glassy eyed, his ankles were grossly swollen, and he had big gaping wounds all over his body. Jim counted twenty-nine wounds, all infected with pus dripping out of them. Ken had been shackled in ropes and irons, stretched out, and beaten. Beanpole used bamboo poles to break all the cartilage down his shinbones. The guards jackknifed him up and dropped him on his spine, repeatedly—ruthless stuff. They wouldn't give him anything for the infection, so the POWs used toothpaste around the edges of the wounds. Toothpaste has some antiseptic value, and it helped somewhat in this case.

George McSwain and Pete Schoeffel also were moved to Jim's room. Fleenor's room was hit hard because he was a communicator at the end of the Garage in contact with the Zoo annex. Fleenor was living with Al Runyan and Red McDaniel. Red took several hundred whacks with the fan belt, which tore him up badly. They also worked McSwain over to teach him a lesson. This terror went on for two months after the escape attempt.

Despite the torture and other recriminations, however, the Vietnamese couldn't stop the prisoners from resuming communications. After the purge, the men in one room were trying to get in contact with those in another building. Needless to say, they were a little nervous. When they went out to wash their dishes, they could hear the men on the other side of the wall. They threw a note over, setting up communication procedures. They waited throughout the afternoon. No answer. The next day they tried again. No answer. The next day they threw the third note, which said, "If your SRO is a lieutenant colonel or above, we respectfully request you attempt to establish communications with us. If you are a major or below, get off your ass and answer this note." That afternoon they were in contact.

To some degree, purging the communication system backfired on the Vietnamese because it caused the prisoners to become even more innovative in order to stay in contact. For example, Kasler and Pete Schoeffel learned real sign language (the deaf code) to transmit out of the building. Previously, they had used a modified form of it. Kyle Berg, whose sister was deaf, knew the system and taught it to other prisoners by using the tap code. The deaf code was useful within a room, too, if a person had been broken and the POWs didn't want to share information.

When things started to cool down again, Rat called Jim in for another quiz, at which he said, "I want you to read over the camp radio."

Jim said, "Negative. I refuse."

So the guards beat him with the fan belt—but only on the left buttock in deference to the stitch marks on the side of his hip. After ten whacks, Rat told him to write a letter about how the Vietnamese July Fourth was just like the American Revolution of 1776, as well as other similar propaganda. Jim said no, but after another thirty-five whacks, the pain was too great for him to hold out, and he was simply tired of being beaten.

By this time, Jim's eyesight had deteriorated, so the Vietnamese put him in a bright room, opened all the windows, and handed him a paper to read. It was from Lawyer Tao, the South Vietnamese leader of the National Liberation Front (NLF). Originally formed in 1960, the NLF was ostensibly a southern movement intended to underpin Hanoi's claim that North Vietnam was not violating the Geneva Agreement by sending forces into the south. One statement was from Madam Nguyen Tai Bien and another was from a woman in California. Two days later they called Jim to read once more, but he had too much trouble, mispronouncing everything he saw. They sent him back to his room and didn't ask him to read again.

After a few days, the guards told Jim the doctors said he should start walking on his leg, so they took away his crutches. Schoeffel, Fleenor, and Kasler had haircuts and were made to shave. Nobody else was getting haircuts in the building then, so they were suspicious of the reason. That afternoon, they moved Schoeffel out and then moved Jim to room one of the Coop, where Rabbit told Jim he was going to meet a delegation. Jim knew he couldn't take more torture, so he decided he could go before the delegation if he didn't have to say anything bad.

Rabbit read a question and showed Jim how to answer, but Jim wrote something entirely different, not giving an inch toward saying anything he couldn't live with. When he finished, Rabbit started ranting and raving about heavy punishment. He threw the sheet at Jim, told him to copy the answers, and said they had better be right. Jim said, "If you lay one whip on me, I won't see the delegation. If you try to make me say one thing I don't agree with, I'm not going to see the delegation." Rabbit picked up the papers and left the room. Soon, he came back and put Jim in leg irons on the floor.

The next morning, Jim was still lying on the floor. Rabbit came in, threw a piece of paper on the desk, and walked out. Jim clanked over to the desk and read the three questions and answers on the paper. One said he had received good treatment from the doctors and now was able to walk again. Another said the Vietnamese had a formidable air defense system with many SAMs and MiGs and much flak (that was true). The third was about how many airplanes the Americans had lost over North Vietnam.

That afternoon, the Professor showed up from downtown

Hanoi. He wanted Jim to tape his answers to these questions. Jim agreed but did so in a monotone. They sent out to get a whip and threw it on the table in front of him. He said, "You put that belt on me one time and I'm not going to tape this. I'm not going before the delegation." So he taped his answers in a monotone, and they departed, leaving him in leg irons for three or four days.

On delegation day the guards sent Jim out to shower. Then they took him into Hanoi to a large French mansion they had converted into their propaganda studio. They gave him beer, cookies, and some cigarettes while he was sitting there. They were remodeling the building and had hung a mirror on the wall. Jim staggered over and looked in the mirror. The face staring back at him was a shock—he looked haggard and gaunt (see fig. 21). About an hour later, they took him into another room. Nearly one hundred fifty people were in two big rooms, one of which contained a camera, a microphone, a few press photographers, and one person with a tape recorder. The person with the tape recorder had eight slips of paper with Japanese writing on them laid out in front of him.

Rabbit sat down and rehearsed Jim on his answers, but he couldn't remember what he was supposed to say. His mind was foggy. After three tries, Rabbit said, "Roll tape." Jim got up and answered the first question. Then he just stood there because he couldn't remember the answer to the second question. Finally, he recited it but then couldn't remember the next one. He actually was having trouble remembering, but he was hamming it up as well. Although he finished with a little prompting, the Professor was angry. The guards took him back to the camp and put him in room one of the Coop.

The next morning, Rat came in and told Jim he had failed the television appearance and now was going to have to write answers to questions about the *Vietnam Courier*. He was to write that the POWs received the paper every week and that it was a fine newspaper. He also was supposed to say that reading the *Vietnam Courier* had taught him about the Vietnamese people and their struggle for food, freedom, and independence. As a result, he recognized the United States had mistakenly intervened in the war. Jim refused to write.

Rat gave Jim time to think about it but came back the next day with the same assignment. He said, "You do this or you will be heavy punished."

Jim said, "I refuse," and waited for Rat to tear into him.

They threw the rubber belt down in front of him. Magoo was there. He said, "You have thirty minutes to write." When Rat picked up the belt, Jim thought he was in for it. But when he looked up, Magoo was behind Rat holding a bowl of soup. Magoo walked over and put it on the table. Both men walked out, leaving Jim there for a few days.

On August 2, 1969, the guards told Jim to roll up his gear, blindfolded him, and marched him through the camp to room five of the Pool Hall, where they left him in solitary. A few minutes later he heard crutches going into the room next to him. It was Ray Vohden moving in. The next day, the POWs learned that all nine men in the building were in solitary. One room was empty because the ceiling had fallen in. The guards posted new camp regulations and required everyone to memorize them.

George "Bud" Day, the Medal of Honor recipient, was behind Jim. An F-100 pilot, Day was the only man to be captured in the north who escaped to the demilitarized zone, only to be captured by the North Vietnamese and returned to Hanoi. He clanked around in irons for three months. Others there included Wendy Rivers, Larry Guarino, Jack Bomar, and Leo Thorsness, an F-105 pilot whose Medal of Honor action occurred before his shootdown. Jim could glimpse them through a crack in his door when they were going to and from interrogation.

After a week, it was Jim's turn for interrogation with Rabbit, who told him he must write out a form for the *Vietnam Courier*. Jim refused. Rabbit said he had violated camp regulations by refusing and put him on his knees for two hours. A week later, Eel called him in. Jim saw a tape recorder on his desk. Eel played a tape one of the POWs had recorded, handed Jim a similar script, and told him to record it.

Jim said, "I'm not going to tape that shit" and threw it at him.

Eel got up, stormed out of the room, and came back about ten minutes later to say, "You will be heavy punished." But when Jim refused again, Eel just sent him back to his room. Later he heard the script on the camp radio, so they obviously coerced someone else into taping it.

KASLER'S FAMILY: A DIFFERENT KIND OF TEMPERING

Although spared knowledge of Jim's horrendous physical torture during the first three years after his capture, Martha and the children had to survive the emotional and psychological pressures of living without him. At first, they concentrated on trying to contact Jim and hoped for his quick repatriation. Nanette was fourteen years old when she learned of his capture—a time, she admits, when you think the world is "all about you." Near Christmas of 1966, she wrote a "letter to God" at the end of which was a postscript: "The one thing I really want most in the world is for you to bring my father home." She knew her mother lived the experience of having a husband who was a POW every day but believed she and brother Jimmy blocked it out of their minds much of the time. Subconsciously, it was always there, of course. During the first few years, they always asked, "Did a letter come?" But there were very few letters, and they recognized that the few they did receive were censored or that Jim was coding them. They tried to interpret what he was saying—what he really meant—but often couldn't make out anything.

The Kasler children quickly became young adults who suffered from conflicting loyalties during Jim's incarceration because nearly all their peers were against the war. Jimmy took it upon himself to defend the nation's policy in Vietnam and had more than one tooth knocked loose in fights. He was small for his age (as his father had been), so he was beaten often. Suzanne attended Butler University for one year and then transferred to the University of Cincinnati's design school to be near Frederick Simmons, an architectural student she had started dating while in high school. His influence led her to become interested in a design career. Students at the University of Cincinnati were liberal and even radical, often marching in favor of the North Vietnamese. Suzanne was almost embarrassed to bring up the fact that her father was a POW. She didn't hide it but was trying hard to understand the other side—to balance Jim's situation with the political climate of the antiwar movement.

Being a POW's children was especially difficult for the Kaslers during the late 1960s, when they were in their teens and in high school or college. They saw the war tearing communities apart, wrestled with the sexual revolution, and observed increased use of "recreational" drugs among their peers. The Kent State demonstration and shootings took place while Suzanne was at the University of Cincinnati, but they were traumatic events for all three young Kaslers. Suzanne called home from college in tears. She said William Kunstler—the lead defense attorney in the Chicago Seven conspiracy trial—was to speak on campus and lead a rally to protest the war. They were going to have a candlelight vigil for him that night, and students were to march with lit candles. Suzanne didn't know whether to follow her feeling that the war was wrong and join the rally or to honor her father's commitment to it. But Martha told her, "Listen, Suze, do what you want to do. Whatever it is, your dad will understand."

The children's anxieties about their father's well-being hung over their lives every day. They tried to consider the feelings of their mother and siblings because they knew each family member harbored similar concerns. As Jim's time in prison wore on, however, Jimmy and Nanette caused Martha more trouble, and their junior and senior years in high school were particularly trying. As a senior, Jimmy took off and went traveling, often not showing up for weeks. Then he would appear at the front door, saying "Hi, Mom," without a dime to his name. Although angry about his behavior, Martha was always secretly relieved that he was still alive.

Martha and the family knew Jim's support of the war was particularly strong, having seen more evidence of it in a trunk containing his personal items, which the Air Force had sent home after his shoot-down. Among the documents was Jim's volunteer statement, showing that he had signed up for another tour in Vietnam—for another one hundred missions. He had promised Martha he wouldn't do that, but he felt compelled to put duty before his own interests and even before his family. He defended his country for a living, and he believed the entire family was part of that commitment. Whenever he wasn't with them for a school play or one of their other activities, they understood why. Thus, although Martha was startled to see the volunteer statement, she wasn't entirely surprised. Jim's devotion to duty and combat was a firm reality that the family had to accept about him.

The people of Indianapolis were exceptionally supportive of the Kasler family, but Martha sometimes felt like a character in *As the World Turns* or a similar soap opera. People regularly called who didn't even know the Kaslers, but who had followed news reports and sincerely cared about them. Even those who were just curious were well meaning and kind. For the most part, these positive feelings were a blessing, but Martha said, only half kidding, "That means I have to be nice all the time. Occasionally, I'd like to go off by myself and be mean!"

By summer of 1968, Martha and Jim had been apart more than two and a half years, with Jim's release from prison still not forthcoming. Martha decided she needed a job to have some regular activity every day that would keep her from dwelling on her circumstances. She had been going out to Fort Benjamin Harrison (the Army post near where they lived) and playing golf with some of the women there. Just talking, she told them she thought it would be interesting to work at the Defense Information School, where they taught broadcasting, journalism, and television to young people coming into the military.

Soon afterward, somebody at the school secretary's office phoned her to say, "If you would like to take the Civil Service exam, we have a job for you as protocol secretary. We need somebody who knows military protocol, the order of ranks, and things like that." Martha decided they had created the position for her and probably would do away with it the day she quit. Still, she thought, *Why not?* Her children were getting into their teens, and she was almost unhealthily focused on their lives, so she needed something else to do. *If everybody else in the world can pass the Civil Service exam,* she thought, *I can, too.* So she passed the exam and worked in protocol for more than five years.

The job as protocol secretary was perfect for Martha because it kept her in contact with the military and informed about the POWs. Many people who visited the school knew Jim or knew of him. For example, Gen. James Hackler had been Jim's wing commander at Bitburg and was then the defense information officer in Washington, D.C. Martha planned visits and speaking engagements at the school. She arranged all the itineraries, made hotel reservations, and planned coffees, luncheons, dinners, and special events for the secretary of defense, several assistant secretaries, and other dignitaries. They all visited with her, often answered her questions, and generally made her feel that she was more a part of the effort to free the POWs, rather than just sitting around, waiting for Jim's release.

CHAPTER 10

The Light of Freedom

THE DEATH OF HO CHI MINH (SEPTEMBER 3, 1969)

ONE morning while Kasler was lying in his cell, he kept hearing "Ho Chi Minh" chanted repeatedly from distant loudspeakers in the city. It sounded like funeral dirges. He tapped on the wall to his neighbor, "Hey Ray, I think something's happened to old Ho." Soon they saw guards with a black-and-red patch on their jackets, so they deduced Ho Chi Minh had died. Somehow, Ho's death cheered them; it seemed from that first moment an important turning point for the POWs. In fact, it began a period of better treatment for them because the North Vietnamese army took control of the prisons from the Propaganda Ministry.

Ho's death was officially announced at the prison that afternoon. The Vietnamese ordered all prisoners to put on their long, red clothes, sit on the end of their beds, and listen to the camp radio. Jim heard phrases such as "beloved leader of the Vietnamese people" and "father of the country" in the broadcasts. Ho's death appeared to upset the guards deeply because they became profoundly quiet but short tempered.

Martha Kasler also saw a change in the United States after Nixon took office and Ho Chi Minh died in 1969. One major difference was public awareness. The government notified Jim's family and those of other POWs to start talking about them to the media and their communities because the Nixon administration had decided that public opinion would be vital to the war effort. Eventually, of course, it was.

Indianapolis continued to be a nurturing environment for the Kaslers, although many people Martha met lacked awareness about the war and appeared disconnected from it. For example, she attended a number of parties on military bases while working at Fort Benjamin Harrison because the commander included her in the invitations. Once, she was standing in a group at a huge cocktail party when a woman asked a typical question wives pose at these events: "And what does your husband do?"

Martha said, "Well, he's a prisoner of war in North Vietnam."

Without hesitation, the woman said, "Well, isn't that nice," and then turned away.

Martha thought, *She didn't even hear me.* Far from becoming angry, however, she thought the woman's response was hilarious. *Oh, isn't that nice,* she mocked quietly, and then laughed out loud. It just proved what she had always suspected: at most parties, nobody pays attention to anything others say.

The *Phil Donahue* show called to ask if Martha would appear in Dayton, Ohio. Suzanne insisted they needed to go because it was a great opportunity to get the news out about the POWs. So they drove to Dayton, and Martha appeared as a "hawk" wife (though she didn't know it at the time). Donahue had scheduled a "dove" wife on the same show, obviously trying to create some controversy. Martha supported what Jim believed in and the country's effort in Vietnam; the other woman thought the United States should not have been there. Still, Donahue protected Martha from any real unpleasantness. For example, one person who called in began to say, "Well, sure, it's easy for her to sit there in her big town house," and the producers cut him off. So Martha never felt threatened. She just assumed that everybody in the audience liked her. That may have been naive, but no one ever bothered her about the Vietnam War, so her naiveté worked in her favor, and she was able to enlighten the television audience about what was going on in Hanoi.

When Martha did encounter attentive, empathetic people, they invariably asked, "How do you do this? How can you live like this?"

And Martha always said, "You know what? You do what you have to do. And you don't know what you can do until you have to do it. You just take one day at a time." She continually assumed Jim would escape or be released any day and lived accordingly. If someone had told her it would be more than six and a half years from the time Jim was shot down before she saw him again, she might not have made it. But thinking that he was going to come back at any time kept her going, just as similar thinking sustained the men in prison.

By 1969, Sybil Stockdale and the wives and parents of other POWs had formed the National League of Families. This group was a strong force that insisted others become aware of what was happening to their husbands and sons. The Indiana chapter contained thirty families who helped each other through the strain and carried out awareness activities throughout the state. For example, they built a prison cage similar to what the Viet Cong confined POWs in throughout South Vietnam and showed it at the Indiana State Fair and other public places to remind people of the prisoners' plight. They petitioned the Indiana legislature to adopt unanimously a resolution condemning maltreatment of the POWs in the north and south. Finally, they began talking publicly about the prisoners and their appalling circumstances.

For the next three years, Martha spoke at every possible organization, such as the Rotary Club or Kiwanis Club, to tell people about the POWs and their horrible treatment in captivity. She also stressed how the North Vietnamese refused to follow the Geneva Convention they had signed and kept the Red Cross from visiting the men under their control. No one tried to censor or guide anything she said. A sponsor, such as the Kiwanis Club, would simply call and say, "We understand your husband is a prisoner of war. Would you come and talk?" Often, she just told them her family's story. Because people typically were uninformed, nearly everything she said was new to them. Some were awed by the Kaslers' experiences, and all were sympathetic. For her part, Martha felt a tremendous release in being able to discuss Jim's situation without restriction, and she found it easy to talk about something she believed in so strongly.

Efforts from the League of Families, the American Legion, and the Veterans of Foreign Wars, as well as the contributions of millions of concerned Americans in many forms, brought the prisoners' deplorable treatment to the attention of the world and forced the Vietnamese to improve their living conditions. Until early 1969, few Americans knew the North Vietnamese were holding U.S. prisoners, and the Vietnamese took advantage of this policy of silence to brutalize them.

At this same time, Ross Perot organized and spent his own money on a national letter-writing campaign. The letters went to the President of North Vietnam, as well as to leaders of the Vietnamese delegation to the Paris Peace Talks. They expressed deep concern about the POWs and urged the North Vietnamese to follow five main tenets of the Geneva Convention: release a complete list of names of all men they held, release the sick and wounded, treat the POWs humanely, permit neutral inspection of the prison camps, and allow the free flow of mail between the POWs and their families. Doing so, the letters added, would enable North Vietnam to take its place in the eyes of the world as a modern civilized nation. Jim later said he imagined few Americans who sat down to write during that campaign dreamed their actions would affect the prisoners' treatment. It was a profound demonstration of what a united citizenry can accomplish.

Ho Chi Minh's death and public opinion led to major changes at the prison. For example, the guards instructed Jim to pull the bricks from his bricked-up window. The mortar was thin, so he could pull them out one at a time and drop them on the floor. Jim heard the men in other rooms doing the same thing. Over in the Pigsty, the guards began tearing down the walls between buildings. They gave the prisoners wicker cobra baskets to keep their water warm in the winter, offered them handkerchiefs, and doubled their cigarette rations. The guards' attitude toward the POWs improved noticeably, and at times smiles even crept over their usually impassive faces.

In early December, they moved Jim back into a double room that had been rooms five and ten. Wendy Rivers and Larry Guarino moved in with him. The Vietnamese gave them a chess set, and Larry taught Jim to play. At the time, Guarino was thin and still a little punchy from the beatings he had taken; fresh lash marks and scars were livid on his skin. Rivers also was recovering from beatings.

About the middle of December, Jim and other prisoners went to the theater to see a propaganda movie. Although they had attended these films before, the Vietnamese had always taken them into the theater in the dark, with blankets as partitions to separate them so they couldn't see each other. They also couldn't speak or communicate by gesture or signal. This time, however, the POWs sat on stools with the lights on. They could see each other because the blanket partitions were gone. The movie was on the antiwar movement in the United States. One sign said, "Spiro sucks"; another said, "Pull out Dick now." In the middle of the screen was the phrase "Communist Party USA." The POWs thought the movie was ludicrous, so they started laughing. The Vietnamese became angry. They said the prisoners were being disrespectful and threatened Guarino, the senior officer, saying he must better control the men or face the consequences.

They managed to get to the end of the movie, which was only forty-five minutes long. But then the guards took them back to their rooms, told them to roll up their gear, and herded them to room six of the administrative building. Strangely, the Vietnamese seemed friendly, chatting with the prisoners amiably until a British lorry-type jeep pulled up. They blindfolded the prisoners, then loaded Kasler, Rivers, Schoeffel, Daughtrey, and Anderson in the lorry and took them to the Hoa Lo prison at night. Jim was heartsick at moving to this depressing place. As the prisoners trudged down the corridors, he thought the guards were going to start pounding them again.

Rivers and Kasler went into room five, west of Thunderbird, where three narrow beds rested in a tiny, dirty space. Schoeffel and Daughtrey were in the room next to them. Anderson was across the hall. Jim climbed into bed and said a few prayers that night as he steeled himself to the terrible possibility of renewed torture. He couldn't see any other reason they would bring the prisoners to Hoa Lo and separate them again, when things were obviously improving at the Zoo.

The next morning, they took Rivers and Kasler for a quiz with the Bug. Cedric—the old whip—was there interpreting. They sat both men at the table and offered them tea and cigarettes. The guards were being too good, so Wendy and Jim were suspicious. The Bug said, "Tomorrow you will start receiving a side dish with your meals, you will get to exercise, and you will get three meals a day." Neither POW could figure out what was going on, but the Bug was true to his word. Food improved dramatically, starting that afternoon. For the previous year and a half, the POWs had received nothing but thin soup, bread, and rice. Now they received a plate of sugar, a half loaf of bread, and a side dish of better soup. The guards began letting them out into the bath stalls. Jim could do some light exercise: sit-ups, push-ups, light knee bends. His leg was improving, and he could bend it more.

Several times near Christmas 1969, Rivers and Kasler were called in at the same time for interrogation and told they were going to meet a delegation. Both men said, "Jam it. We're not doing anything." The Vietnamese threatened them with heavy punishment and then sent them back to their room. The Vietnamese wanted Jim to meet with one of the Americans in the delegation and say that their policy toward prisoners was lenient. They urged Jim to say they had given him immediate medical attention after his shoot-down and had offered him beer and other amenities. Jim steadfastly refused.

On one occasion, as Jim came out of his cell, he stopped midstride because he saw a Christmas tree standing in the corridor. The man other POWs called "Stoneface," who never uttered a sound or shed a tear during hundreds of hours of abject torture, broke down and cried at this bright reminder of better days.

With food and conditions improving, some prisoners made tapes and helped the Vietnamese in other ways. Jim passed the word to knock it off, but some ignored him. He couldn't fathom why they were cooperating with their captors. The torture had stopped by this time, but they went right on aiding the Vietnamese and their propaganda campaign.

After Christmas, treatment started going downhill again. The POWs still could leave their rooms each day, but the guards limited communication and pressured them to make concessions. Somehow they found out Jim liked to paint, so they insisted he accept materials and take it up again. He refused. Although he very much wanted to paint as a mental release and a way to pass the lonely hours, he was afraid they would use the paintings for propaganda. Later he learned that was indeed their purpose: a way to claim lenient treatment for POWs. The Vietnamese never gave the prisoners anything for nothing.

In June 1970 the Vietnamese increased the size of the exercise compound and started letting a few more people out for longer periods. One day, Rivers and Kasler were out in an area about ten feet by twenty feet, next to the bath area, when they saw a finger moving at the covered window in one of the solo rooms. It was Larry Guarino. He could stand on a box and peek out through the top of the shutters. Jim hadn't seen or heard of Guarino since the movie incident, so he had been concerned about him.

Kasler and Rivers started communicating with Guarino (using sign language) each time they were able to get out for exercise. Larry had come over from the Zoo. The Vietnamese had put him in solitary confinement at the Mint as punishment for allowing the prisoners to laugh at the movie. After a while, they moved him out to another room. Then, a month later, they moved him in with Wendy and Jim. They began combining rooms, which meant Anderson, Daughtrey, and Schoeffel joined them in a larger space. The six men could visit, so they started playing bridge and typically exercised together in the compound for three or four hours at a time.

In August 1970 the food took a fantastic turn for the better and continued that way for three months. The POWs started looking forward to three meals a day. In the mornings, they often received marmalade instead of sugar with their bread. They stopped eating bread at other meals because the soup had so many vegetables, they didn't need it. They also had potatoes and lots of fresh fish. The improved food made them think their release was imminent; they didn't know that their treatment had changed because of a tremendous outcry in America.

Near the beginning of that period, Jim first contacted John McCain, now the senior senator from Arizona. Jim was standing in the bath area, and Wendy Rivers was carrying water in from the wash area. McCain was in the Golden Nugget, with the flap open on his window, so Jim could see his head bouncing up and down.

Jim used flash code to ask, "Who are you?"

He replied, "John McCain." Then he asked, "Are you Jim Kasler?"

Jim said, "Yes. How did you know that?"

McCain said he recognized Jim from a photograph he had seen in Frank Harvey's 1967 book on the war, *Air War—Vietnam*.[1]

Jim talked with McCain for a few minutes until Rivers returned with the water. McCain was in good mental condition at the time but was physically beaten up. He had been near death after his shoot-down, and the Vietnamese didn't recognize who he was at first, so they almost let him die. Jim was impressed that McCain never accepted special treatment because of his father's position as boss of the air war. (Later, in better times, he supported the senator's bid to become President of the United States.)

But McCain was far more impressed with Jim's conduct throughout their imprisonment. During a 1999 interview Geraldo Rivera called McCain a hero, which truly embarrassed him. He responded,

> I mean this in the utmost sincerity. I was no hero. I was privileged to serve in the company of heroes. I witnessed a thousand acts of courage and compassion and love, and I did not measure up to the standards that were set for me by others—people like Jim Stockdale and Everett Alvarez and John Dramesi and Jim Kasler and Robinson Risner. . . . They were the ones who sustained me . . . who will always be my heroes.[2]

Shortly afterward, the POWs heard Ramsey Clark and Jane Fonda when the two visited Hanoi. Fonda announced on the public-address microphone that the POWs should study while they were there to learn the ways of the Vietnamese people. By doing so, she said, they would be better citizens when they went home and wouldn't commit crimes such as they had committed in Vietnam. Ramsey Clark offered the POWs who accepted the justness of North Vietnam's cause legal help when they got home. That behavior also resonated in Jim's memory, causing him to form a lifelong enmity for both Clark and Fonda.

1. The book doesn't contain Kasler's picture. McCain may have been thinking of the article Harvey wrote for *Argosy* magazine, "Thunderchiefs under Wraps," which was published in January 1967. It included a picture of Jim, featured his strike on the Hanoi POL plant, and discussed details of his shoot-down and incarceration in Hanoi.

2. *Rivera Live*, CNBC, September 9, 1999.

THE SON TAY RAID (NOVEMBER 21, 1970)

One day that fall the prisoners heard a commotion. It turned out to be the Vietnamese packing up all the dishes and food racks in order to move them out of the camp. The POWs received packages from home, after which the guards took them back to their rooms. That night, they suddenly were told to roll up their gear. The guards stacked everything on the floor of the Christmas room with the prisoners' names on the piles. Then they lined the POWs up between the Golden Nugget and the washroom and searched them thoroughly, including their body cavities. They found razor blades, pencils, string, and needles hidden in clothing, then handed back the prisoners' clothes.

Twenty-six prisoners were gathered in the Golden Nugget, which allowed Jim to see men he hadn't seen in years. He was able to talk with others, so he again speculated that his release was imminent. Soon, the guards blindfolded everyone and marched the group out. As they were leaving, Vietnamese prisoners were coming in—maximum-security hard cases being incarcerated for typical criminal offenses. The POWs marched blindfolded to the Hilton compound across the camp and stopped outside room seven, where the guards removed their blindfolds and put them in the big room together.

The next night, they moved in the full colonels. By that time, Jim understood that they were moving in the POWs from other camps all over North Vietnam. Jack Fellowes, Bud Day, and Ben Pollard moved out of Heartbreak on the night of November 25. They told Jim that Connell, Cameron, and Cobeil were there and in very bad physical and mental condition. Jim and others talked to Mumbles and the Bug, who were in charge of their compound, to see if they could get those three men moved in with them. The Vietnamese said, "We'll study it"—one of their favorite expressions. But they never did anything. The three eventually disappeared and, presumably, died in captivity. They didn't come home with the rest of the POWs in 1973.

The Vietnamese had a number of prisoners in a room that had gone by various names but was called "Double Zero" at the time. These POWs had been at the Plantation and had capitulated. Now they were antsy and wanting to fight back. They yelled and swore at the Vietnamese, which made the guards nervous about having everyone together. As a result, they tightened control over the group, commanding them to go to bed, keep silent, and otherwise avoid demonstrative behavior.

Jim was puzzled about why the Vietnamese had moved everyone together in Hanoi. He wanted to believe it was to gather them for release, but he had been down that road often enough not to get his hopes up. Then he learned from the POWs in room four, who had heard from the Vietnamese prisoners, about the Americans' November 21 rescue attempt at Son Tay. Men who had been at Camp Faith also reported that they had heard about the activity. Hearing about the raid boosted Jim's morale because he knew his country had not abandoned him. But he couldn't help thinking, *Why an attempted rescue if our release was on the horizon?* He also thought, glumly, *What kind of intelligence did our government have if they raided an empty camp?*

Although Son Tay had failed, other efforts to free the prisoners continued, including massive letter-writing drives. Martha Kasler and other wives in the League of Families helped gather 115,000 letters from citizens in Indianapolis alone. They arranged to have the letters delivered to the North Vietnamese delegation at the Paris Peace Talks. Their idea was to show Hanoi with a continual stream of letters that ordinary, grassroots people cared about the prisoners. Remarkably, the stream did impress Vietnamese leaders in Hanoi; they were amazed that so many people were concerned about so few men.

On Christmas Day everyone in Jim's room except Rivers had to report for a quiz in the Ping Pong room or Christmas room, but no one received physical punishment. They each were able to write a letter that day. Although letters were usually restricted to just six or seven lines, mail from the prisoners had increased considerably during 1970. In a letter to POW families on December 26, 1970, President Nixon noted that 332 families had received more than 3,000 letters during the year—far better than the total of 100 families and 600 letters at the start of 1969. During this period, the letters from families had to fit on the same size forms, and packages could be sent only every other month. Of course, those were the official numbers; in fact, few letters or packages from home ever reached the POWs. For example, although Martha was writing often, Jim received only thirteen letters during the entire six and a half years of his imprisonment.

THE CHURCH RIOT (FEBRUARY 7, 1971)

The POWs held a church service on February 7, over objections from the Vietnamese. George Coker, Robbie Risner, Nels Tanner, and a few other men led the service. The Vietnamese tried to break them up as soon as the service was over by taking the leaders out one by one. But Bud Day started singing "The Star Spangled Banner" as loudly as he could. Larry Guarino jumped up and helped lead the singing. Next they sang "God Bless America," with everybody joining in. They continued singing—patriotic tunes, popular songs, and hymns—as other rooms around the camp lent their voices to the effort. The Vietnamese called it the "church riot."

The guards came out armed, and administrators from downtown Hanoi came, too—all trying to quell the riot. The next morning, the POW Committee decided to escalate their fast in response to the removals and restrictions. Vern Ligon, the POW commander at that time, was working with Stockdale, Denton, and Risner. Guarino sat in as liaison. The men didn't like the idea of a fast and said so, but they followed orders. The next morning they started chanting, "no church, no eat." The Vietnamese took away their water, and two days of no food or drink left many of them weak and ill. Three-quarters of the men in the room were sick. Some were essentially dying of thirst, and many were running fevers and shaking under their blankets.

On the morning of the third day, the POWs sent a delegation to ask for food, and the Vietnamese did feed them rice mixed with canned meat. Almost immediately, they began pulling POWs out of the room, starting with lieutenant colonels and above, to punish them. They continued for weeks as they worked down through the ranks. Some of the prisoners went to isolation. Others were locked in stocks at the ends of their beds. Sometimes, two men were locked to one bed, with each man's foot in a stock for a month or longer. McCain, Fellowes, Day, and twenty-seven others went to Skid Row and remained in isolation for three months. Eventually, the Vietnamese reduced the original fifty-six prisoners in the room to just seventeen. Jim was still there. But they gradually brought people back, so about forty-five were there when American bombing started in April 1971.

Soon after the bombing started, a guard climbed up into Jim's window one night and in very precise English told the POWs that Americans were committing acts of aggression against the North Vietnamese. As a result, the prisoners' lives were in jeopardy, so they must move. In early May the guards read out a list of names (mostly of the younger prisoners), loaded them into trucks, and moved them out at night heading north. They left behind most of the sick and all the colonels, as well as other higher-ranking officers. Jim expected to go, too, because the Vietnamese were taking prisoners up near the Chinese border, where they would be less accessible to potential rescues. Two days later, they moved twenty-six of the prisoners across the compound to room one.

Negotiations continued very slowly in Paris, and the prisoners' families remained uncertain whether the men would be alive by the time they achieved peace. Meanwhile, Martha had to deal with her own uncertainty while holding the family together. Jimmy and Nanette had become more difficult during their high school years and were always in trouble, so she was ever anxious about what they would do next. One winter day in early 1971, Suzanne arrived home from college and was stunned to see that one whole side of Martha's face was paralyzed with Bell's palsy, a sudden viral disease that causes the facial nerves to swell and stop functioning. Its cause is unknown, but one can imagine it had something to do with the tremendous stress that had built up over the years. Although the condition eventually subsided, it was a low point for Martha and the children.

Soon after that, on June 8, 1971, Suzanne married Frederick Simmons and left home for good. She was barely twenty-one, but she didn't want to live at home and deal with continual reminders of her father's imprisonment. The only positive thing she could imagine coming out of his experience was that the family would see what the human spirit could handle, that her father would have a unique experience by maximizing human endurance in a way no one would ever otherwise have put himself through. Suzanne felt guilty about getting married because Jim didn't know her fiancé. Yet, she was too conservative just to live with someone, even though that was the rage at the time. So the immediate family was diminished by one as Suzanne moved on to her new life. She and Frederick both finished college while married and graduated after Jim returned from Vietnam.

ESCAPE COMMITTEE (1971–1972)

By late 1971, many of the POWs had already been held longer than any other U.S. citizens in history and saw no hope of release any time soon. As a result, even though the last escape attempt by Dramesi and Atterberry had brought harsh repercussions in 1969, some of the POWs decided to organize an escape committee. They came to Jim and asked him to take charge.

Various people were involved over time, but mostly the committee included John Dramesi, Ted Kopfman, George McKnight, and Kasler. Dramesi and Kasler started gathering food and supplies: ropes and a ladder, containers for food, a mirror for signaling, Vietnamese-style clothing, conical hats, and a pole to carry baskets. They planned to color their skin and dress like Vietnamese peasants. They hid their supplies in apertures at the bottom of the wall or in the ceiling. Then they concealed the openings with a plaster made of bread dough or of lime mixed with toilet paper, colored with charcoal to match the wall. When they were done, nobody could see the openings. They also received a tiny map of the area from the United States that showed the easiest way to get to the river and to an island rendezvous point at the mouth of the Red River.

The escape committee developed and rejected several plans. For example, the "mole plan" involved tunneling under the wall and then underground to the Red River. The escapees would then float down the river to the Gulf of Tonkin, where a rescue helicopter would pick them up at one of four designated locations. The mole plan reached the Pentagon in late January 1972; the military called it *Operation Diamond*. Secretary of Defense Laird at first rejected this plan but later approved it. However, the POWs eventually had to abandon the mole plan because they determined that concrete under the floors made it impossible. They finally decided they would go out through the compound's roof and over the wall. The

Vietnamese had abandoned the guardhouse closest to their compound, so the POWs thought they could get out from there on the shady side of the roof by removing tiles and going up through the ceiling.

By April 1972 the group was ready to go and had a plan well formed. Once over the wall, they would head to the river and follow the water downstream to the island rendezvous. On arriving there, they planned to use the mirror they had hidden to signal a rescue team. An alternate method would be to steal a boat and then fly a red or yellow flag from the mast. Through prisoners who were writing letters, Jim's team sent primitive coded messages to the United States about their plans and requested a signal of two sonic booms over Hanoi if their plan was approved.

On April 28 Admiral McCain (Commander of Pacific Forces and John McCain's father) approved the escape, partly because the military command had gotten the idea from the prisoners' coded messages that Jim and his team had inside help from the Vietnamese. Kasler and Dramesi insisted they never sent such messages and never meant to imply any Vietnamese were helping them. In any case, Admiral McCain directed the Strategic Air Command to perform the sonic booms by sending two SR-71 Blackbirds over Hanoi. At the same time, however, he delayed the recovery plan to mid-May. The escape committee needed the sonic booms to show that outside help was available and that the Navy would be waiting for them at the mouth of the Red River. They decided to leave during the flooding season, between June 1 and 15, when the river would be moving at a speed of seven to twelve knots.

Meanwhile, the military was planning how to accomplish the recovery operation, which they nicknamed *Operation Thunderhead*. They intended to use search-and-rescue (SAR) helicopters to inspect the smaller rivers at the Red River delta. At the same time, a SEAL submarine, the USS *Grayback*, would launch the Navy's SEAL teams in small, motorized vehicles to cover the back side of Point Delta—a small island considered to be the main rendezvous point.

On May 31 they set everything in motion by launching the Navy's HH-3 SAR helicopters to start searching the delta three times a day. Surprisingly, the North Vietnamese air defenses didn't fire on these helicopters, even when the latter pushed inside their airspace. They may have expected an amphibious assault and therefore refrained from tipping off U.S. forces by firing on the surveillance craft. In any case, the helicopter operations went smoothly through June 4, although they saw no escaped POWs in the area.

Other parts of the plan began running into problems. For one thing, the Navy had heavily mined the mouth of the Red River. Once informed of the *Thunderhead* operation, they immediately stopped mining, but it was too late. Because of the primitive, slow nature of the prisoners' communications with the outside world, no one could warn them of the danger. The Navy judged that, if the escapees had stolen a boat to get downriver, U.S. mines almost certainly would have killed them.

Key problems surfaced on the nights of June 4 and 5. SEAL teams from the *Grayback* tried to get to Point Delta in their motorized vehicles, but the current from the river's mouth was so strong that the vehicles couldn't make any headway. Their batteries eventually died, or the vehicles capsized, stranding the SEALs in the open ocean. On June 5 a SAR helicopter quickly picked up the SEALs who were stranded the night before. That night, the helicopter crew tried to put the team back in the water near the *Grayback*. But they mistook a second stranded team's flares and signals for the *Grayback*'s and dropped the first team from thirty feet onto heavy equipment floating in the water. The drop killed one SEAL and broke another's rib. The other seven managed to survive the night and were rescued the following day, but the military command understood that this part of the plan was not likely to work as long as the flood current continued.

Despite these setbacks, *Operation Thunderhead* persisted with surveillance flights through June 15. At that point, they had found no POWs, so the military command reluctantly called off the mission, assuming the escape attempt either hadn't occurred or had been unsuccessful. What had happened to Kasler and Dramesi? Three days after the second sonic boom, Jim told their senior ranking officer, Colonel Flynn, they were ready to go. They were within a few hours of leaving when Flynn and other senior officers decided the repercussions would be too rough on the rest of the prisoners if they escaped at that time. The senior leaders believed retaliation from the North Vietnamese would disrupt their new, hard-won communication system, so they ordered Jim not to escape. Though furious, he followed orders.

The senior staff also asked Jim to put a lid on Dramesi because the latter was creating a problem with the command structure. He was a zealot about the Code of Conduct and the necessity of escape attempts, so he considered the senior officers' "softness" a reason to argue with them over issues large and small. Although Jim had several talks with Dramesi—asking him to cool down—he had to admit his heart wasn't entirely in the admonishments. He also did not understand the senior officers' willingness to flush long months of planning and preparation down the drain. He had been willing to risk death to escape because he had no hope of getting out by other means.

The cancellation became more poignant when the POWs eventually learned the Navy had been waiting for them, although they never heard about the deadly mines that might have killed them outright if they had sailed or drifted by boat into any of the rivers laced with mines.

LINEBACKER II: THE ELEVEN-DAY WAR

In October 1972 the Vietnamese guards had become very optimistic about the war, believing the Paris Peace Talks would resolve it in their favor. The guards removed the screens from the prisoners' windows and the fences separating their compounds, unwittingly giving them a ringside seat to one of the most awesome, terrifying spectacles in modern military history. In December, after the Vietnamese again decided to delay the Paris Peace Talks, the Nixon administration determined something had to move them to serious negotiations by showing them the consequences of delay. Nixon sent B-52 bombers to North Vietnam in a sustained bombing campaign.

On December 18 the Vietnamese held a practice alert in the camp—the first since just after the Son Tay raid in 1970. That same night, camp sirens signaled that bombing was under way. Bomber and attack aircraft came hour after hour, day after day, without letup from December 18 through 29—except for a pause on Christmas Day. (Antiwar protesters who said the aircraft bombed on Christmas Day were mistaken.)

This was the only time in the war that the United States went after the enemy in a determined, effective way—finally demonstrating the country's power and resolve. It was not, as some claimed, carpet-bombing of cities and civilians, as had been done in World War II. All the targets were military. But neither Hanoi nor any other city was off limits, so the Vietnamese had no sanctuary. In fact, the POWs were amazed at the bombers' accuracy. News reports about their being injured by the bombing were phony; they sustained no damage more harmful than cracks in the plaster.

The B-52s' coming to Hanoi was the most electrifying experience of the Vietnam War for the POWs because they knew the war was all but over. The Vietnamese also seemed to know it and obviously were scared. Each guard had his own little Ho Chi Minh sewer-pipe hole in the courtyard. They spent each of the eleven days reinforcing them and piling more bed boards and cement covers on top of them. Oddly enough, their attitude toward the prisoners improved during this period, perhaps to create goodwill at Paris. They brought the POWs a little coal-oil lamp to burn in the room so they could light their own cigarettes. The guards even gave the POWs a traditional turkey dinner at Christmas time. They reduced the prisoners' outside time, but that was understandable considering the number of alerts they were having.

For eleven nights the POWs hung in their windows watching an unbelievable spectacle. The city rang with explosions and fires that burned all night; shock waves of fantastic intensity rolled over the camp, and hundreds of SAMs rose out of the city by twos and threes. The POWs could see the missiles going up and, unfortunately, some B-52s being hit and going down in flames.

Jim's emotions were mixed during the campaign. On one hand, he knew his chances of going home soon were better than they had been in a long time, and he was happy to see the B-52s being brought to bear against the enemy. On the other hand, he hated to see bombers shot down. To a pilot nothing is more awful than to witness the destruction of an aircraft and, especially, the death of its crew whenever men can't get out before an explosion. Jim could see fires burning around Hanoi for all eleven days of the bombing campaign—some ignited by bombs and others by the fallen wreckage of the bombers. Worse still, the B-52 losses weren't inevitable—proper planning could have decreased them significantly. Mission planners in Washington insisted on lining them up on specified routes and headings, at regular intervals, turning the bombers into clay pigeons in a skeet shoot. Later Jim learned some of the B-52 crews were in virtual revolt over not being able to do evasive maneuvers during the bombing runs. That they didn't suffer even more losses was testimony to the crews' exceptional skill.

In all, nearly thirteen hundred SAMs were fired, knocking down fifteen B-52s and a pair each of F-4 Phantoms and F-111As. Some pilots reported seeing volleys of a dozen or more SAMs in the air at one time. Although MiGs came up to meet the bombers, they didn't shoot down any U.S. aircraft during the eleven-day campaign. But two B-52 tail gunners received official credit for a MiG each—the first such kills by tail gunners in the war. The Air Force disallowed several other claims by B-52 tail gunners because they didn't have enough evidence to support them.

On December 26, the POWs watched as tactical fighters struck Little Detroit south of Hanoi. Suddenly, a blinding explosion filled the sky in front of them—a B-52 exploding at eight thousand feet. They watched in horror as the flaming wreckage and engines fell to the ground, and they went to bed sadder that night. But the following morning at dawn, one of the men in Jim's room—who had gotten up early to exercise—let out a shout. Everyone jumped to the windows. Entering through the Heartbreak courtyard were eight injured men, several of whom were on stretchers. The Vietnamese moved the men into an empty room they had kept vacant to prevent communications with senior officers across the camp. To the prisoners, this episode was additional proof that the war was almost over, for the Vietnamese had never before exposed new shoot-downs to the older prisoners.

The Vietnamese made a halfhearted attempt to keep the POWs from communicating with the injured men by telling the latter to stay away from their door. Jim told them to go into their toilet area and talk through a hole they had drilled through the twelve-inch wall two years earlier. Usually, the first thing a recent shoot-down would ask was, "When do you think the war will be over?" This time, however, they sent a different message: "The peace treaty is 99 percent complete, and it's only a matter of days before the war will end." After six and a half years, those were heartwarming words to Jim. He also was delighted to discover two of the men in the room were from the B-52 that had exploded the night before. The crew had bailed out well before it blew.

At that point, the United States was past ready to end its involvement in the war. Many war protesters were upset with Nixon's use of heavy bombing to end it, but Jim considered the bombing effective, necessary, and long overdue. In fact, he has always wondered if some analysts were correct in believing the United States should have asked for North Vietnam's surrender. By the end of the campaign, the Vietnamese had shot all their SAMs, and their air force was essentially neutralized. They had no way to defend themselves against attacks. On the other hand, the United States could sustain the bombing indefinitely. Instead, the United States demanded a negotiated settlement and the return of all POWs preparatory to withdrawing from the war.

Jim's family also was becoming more optimistic that he might be returning soon. Although Martha had learned over the years to temper her optimism, at Christmas 1972 it was hard not to get her hopes up. No year of their long separation was easy for the family, but 1972 was better for Martha because she received ten short letters from Jim. The tone of those letters was much more positive, reflecting his improved morale, so Martha drew comfort from believing that he knew peace was on the horizon.

Every year since Jim's capture, she had bought him a special Christmas present and stored it away for his homecoming. A few weeks earlier in 1972, with the peace negotiations looking especially promising, she had bought a sweater the exact color of Jim's eyes for him to wear on Christmas Day. She even started getting some of his other clothes ready for dry cleaning, so all would be ready on the day he returned. She vowed that when he did return home—even if it were in the middle of July—the family would hold a Christmas celebration to make up for all the years they had missed. Of course, the sweater had additional significance because Suzanne had found a sweater of the same color on the shopping trip she shared with her father the day he left for Vietnam in 1966.

Fortunately, the Nixon administration didn't rely on North Vietnam's goodwill as an impetus to peace. Instead, when the Vietnamese appeared to be stalling again, he continued the aggressive bombing campaign that began with Linebacker II. During the first two weeks of January 1973, U.S. pilots flew another twelve hundred sorties against North Vietnam, with more than five hundred by B-52s. The bombing stopped only when the North Vietnamese began sincere peace negotiations and—within two more weeks—signed the Paris peace treaty on January 27, 1973. According to the treaty, all American troops would withdraw from South Vietnam within sixty days. By that same deadline, the Vietnamese would release all American POWs. Kasler's long tour of duty with the Fourth Allied POW Wing was about to end, but his captors didn't tell him immediately, so he wasn't aware that his freedom was at hand.

Still, in the midst of the intensified air war, some optimism and humor had returned to the POWs. For example, one man went in for interrogation, no longer fearing the brutal treatment he would have received earlier. When the man returned, he said to Jim, "Good news. The 'V' aren't going to give us any more pig fat to eat."

"Why not?" Jim asked.

"Because the Marines have landed and taken all the pigs home as war brides."

CHAPTER 11

Home

RELEASE AND HOMECOMING

ON March 1, 1973, Martha Kasler found out that Jim would be released three days later; she reflected on their long separation to an *Indianapolis Star* reporter. Asked how she had managed, Martha repeated what she had said often: that she and Jim were luckier than other POW families because they had years together before Jim was captured and had already developed a strong relationship. She told the reporter, "No one can judge any wife who divorced her POW husband. Unless you've lived in this particular situation for years, it would be almost impossible to understand." She observed that one wife who eventually divorced her husband had been married to him only two months before he was captured and had heard from him only once or twice over the years. Others didn't even know if their husbands were alive. She had outlasted those pressures through her commitment to Jim, having a job that gave her a sense of identity, and, of course, being responsible for children and running a household. Now, after seven years, her steadfastness would be rewarded by Jim's homecoming.

Starting on February 12, 1973, American POWs began leaving North Vietnam in the order of their shoot-downs. Those who had been held the longest started the exodus, except that Army Special Forces captain Jim Thompson, who had been held captive nine and a half years, insisted on departing on a later plane, after the junior Army men. Otherwise, Everett Alvarez was first, Bob Shumaker was second, and 114 others were in that first planeload. A few sick or injured men went out of order for obvious reasons.

After the first releases, however, there was a pause until March 4, 1973. Even though Kasler had been a POW for six and a half years, he fell just over the cutoff into the later release group. The Vietnamese gave him "going home" clothes: shoes, shirt, and pants. (They had kept his flight suit and later placed it on display at the Hanoi Army Museum, illustrating how much his capture had meant to them.) Anyone who has seen a set of the clothes POWs wore on their last day in Hanoi recognizes just how much weight they had lost and how thin they were, despite the North Vietnamese captors' efforts to fatten them up before their release.

Kasler placed his group in military formation to leave the Hoa Lo prison, but the Vietnamese protested. He told them, "Go to hell," and marched the men out to the buses single file. Thousands of people were standing there watching them, not making a sound. Once on the bus, the POWs rode through Hanoi to Gia Lam Air Field. Despite the torture and ill treatment Jim had received from the Vietnamese, he pitied the people of Hanoi for the way they were living. Many used lean-to shelters laid against building walls as permanent homes. It depressed him to see what long years of war and deprivation had done to them.

At Gia Lam the weather ceiling was down to one hundred fifty feet. It was gray and overcast. Jim worried that an airplane might not be able to land with such limited visibility. Could they get in to pick up the prisoners? Obviously, so close to freedom, a delay would be very tough to take. Then, suddenly, a gleaming white C-141 popped down through the clouds—*a wonderful, friendly monster*, thought Jim. His eyes filled with tears when he saw the large U.S. flag painted on the side of its fuselage. *What a big moment!* he thought. The C-141 glided to a stop, and soon they started to board.

President Nixon had set up a state-of-the-art, closed-circuit television system for all families of the POWs, so they could watch the arrivals at Clark Air Force Base in the Philippines. Jim's family gathered in Indianapolis. Because no one knew when the arrival would occur, his son Jimmy was tasked to watch a test pattern with a tone until the live feed came on. He was lying on the couch at 3:00 A.M., trying to stay awake, when an image appeared on the television. The plane had already landed, and they were opening up the door. He yelled, "Mom! Suzanne! Nan!" Within seconds, all three hit the doorway into the den at the same time. Like something out of a cartoon, they remained suspended there for a moment, unable to get through the doorway, with all eyes riveted on the screen.

Jim had been promoted twice during his POW years, but he didn't know he had made colonel until that day. An American officer met him in Hanoi and said, "Colonel Kasler, you are in charge."

Jim asked, "I'm a colonel?"

The officer affirmed, "Yes, sir. You have been a colonel since 1969."

As a result, when the POWs arrived at Clark, Jim was the spokesman for their release group. He made his way down a steep, yellow-painted ramp, clipped off a brisk salute to the U.S. and Philippine flags held by a color guard, and then exchanged salutes and handshakes with two high-ranking officers and an ambassador. He spoke briefly:

> We went to Vietnam to do a job that had to be done, and we were willing to stay until that job was complete.
>
> We wanted to come home, but we wanted to come home with honor. President Nixon has brought us home with honor.
>
> God bless those Americans who supported our President during this long ordeal. We know better than any other citizen has ever known how great it is to be an American. It's good to be home.

Then, calmly, with eyes straight ahead, he walked down a red carpet to board the blue ambulance bus that waited to take him to the hospital for a battery of physical examinations and medical treatment. Those who followed kept to protocol—they debarked in shoot-down order, by date of capture.

Like all other POWs, Kasler spent a few days at the Clark Air Force Base hospital, which had been elaborately prepared to create an understated, homelike atmosphere. Gaily colored Valentine's Day decorations lined the corridors, along with posters made by schoolchildren at the base that contained such statements as, "Welcome home, we love you" and "Do you laugh inside all over?" The medical examinations were as gentle as possible, and a personal aide helped each prisoner adjust to his surroundings.

When the POWs weren't undergoing examinations, they mostly just ate—casting aside their prison diets of pumpkin soup and banana peel stew for steak and eggs, fried chicken, Cornish game hen, corn on the cob, french fries, and extra helpings of ice-cream sundaes. One POW called his fried egg "beautiful," and many downed several sundaes while drinking glass after glass of milk. Navy commander Richard Stratton told a photographer he had eaten a dozen eggs at one Sunday meal. The men gained an average of more than five pounds during their stay in the hospital; one gained fifteen. Despite problems with his teeth and the effects of his injuries, Jim held his own at the table.

Once the medical exams were complete, Jim went through official debriefing, mostly about his treatment in prison. Some news correspondents interviewed him as well. When they asked if the POWs had been tortured, he said, "Absolutely." He also talked in detail about the torture to *Time* magazine's Don Neff, even though the Air Force immediately put a muzzle on any mention of torture or other atrocities. The Air Force's position was that nobody should talk until everyone was out and back in the United States.

Gen. Daniel "Chappy" James Jr. told the *Time* reporters that information about mistreatment in the prison camps was off limits in the Philippines. But the reporters kept digging anyway and were poised to break an exclusive story on the following Monday, so the Air Force reversed its position and authorized press conferences with POWs all around the country. Although Air Force leaders were upset with Jim, he thought the story needed to be told. Eventually, after Jim had discussed his torture at several appearances, his candidness turned out all right. General James told the *Time* reporters, "You guys were right. It's all out now, and we're glad that it is. I don't see how anybody's going to get hurt. We've got them all back home."

After debriefing, the POWs flew to Hawaii for a stopover. They were supposed to land at Travis Air Force Base in San Francisco, where Jim was to meet his brother and his brother's family. But that didn't happen. Instead, they flew on to St. Louis and then to

Dayton, Ohio, where his family was waiting for him. He had talked to Martha and the children by phone from the Philippines, but Dayton was his first chance to see them.

Jim spoke briefly when the group landed in St. Louis and again when they arrived at Wright-Patterson Air Force Base in Dayton on March 8, 1973. He was bone tired by that time, and his family was in a staff car across the tarmac, waiting to greet him. His eyes wandered toward them and his voice broke with emotion several times as he delivered a short speech to a crowd of six hundred; it nearly deserted him with the last few words:

> We are not bitter men. We are proud men, but no prouder than any loyal American has a right to be.
>
> During our darkest hours in Hanoi, we maintained our faith in our God and our country. This was our strength, and we were not denied.
>
> I want to take this opportunity to thank those millions of Americans who participated in the 1969 letter-writing campaign and those who in other ways brought our deplorable treatment to the attention of the world and forced the North Vietnamese to improve our conditions. Had it not been for your efforts, many more of us would not have returned today. We are overwhelmed by the concern and the love which has been showered upon us on our return trip. We are so proud to be Americans.

At that point, Martha and the children broke away and sprinted toward Jim, as he ran toward them. The press cameras caught this long-awaited, joyous reunion (see fig. 22). Tears welled from Martha's eyes, and Suzanne and Nanette kept repeating: "Oh, daddy! Oh, daddy! Oh, daddy!" Martha had worried about what she would wear and how she would appear to Jim after aging seven years and still showing slight effects of the Bell's palsy that attacked her in 1971. But any anxieties either partner had felt concerning this first meeting immediately melted away. After all, they had changed physically, but their feelings for each other had not changed, and both recognized that was all they needed to start again.

On the other hand, Jim's children had grown so much in his absence that he barely recognized them. During their first meeting, he thought his son Jimmy was his son-in-law (Suzanne's husband).

Jimmy was a boy when he had last seen him; now, he was a six-foot-three-inch-tall young man. His daughters had become young women.

Although Jim's family had no trouble recognizing him physically, he also had changed in a very important way. As Sandy Vandenberg said in an interview:

> I had the feeling he had really come to terms with himself. He was relaxed. . . . In the military and in war you come to terms with danger, mayhem, and pathos all by yourself. Your priorities get properly aligned and the unimportant things start dropping off. You are left with the most important things, which quiets you psychologically. Some of what you have learned wears off, but you are a different person because you have learned yourself.

A clear example of Jim's self-learning occurred that night at the Wright-Patterson Air Force Base officer's club. When he sat down with his family for dinner, they were the focus of attention, as though they were national celebrities. They were seated at a huge, round table with a general and his family. Suddenly, Jim said, "I'd like to say something." Everybody hushed. Then he said, "I want to apologize to my son. I had a lot of time to think, lying there in prison for years. I went over every aspect of my life. I made a lot of mistakes. I know one mistake I made was being physical with you when I disciplined you. I want you to accept my apology."

At the time Jimmy thought, *No big deal, Dad, because seven years have passed while you were away, and I'm grown up now.* Later he recognized how much it took for his father to apologize in public. Jim didn't take his son aside and say, "Sorry about that, kid." He did it in front of people because he wanted Jimmy to know how important it was. His son called it a brave act—and well done.

While Jim was still at Wright-Patterson, he met with the press and delivered a speech at the press conference. The speech illustrates Jim's powerful belief in his country and in his fellow servicemen, despite his having suffered the most intense test of those beliefs anyone had ever encountered. In part, he said:

> American prisoners held by a foreign country, whether they are prisoners of war or civilians being detained, are never forsaken. Our country more than any other in the world never forgets nor ever

ceases in its efforts to protect its citizens or its soldiers abroad. The citizens of the United States are this country's most valuable resource, and this fact sustained us.

We never felt we were forgotten men because we knew that our government was doing everything in its power on our behalf. During this long war we never lost faith in nor doubted the actions of our government. We went to Hanoi believing in the Vietnam War. We were willing to remain until a successful and honorable conclusion was reached. Our wait was not in vain.

Kasler and his family stayed in Dayton for a few days while the Air Force's dentists worked on his teeth. Decalcification and beatings during his POW years had taken a toll. Many of his teeth in the back, those with fillings, had broken off. Other teeth had lost their enamel. Jim had thought he would lose some and perhaps all of them. Fortunately, the roots were still good, so the dental specialists were able to cap and save them. That he still has them today is a testament to his own constitution and the skill of those who did the work. Within a day or two of his return, Jim also insisted the children get their wisdom teeth pulled—all four of them. Although it seemed bizarre to them at the time, they knew he was focused on their teeth because of problems with his own, so they went along with his decision.

When the Kaslers left Wright-Patterson, they went back to Indianapolis, where people had been so gracious to the Kasler family during Jim's POW years. They couldn't get the front door of their town house open because letters and prisoner-of-war bracelets (see fig. 23) were piled four feet high on their entryway. They had to shove their door open in order to get in. In the coming weeks the Kaslers responded to every letter, as they still do today.

The bracelets with Jim's name and capture date on them were the brainstorm of Voices in Vital America (VIVA), an organization of concerned citizens who inscribed bracelets for all the known POWs and MIAs. They considered these simple metal bands an emblem of human understanding and caring for each man in captivity, often worn by people who had never met or known "their" POW or person missing in action. VIVA was a major contributor to bringing the POWs home by distributing bracelets, maintaining symposiums and support for families, advertising, issuing brochures and other information, and operating a newsletter, *The Voice*, all free to recipients.

Besides all the mail and bracelets, a box of roses for Nanette had arrived from John Brodak. Later Brodak invited Nanette to be his guest when he threw out the first baseball of the year as a returning POW in St. Louis. Brodak had kept Jim alive in prison, of course, but he also kept in his mind nearly everything Jim had said to him while they were in the cell together. His incredible memory helped restore some of the experiences and observations the family had missed during those years of separation.

The city of Indianapolis also continued to welcome and honor Jim when he came home, which helped greatly with his transition into normal life. The honors began with a huge welcome-home parade on a route published in the newspaper. It ran from the Kaslers' town house all the way to the city-county building in downtown Indianapolis. People with little U.S. flags in their hands lined the entire route. Mayor (now U.S. Senator) Richard Lugar was master of ceremonies at the event, and Indiana's governor, Otis Bowen, attended. Lugar's limousine picked up the Kaslers at their home and carried them through the parade, after which Lugar gave Jim the key to the city. Jim delivered a public address that included these remarks:

This is the third time I have returned to Indianapolis after fighting in a war in the Pacific. The war we are concluding there now is our best insurance that our sons will never have to fight there again. We went to Vietnam to stop the spread of Communism in Southeast Asia. In this we succeeded. The reason for our presence in Southeast Asia is just as valid today as it was when we first committed ourselves.

This great country has made many sacrifices during the past decade. To some, these sacrifices seemed too great. Because of the length of the war, some people despaired and became disillusioned that their government was not pursuing the correct path in Southeast Asia. Now I believe that most of these people will be able to reevaluate their judgment and recognize that our involvement was necessary and justified.

Every American has a right to express his opinion on matters of state: that is one of the freedoms for which we were fighting. But for those people who, while our boys were dying in Vietnam, carried the flag of our enemy through American streets; for those politicians and personalities who used their names to influence and encourage our young men to burn their draft cards, to desert or flee this country in order to escape the draft; for those who came to Hanoi and broadcast for the "Voice of Vietnam," telling our soldiers to desert and lay down their arms . . . for those people, I feel nothing but contempt.

Yet, for these individuals, who forsook their American heritage and worked against their country during this war, I also must have a sense of compassion. They, I cannot help but feel, have lost forever some of that godly gift of immense pride for being born American citizens. They can never again feel the tingling thrill when seeing the American flag unfurled and upon hearing our National Anthem played.

History will applaud this era of American loyalty and determination to support our allies in the free world. It will applaud our great President for his courage during these trying times, and it will forever reward those Americans who never wavered in their loyalty or support.

I want to thank you, Mayor Lugar and the citizens of Indianapolis, for the great honor you have bestowed upon me today. We, the POWs, do not feel that we are heroes. But America has every right to feel proud of the prisoners who were interned in North Vietnam. Our life was difficult, and for some brave men, too difficult. But we maintained our faith in our God and our country. Our return to freedom is our reward. It is full payment for our service.

This speech captures several of Jim's unwavering beliefs. He remains committed to a citizen's right to protest government policy but doesn't tolerate what he sees as outright treason or attempts to undermine that government. Also, he suffered personally as a POW from visits by delegations of peace advocates, whose pronouncements about North Vietnam's peaceful, agrarian society were unsullied by knowledge of the prisoners' torture and deprivation. So he has an enduring contempt for Jane Fonda, Tom Hayden, Father Berrigan, and others who (he believes) took the right to free speech to mean direct support for the enemy. And he still can "cry like a baby" when he hears the National Anthem or become "misty" over an unfurled U.S. flag because he gave so much to enjoy the freedom and humanity they represent. Finally, although he hopes humankind can find a way to end all conflict, Jim believes we must defend ourselves and our way of life against those who would take everything from us. Although others may debate the Vietnam War's efficacy in history, these core values of American democracy endure.

Once Jim was back in Indianapolis, television producers began to call him for interviews on their news and information programs. He had been on Phil Donahue's show in Dayton and was supposed to interview on the *Today Show,* but the Air Force tried to keep him out of the public eye whenever possible because of his strong views about his treatment in prison and the Johnson administration—especially Robert McNamara. Some of his appearances occurred before the last planeload of POWs came out of North Vietnam, so the authorities had some reason for circumspection. Comments about torture in Hoa Lo prison could anger the publicity-sensitive Vietnamese and endanger the remaining POWs. But that may simply have been an excuse to keep Jim from speaking about the stupidity of letting civilians run the war.

Whatever the Air Force's rationale, they assigned Gen. Chappy James to pick up the Kaslers in Indianapolis and escort them to Jim's appearance on the *Today Show* in Washington, D.C. General James flew into Indianapolis in an Air Force T-39 and took them to Bolling Air Force Base, where they landed at about 6:00 A.M. They went on short notice to a woman colonel's house on the base. She schlepped around in her bedroom slippers and bathrobe, trying to get a pot of coffee going while wondering where these interlopers had come from. The Kaslers stayed there quite a while before going to Washington, where they soon discovered that Jim would not appear on the *Today Show.* Instead, he was scheduled to interview with Howard K. Smith. Smith was a respected journalist and a good interviewer, but his show had a much lower profile—and a much smaller audience. Jim took the change in stride but always thought the Air Force had engineered it to temper his potential impact on public opinion.

Perhaps the most dazzling speculation about Jim's future focused on the possibility that he would run for the United States Senate by opposing Birch Bayh in the 1974 election. That speculation arose over the weekend of April 7, 1973, and the Indiana newspapers carried headlines about it on April 9. Republicans had stated they were looking for the best possible candidate to oppose Bayh and included Jim on the list.

In response to the news, Jim said he might be interested, although he emphasized that he had not been consulted by any official in Washington or Indiana about running for the Senate nomination. He said, "The thought of campaigning does not frighten me, but I would have to consider whether I could serve my country better by staying in the Air Force or by making the Senate bid, if the GOP really wants me to run." The previous Saturday, he had made a speech to the press association of Fort Wayne, Indiana. Although he didn't talk about the Senate race, he said returning POWs intended to be heard in political circles. He mentioned that the POWs were planning a coalition oriented toward political activities and working against communism in the United States.

Political analysts in Indiana and Washington gave Kasler's candidacy serious attention. Jim observed that he had been out of the state for a long time and didn't know if he could come up to speed on the state's needs and wants. But the *Indianapolis Star's* political columnist, Raymond Mooney, said the "colonel shouldn't worry. Some who have been in Washington several years still don't know." Mooney related that one longtime Republican who was not aligned with any GOP faction and who was asked to study the Kasler candidacy said he would make a positive report for several reasons. First, Jim had handled himself well in public appearances and had emerged as one of the leaders of the returning POWs. Second, Indiana's governor, Otis Bowen, had taken a strong liking to him. Many state legislators who would be on the ticket in 1974 also appeared impressed when the 98th General Assembly of Indiana honored Jim a few days earlier. Third, Republicans saw Martha Kasler as a definite asset: she had been named Indiana's "Mother of the Year" and was peppy, bouncy, and a quick learner.

Commentators also cited Jim's strong ties to Indiana communities, which might cut into traditional Democratic voting blocks. The influence of the American Legion and the Veterans of Foreign Wars in the state couldn't hurt his chances, and a Kasler nomination could relax the Republican Party's internal rivalries, while creating a chance for real unity among the leadership and the rank and file.

With so much positive press and a real interest in politics influencing him, Jim carefully considered the possibility of a Senate run. When he consulted the family, however, he heard a unanimous no! Whatever Martha may have thought about descriptions of her "peppy and bouncy" personality, she was clearly against Jim's going into politics. She and the children had been in a negative political state for years and had been apart from Jim too long to welcome the pressures and separations a Senate race would have entailed.

Although Jim loved a challenge, deep down he knew that he was too honest and direct for politics. He always said what he thought and had no tolerance for political "spin," which he called "lying." That kind of directness was seldom an asset in Washington, D.C. Also, despite his own popularity and growing public recognition, Jim would have faced a very steep climb to the nomination and an even tougher test against Indiana's longtime favorite son, Birch Bayh. Though he felt up to it, the months of campaigning would have taken a toll on him and exacted an even greater levy from his marriage and family. He hadn't looked forward to his return all those years only to place more strain on his loved ones. He also said it wouldn't be right to exploit his notoriety as a returning POW by running for office. He was proud of his record but would not want anyone's "sympathy vote" because he had been a prisoner. Thus, in the end, Jim decided against the Senate run in favor of staying in the Air Force and continuing his military career.

Jim's decision turned out to be a good one for personal and political reasons. Birch Bayh's hold on Indiana was too strong in 1974 to be broken by the Republicans. Bayh won another term in the Senate, was a candidate for the Democratic presidential nomination in 1976, and eventually left his Senate seat in 1981. The man Jim would have opposed for the Republican nomination, Richard Lugar, became even more formidable. He defeated Senator Vance Hartke in 1976 and began serving in the Senate in 1977 (Hartke had held office since 1959). Lugar eventually became the senior U.S. senator from Indiana. He shattered all statewide U.S. Senate election records in 1994 by more than doubling his Democratic opponent's vote and being elected to a historic fourth term. In 2001,

Lugar began serving his fifth term and is the longest-serving senator in Hoosier history.

Having decided against politics, Jim began looking forward to his next assignment at the Air War College on Maxwell Air Force Base, Alabama. Fortunately, he wasn't scheduled to report until September, so he had plenty of time for rest and recuperation on leave. The Kaslers traveled a lot, which included taking a family trip to Disney World. They also attended many events to which they were invited. Martha told everyone, "We are not going to just sit around and stare at each other. We can't make up for those lost years." She was right. Time had moved on, and the family had transmogrified in Jim's absence. No one could go back to recapture what they had missed.

Jim's approach was to put bitterness and hatred behind him so he could concentrate on the future. He also did not try to make up for being away during the children's formative years by buying them things or interceding in their daily lives. Two weeks after he came home, they all went back to what they were doing before—college or careers, their own circle of friends, and normal activities. He didn't ask them to skip anything. He said, "It happened. We've got to live with it. Let's deal with it. Let's move on." A few months after he returned, it was as though he had always been there, so he was a strong, stabilizing influence on the family, not a disruption.

Jim's decompression period also gave him a chance to adapt to the new culture around him, some of which had permeated his own family. One night, shortly after his return, he and his wife were dressing to go out.

Jim looked at Martha and said, "What's that?"

She said, "What's what? You mean my panty hose?"

Jim said, "I think they're great, but they make it awful tough. In medieval days they used to put locks on those things!"

Styles and language had also changed in ways that others took for granted but were foreign to Jim. Long hairstyles on men and bell-bottom pants were two examples, but even such mundane things as product packaging could be frustrating, especially when Jim didn't have his glasses handy to read the detailed instructions on how to open a plastic container or box.

With two twenty-year-olds still at home, Jim found the language equally puzzling. Knowing that it might be a problem for the

POWs, the Air Force had prepared a guide on current slang expressions based on interviews with young people around the country. They ended the guide by saying, "So Big Daddy, when your son or daughter comes to you and says, 'Do you dig?' you can say, 'Right on. Lay it on me, dude.'" Jim noticed that people had acquired "lifestyles" and were "doing their own thing." Other odd-sounding words he noted were "polarization," "rhetoric," "opted," and "ecology"—and he was especially amused by the new ecology slogan: "Eat a beaver. Save a tree."

Changes in Martha also demanded adjustments in the Kaslers' relationship. Circumstances had forced her to become much more independent. She had been one of that generation of small-town girls who believed they were supposed to be pleasers—to keep everybody happy and be nice and not get anybody mad at them. Suddenly, she was left to handle everything without consulting Jim. She had to make major financial and family decisions, such as where the children were going to college, where and how they would be married, and whether they would buy a car, a house, and various kinds of insurance. Gradually, she discovered an assertive personality that had always been there, lurking below the surface. As a result, she affirmed her leadership of the Kasler household and, by her own admission, became much more controlling. As Jim and Martha came to know one another again, each had to concede some authority to the other—a process that, in the end, brought them even closer together.

While waiting to move to Maxwell Air Force Base, Jim gave a number of speeches, especially around Indianapolis. Although he wasn't a natural-born speaker or a loquacious person, several experiences had prepared him for this role. He had taken public speaking courses at Las Vegas College while stationed at Nellis Air Force Base but was initially very nervous and ineffectual. One early classroom speech about world resources concluded with a less than earth-shattering observation—something like, "If we keep this up we're going to run out of resources." Jim thought he had presented it fairly well, but the instructor berated him for the poor content.

Jim gradually improved his public speaking through classroom practice and later increased his skill during his exchange tour at New Brunswick, Canada. There, the Canadians had impromptu contests in the officers' mess. They would call on somebody, give him a subject, and require a speech of two to five minutes. Although Jim had taken speech courses so he wouldn't go into shock when required to speak, he eventually became skilled enough to talk from a few notes on a wide range of subjects.

A particularly significant speaking opportunity came on his forty-seventh birthday—May 2, 1973—his first birthday in the United States in more than ten years (including his tour in Bitburg, Germany). His words reveal the emotional effect of his internment in North Vietnam but also show that, for the most part, the POWs endured and prevailed over their enemy:

> As military officers, we expect to be pressured or even tortured for military information. We are taught to resist to the best of our ability. If forced to give anything, we try to negate its value through lies or delays. Delays because we know that most military information we have will lose its value in a matter of weeks.
>
> We knew our internment would not be pleasant, but little did we imagine that we would be subjected to years of torture accompanied by continual pressure. It's difficult to imagine the mental anguish that we went through—waiting in isolation for them to come after us and fearing that we would not be strong enough to resist being forced into taping or writing something that would harm our country or its cause.
>
> During those early years we were kept in isolation much of the time and denied anything with which to occupy our minds. We were never allowed to see or communicate with other prisoners and never allowed out of our cells except for an occasional bath. The Vietnamese used these techniques for good reason: when a man living under these conditions is subjected to any mental inputs or torture, it remains vivid in his memory for months.
>
> Brainwashing has been described as torture, fear, and relief—repeated until the individual becomes receptive to, and is willing to parrot, anything he is told. Isolation, starvation, and denial of sleep are used with brainwashing to reduce the individual's resistance. The Vietnamese employed all of these techniques, but they were crude and ruthless in their approach. They were impatient for results and, when the results were not forthcoming, they became even more ruthless.
>
> Their biggest mistake was in underestimating the men with whom they were dealing. The POWs in North Vietnam were a unique group. All but three were rated officers (pilots or naviga-

tors). Most had college degrees. Many had master's degrees. For the most part, they were career officers who believed in the Vietnam War. Our mistreatment in Hanoi only strengthened that belief.

Jim considered one of his most important public appearances to be in Denver, Colorado, at the national convention of the "Mother of the Year" award recipients from each state. After things had settled down a bit, Martha and he decided to go through some of the hundreds of telegrams and letters they had received. The first telegram Jim picked out of the bag read, "Congratulations. You have just been selected as Indiana's mother of the year." He handed the telegram to Martha, suggesting dryly that it probably was for her. Although the event's organizers asked Jim to speak, he observed that Martha was the true Kasler of honor at that national event. He greatly admired her for taking such good care of the family while he was incarcerated and relished her recognition as "Indiana Mother of the Year" for 1973.

The honors and acknowledgments Jim received were typical for most of the returning POWs. In contrast to the cool or hostile treatment many veterans received when they returned from Vietnam, people typically welcomed home the former POWs with warmth and enthusiasm. Kasler and others received extraordinary treatment. For example, President Nixon honored 676 former POWs and their guests at a White House welcome-home dinner on May 24, 1973. All told, some 1,280 people attended. A huge red-and-yellow striped tent was erected on the White House lawn to host the dinner, but the President opened the White House itself—including the Nixons' private quarters—to them and their guests. They received the grand tour and were allowed to roam throughout the building.

Notable guests attending included the nation's leading political figures, such as Henry Kissinger, Defense Secretary Melvin Laird, Vice President Spiro Agnew, and the Eisenhowers. The entertainment world's rich and famous also were well represented by John Wayne, Jimmy Stewart, Bob Hope, Roy Acuff, Sammy Davis Jr., and others. Air Force captain Galand Kramer created a stir when he appeared with Miki Garcia, a *Playboy* centerfold model, on his arm. Kissinger followed his usual practice around beautiful women by sitting at her other side throughout the banquet. Bob

Hope, who had entertained the troops in Vietnam for the past twelve years, was master of ceremonies for a star-studded show. He drew good-natured boos from the guests when he referred to them as a "captive" audience.

It was the social gathering of the year, and President Nixon must have particularly enjoyed the heady atmosphere because he was in the midst of the Watergate scandal, with G. Gordon Liddy, his former aide and campaign official, already convicted and sentenced to up to twenty years in prison for conspiracy, burglary, and wiretapping. He could put those worries aside as the POWs showered accolades on him for ending the war and bringing them home. They presented him a wooden plaque that dubbed him "Richard the Lion Hearted." The POW Chorus, which had organized in the prison camps, sang a special POW hymn they had written and sung in North Vietnam. Finally, the honor guard hoisted a foot-long U.S. flag over the stage, accompanied by "The Star Spangled Banner." The POWs had crafted the flag from fiber fragments—blue from snippets of uniform, white from twine or Red Cross packages, and red from someone's underwear. They had raised it every night so they could salute it when their captors weren't looking. The program ended with everyone singing Irving Berlin's "God Bless America." The POWs received various gifts, including a set of Congressional cuff links, which Jim still has.

After the White House party, Jim also was honored as the grand marshal of the Indianapolis 500 Festival Parade. The organizers gave him a "street-legal" copy of the official pace car—a red-and-white Cadillac Eldorado convertible with his name painted on the side—to drive for a month. About one week before the race, Nanette had a little accident with the car while Jim was off speaking. Because she was the only one home, she thought she could drive it. Whereas before Vietnam he might have gotten upset, Jim remained calm about the accident and simply had the car repaired.

The day before the race, Jim rode in the parade in Indianapolis. That night, the Kaslers attended the 500 Festival Gala Queen's Ball in the Civic Center. The POWs and their guests included George Coker, Lewis Shattuck, John Brodak, Ben Pollard, and Hubert Buchanon. Later on, Jim accepted the 1973 "Liberty Bell Award" from the Indiana Bar Association on behalf of the nineteen Indiana Hoosiers who had been POWs.

On the day of the parade, Jim attended the driver's meeting, where all thirty-three Indianapolis 500 drivers signed a helmet for him as a souvenir to honor his selection as grand marshal of the parade. But Jim didn't drive the actual pace car for the race. In 1971 a nonprofessional driver had lost control of the pace car and injured some people. With an occasional exception, such as for Chuck Yeager, professional drivers handled the pace car for years afterward. Still, Jim and Martha rode in the car and waved to the crowd as Jim received their cheers.

After the race, the Kaslers traveled to the Doral Beach Club, a five-star hotel in Miami, Florida, for a week of royal treatment. The owner of the hotel gave them the use of his personal yacht and wouldn't allow Jim to pay for anything—not even tips. The owner also put Jim and Martha in a cabana on the beach. They had a marvelous time. While they were there, Jim's brother and his wife joined them. Any guest of Jim's was a guest of the hotel owner, so they also paid nothing for their stay. The entire party had golfing privileges at the owner's other club and, although they didn't golf, they went there for dinners.

From Florida, the Kaslers spent the summer traveling. Often, they stopped for lunch along the way and found that restaurant managers also wouldn't let them pay for anything. One evening, they were in Stouffer's (a fancy restaurant) and, instead of getting a bill, they received a card with all the employees' signatures and a message of gratitude for their service to the country. Invitations to country clubs and festivities nearly overwhelmed them. Although being in the limelight was fun for a while, Jim and Martha agreed they would be glad to return to a relatively normal life.

FROM AIR WAR COLLEGE TO MOUNTAIN HOME AIR FORCE BASE (1973–1975)

For the first few years after Jim was shot down, he wasn't too concerned about fitting back into the Air Force. He remembered his two-year exchange tour with the Canadian Air Force (1955–1957), during which he had been anxious about getting back because he believed he was missing out on something. In fact, little or nothing had changed when he returned except that he had gained some valuable experience. But as their time dragged on in Vietnam to four, five, and then more than six years, he and the other POWs became greatly concerned. They were sure their contemporaries were gaining valuable experience and passing them by—that on their return they would be out of tune with the times. They didn't know to what lengths the Air Force would go in order to update them and help them get rolling (and flying) again.

Nearly all the POWs wanted to get out of the returning-prisoner syndrome of debriefings, fêtes, and speeches so they could return to work. All they asked for was a chance to compete in the mainstream Air Force, and they received that opportunity. As a first step, Jim and others reported in September 1973 to the Air War College at Maxwell Air Force Base, where they spent a year studying contemporary defense policy, force structure, and strategy. Because twenty-six former POWs were enrolled in the War College, the Kaslers were not extraordinary at Air University, so no one paid them special attention. That was fine with Jim and Martha. The relative anonymity helped both of them relax and ease back into Air Force life.

By Thanksgiving of 1973, Jim's first Thanksgiving at home since 1965, they had settled into a comfortable academic lifestyle, embellished by the military courtesies and routines they had always enjoyed. In fact, Jim slipped away while the turkey was baking to play a round of golf on the course that nearly adjoined his on-base house at Maxwell. As he stood on the last hole, he contemplated the long, peaceful day ahead and checked off some things he had to be thankful for.

On the lighter side, he had rediscovered professional football on television and especially enjoyed the new (to him) instant replay. He had pushed his golf scores down into the low eighties, despite having to adjust his swing to accommodate lingering problems with his knee and back. More importantly, his family and children were with him again. He was in relatively good health and had resumed his Air Force career. But most of all, he thought suddenly, *I'm free!* A joyful mist clouded his eyes at that simple but profound thought, as he walked back not to a dank, narrow cell but to his home and family.

December 1973 was particularly eventful for Jim. In a ceremony at Maxwell, he received his first and second Air Force Crosses, as well as sixteen other medals. Then he had an exceptionally joyous Christmas celebration (after seven Christmases in prison). Jim's parents came in from Indiana, and his children gave him a calculator made by Ross Perot's firm to commemorate Perot's personal expenditures and efforts to obtain humane treatment and ultimate release for the POWs.

Perot traced the whereabouts of each returned POW for Christmas and sent each man a personal letter. It said, in part, "On your first Christmas back home, we celebrate with you and thank you for all you have done for our country. Keep your high ideals and patriotism untarnished over the years. May the future bring you added happiness and joy to offset the years you gave up for us." Perot also gave everyone special attention whenever possible. For the Kaslers, he arranged carols on Christmas Eve, sung by a Catholic youth group.

While Jim was at Air War College, he wrote an account of the June 29, 1966, strike on the Hanoi POL facility that made him one of the most famous pilots in Southeast Asia (adapted closely in this book). When the year was over, he reported to Mountain Home, Idaho, as vice commander of the 366th Tactical Fighter Wing, which flew the F-111 Aardvark (see fig. 24). Jim hadn't flown for almost eight years and had just emerged from years of physical abuse. That could have discouraged a less skilled pilot from trying, especially in a new aircraft, and a number of the POWs had not gone back to jet aircraft. Yet, the only thing that worried Jim was his right leg. It was now shorter than the left from his shoot-down injuries and poor medical treatment in North Vietnam. He wasn't sure he could get full deflection on the right rudder pedal.

But once Jim buckled in, his leg didn't prove to be a problem. His transition from the F-105, the Air Force's largest single-engine fighter, to a twin-engine, medium fighter-bomber was remarkably smooth. He took two simulator rides, learned how to start the airplane, and flew. Earlier in his career he had flown many different aircraft types, including various multiengined ones. The F-105 wasn't that much smaller than the F-111, and it had an internal bomb bay. For the most part, Jim liked the F-111. The swing wing was new to him, but he could watch his airspeed or just feel where he needed to set the wings for best performance. It cruised very well just below the speed of sound. A few times he kicked it up past Mach 1 with no problem.

Kasler's wing did a lot of night flying at Mountain Home because the F-111 was a highly automated, electronic airplane. Jim plugged in the mission information and then took off. He set the automatic system at thirty thousand feet, after which the airplane would dive down toward a black desert and level out at five hundred feet. He could go even lower, whistling across the desert, automatically following the terrain. If he came to a hill, the F-111 would rise up to clear it and then drop back down again, taking him right where he wanted to go. It was an amazing piece of machinery.

Jim was very pleased to be flying again, as well as leading others in an important mission with state-of-the-art airplanes. After six and a half years of living in suspended animation, his life and Air Force career were back on track. Robbie Risner, fellow Korean War ace and Vietnam POW, was boss of the 832d Air Division, which included several wings of F-111 aircraft. In that capacity, he often visited Mountain Home. Jim had a great rapport with Risner, partly because of their common Air Force background and partly because they both had some Indian blood in them and considered themselves warriors, as most successful fighter pilots do.

Kasler and Risner both flew the F-105 in Southeast Asia, Jim out of Takhli and Robbie out of Korat, but their paths didn't cross until they ended up in prison. Risner was shot down on September 16, 1965—nearly a year before Jim. Risner always believed the two toughest men in captivity were Jim Kasler and George (Bud) Day. "As tough as pine knots," he said. Risner said Jim would fill one of the division's wing commander positions as soon as it became vacant. He firmly believed Jim would be a three- or four-star general if he stayed in the Air Force, telling Jim he had all the makings for senior rank.

As a future wing commander, Jim certainly would have made brigadier general had he stayed in the Air Force for one more promotion cycle. But life had a way of hurling challenges at him whenever he thought his course was set, forcing him to rely on instinct and determination to mount the next hurdle. This time, the challenge took a strange form: more than six thousand yards of turf, sand traps, and trees called South Shore Golf Course—tenuously carved out of cornfields near Momence, Illinois.

GOLF COURSE OWNER AND AIR FORCE RETIREE

Jim's new crossroads—Air Force officer or businessman—didn't arrive out of the blue. He first became a golf course owner in 1957, when he partnered with Martha's brother, Marc Rankin, who was a Professional Golfers Association pro at several courses in northern Indiana. Marc found a little nine-hole course for sale at Bass Lake, Indiana, which he wanted to buy in partnership with Jim and Marc's brother, Jimmy Rankin, who would run the place. The price was reasonable, so they bought the course as a three-way partnership.

In 1959, when Jim was home on leave, his partner joined him to look at South Shore Golf Course—originally built in 1928. The owner had died, and the course was tied up in litigation. They made an offer to the heirs, but it wasn't until 1963 (when Jim was stationed at Bitburg, Germany) that the heirs finally accepted the offer. Meantime, Marc Rankin decided to get out of the golf business, so Kasler and Jimmy Rankin bought him out. They owned both Bass Lake and South Shore at one time, but while Jim was gone, his brother-in-law sold the Bass Lake course.

Meanwhile, during Jim's long years in prison, he had developed the course in his mind, especially during the two years he spent in solitary confinement and after conditions began to improve in 1971. He had little to do and nothing to read, so he visualized improvements to South Shore. When he came home from Vietnam in 1973, he didn't necessarily believe those improvements would be in place, but he thought the course would be in good condition. It wasn't. Not much progress had been made, so he invested a lot of money, made his intentions clear to his partner, and assumed things were squared away. Again, he was mistaken. The following year, when he was at Mountain Home Air Force Base, he received a letter from the bank stating they were going to foreclose on the loan against the course. He flew home, talked to a banker, and then made an offer to buy out his brother-in-law. After refusing at first, Rankin finally accepted.

That's when Jim had to make a tough decision about retiring from the Air Force and giving up an excellent chance for star rank. He knew he might regret retiring short of his goals, but he needed something to do when he left the Air Force. Although he had some years left, they wouldn't let him fly or lead flying units forever. After agonizing over his options, Jim finally decided to retire from the Air Force and settle into rebuilding the golf course and the business. When he retired on May 1, 1975, he had served in combat or combat-related actions under seven presidents: Roosevelt, Truman, Eisenhower, Kennedy, Johnson, Nixon, and Ford.

The officers planning Jim's retirement had some fun with it. Lt. Col. Ronald Strack, the deputy base commander at Mountain Home and project officer for the retirement, wrote Jim a letter to let him know he would "strive to make it a dignified event, but with a flair befitting your stature and fully expressing the sorrow we feel at your departure." He went on to request approval for the main events:

Lead off with twelve virgins in white gossamer gowns scattering orchids along the line of march (there may be some difficulty in obtaining sufficient qualified applicants—only Barbara has volunteered so far).

The three Fighter Squadron Commanders line abreast in sackcloth and ashes rending their garments and wailing appropriate laments [over your departure].

A wheeled platform with five gallows from which sway five former Inspector General complainants of your choosing. Only one hanging per complainant regardless of whether his name begins with "F."

Six members of the Social Actions Staff, with each lashed between two Anheiser-Busch Budweiser horses and torn limb from limb in front of the reviewing stand on command of Ed McMahon.

Another wheeled platform on which Colonel Walborn and Colonel Hubbard engage in mortal combat to determine succession to your vacated position.

Lastly, you will bring up the rear on an elephant dyed Air Force blue and in silver trappings. In place of the usual awards and decorations, we will match your weight on a set of scales in 24-carat golf balls.

Getting into the spirit, Jim replied, "Because of my quiet nature and inclination toward a low profile, I feel that the rather modest retirement parade you propose would be very appropriate." He expressed some reservations about Barbara's qualifying for the first group but recommended several other candidates. He added that it might be fun to have a flashback to his first entry into the Army Air Corps. They could pick one of the participating squadrons, shave their heads, have them dressed in raincoats, and let the nurses give them a "short-arm inspection" in front of the reviewing stand.

The actual retirement ceremony was less ebullient, but equally moving. In his parting remarks, Kasler said that he no longer believed war was the "glamorous thing" he thought it was in his youth. Yet, the courage and gallantry displayed by men in battle and while suffering under adversity was an inspiring, strangely beautiful thing to behold. He asserted that the human mind tends to retain only the good and reject the bad, which may explain why mankind is so fascinated by the glamour of war. Still, were he to have a chance to live his life to date over again, Jim said he would change little. He would be a fighter pilot in the United States Air Force, jink harder at a certain moment in Vietnam, and marry the same woman. He didn't elaborate on Martha's attributes, except to say that she was a superior woman who had played an important role in his career and was the source of much of his confidence.

Although Jim's words of tribute pleased Martha, his decision to retire had shocked her. She was enjoying her return to Air Force life as a vice commander's wife and president of the officer wives' club at Mountain Home. She had missed all the middle years as an officer's wife during which she would have related to younger people. Being back in the military society enabled her to start making up for lost time with a very nice group of women at the flying base.

Given her enjoyable surroundings at Mountain Home, Martha couldn't help feeling some trepidation about their change of lifestyle. Although Momence was just a few hours away from Indianapolis, where the Kaslers' children lived at the time, it wasn't the kind of place most people would pick to live. Nearby Kankakee had made the bottom of a list of the "least livable" cities in the United States. One commentator summed it up by saying, "If you want to live in the middle of the prairie with absolutely nothing but open space around you and no place to go, then move to Kankakee."

Martha knew the area from visits to her brother and sister-in-law while Jim was in Hanoi, so she remembered it as a drab, dusty place. She easily could have imagined herself sitting with locals at the country store discussing crops and prize bulls. But when Suzanne told her mother she couldn't believe her parents had decided to live there, Martha just said, "We have been to the White House for dinner." They had done so much and knew so many famous and important people that they could be comfortable anywhere. Once in Momence, of course, the Kaslers found the quality and genuineness of people in their township made their transition much easier.

Despite her concerns, Martha knew Jim would press forward once he made up his mind to retire and move to Momence. She had seen his determination too often to doubt his intentions. In an interview she reflected on Jim's life-changing retirement:

> Jim has always been able to get from point A to point B by just pointing in the right direction and going straight there. When I was younger and a little more naive, I thought he knew everything. I had never been anywhere, so his experience and confidence were impressive. In retrospect, I think we were lost an awful lot of the time while we were traveling across country with our kids and our dogs and all our personal belongings.
>
> But Jim has always thought that if you just go in the right direction, you will get where you want to go. We always did, sooner or later. He has always lived his life like that—staying on course, heading in the right direction.

CHAPTER 12

Businessman and Citizen

WHEN Kasler came to South Shore after retirement and looked closely at his golf course, his famous confidence faced a stern test. In fact, he wondered if he had made a huge mistake. Willy Wilson, a famous early designer of golf courses, nicely designed the original nine holes at South Shore in 1928. But the owners had added a back nine after World War II and never developed it much, so a golfer could walk fifty feet from some locations to find one weed on which to place a ball. Also, the sand traps had been filled in. Jim asked his former partner why.

"Oh," Rankin said, "We filled those in to speed up play."

Jim replied, "You don't have to worry about speeding up play here: you don't have any." The course needed everything immediately. It had no watering system and, consequently, very little grass. There were no traps, no tee boxes, very few trees, no carts, no maintenance building, and no cart barn. Who could blame people for staying away in droves?

Jim started from scratch and worked like a longshoreman for five years to build up South Shore. Early on, he asked his son, Jimmy, who was undecided about his future, to drop out of college temporarily in order to help with the golf course. He knew Jimmy wasn't happy with college. In fact, the university had told his son that if he didn't declare a major by the next semester, they weren't going to let him enroll. Meanwhile, he had taken courses from beginner piano to science, searching for something he could enjoy and do well.

Jimmy jumped at the chance to help but soon found he had sentenced himself to hard labor. Jim worked with his son seventeen hours a day, seven days a week, for nearly two years. Jimmy couldn't complain, though, because his father did any kind of work necessary to achieve his vision for the course. If Jim expected others to dig ditches, he dug ditches. When they pushed earth to sculpt a fairway, Jim was there, pushing and carrying with them. He plunged right into the lakes to pull weeds and into the bathroom to clean. His entire life, and especially his years of hardship as a POW, had taught him that few people die of hard work—and few succeed without it.

One event at the time showed Jim's character, despite significant money pressures that might have tempted him to compromise. A family member had learned of a scheme by which he was going to make a lot of money quickly. He sent a letter to Jim proposing that he get involved. The Kaslers were struggling financially, and the scheme promised to return fifty thousand dollars in profit— rapidly and with very little risk. However, the ethics were questionable. Jimmy thought it was a great idea, but Jim said, "Nope. We're not going to do it. I wouldn't feel good about it." Although that decision meant his own enterprise would remain in jeopardy, the philosophy behind it eventually made his entire business a success: never harm others to benefit yourself. In fact, he went out of his way to make sure no one could even perceive that he had harmed anyone in a business deal.

To improve business, Jim decided to cut the cart and greens fees drastically on Mondays and Fridays. Although the fees were too low to support his operations, he knew the key to survival would be to win back customers who had migrated to other courses as South Shore deteriorated. As soon as people began to snap up tee times on those days, he bought twelve more new golf carts, which further enhanced play. Golfers who returned began to love playing there. Nearly every outing revealed some new feature at the course, and they especially appreciated seeing the owners at the club, working hard to improve things for them.

The Kaslers had built their own home on the course—nestled under shady maple and oak trees just off the fourth green. As a result, they were always available. Martha tended bar and waited on tables, considering it her mission to straighten out the "den of iniquity" that the clubhouse had become. She improved the decor, shushed the men who enjoyed saying "bad words," and tried to keep them all in line. Everyone tolerated her leadership fairly well, although Jim told her she couldn't tend bar anymore after she mixed someone a scotch and lemonade. She continued working for ten years to get everyone straightened out and then retired. Since 1985, she has popped in and out of the clubhouse, but paid no attention whenever behavior has seemed to slip below her high standards.

Meanwhile, Jim helped with every aspect of the course's operation and even cooked steaks at weekend barbeques for members. Gradually, golfers bought club memberships or played at higher daily rates, which eased Jim's cash flow and increased his bottom line. More cash brought further improvements because he plowed all his profits back into the course for the first decade.

Thanks to Jim and Martha's diligence and hard work, a skilled course superintendent, and a savvy, attentive club manager, South Shore's entire character and appearance have changed. The course has five small lakes that Jim dug for irrigation, a watering system complete with an automatic deep-well pump at the main lake, six stone bridges over a meandering creek, and many little mounds built with the dirt dredged up from the lakes. It has seventy-five carts, a cart barn to house them, and a maintenance barn Jim acquired from a neighboring landowner. He and his staff have planted more than one thousand trees. When they lose a few trees every year to weather or insect damage, they replace them. During the Labor Day weekend of 2004, they celebrated their thirtieth South Shore Open—a two-day event that wraps up the summer with a cookout and band under the pavilion, while contributing a significant amount of money to charity.

Jim and Martha also are members of the Kankakee Country Club, which they joined when Martha retired from South Shore. That turned out to be a smart personal and professional move because they became acquainted with all of the Kankakee city fathers, who now play golf and socialize at South Shore. The decision opened many doors for the Kaslers and gave greater dimension to their overall life. In addition, they have a home on a golf course near West Palm Beach, Florida, where they spend a few months each winter to escape the sometimes brutal weather in Illinois.

BANK DIRECTOR, DEVELOPER, AND GOOD SAMARITAN

Today, James Kasler is a financier, landowner, and leading citizen in Kankakee County and its environs. Shortly after he came to South Shore, Jim asked the manager at the Bank of Momence about getting on the bank's board of directors. At the time, Merlin Karlock owned the bank, as well as thousands of acres in Indiana, which he eventually sold. Karlock was the largest landowner east of the Mississippi, but his bank had only about $17 million in assets then. When the manager mentioned Jim's interest, Karlock offered Jim a directorship, and Jim accepted. As a consequence, he became very involved in the bank's operation.

The board decided to reorganize and build another bank in the nearby town of Bourbonnais, so they asked Jim to be one of the organizers. Recognizing an opportunity to help secure his future, Jim also bought shares in the Bourbonnais project, which began with $2 million in capital. Since then, the group has added a bank in Manteno in a new building very similar to the new bank they built in Momence. The latter's assets went from $17 million to $250 million during the first fifteen years of their management and are still climbing. Jim has found the banking operations very interesting and highly lucrative. His decision to become involved was another instance of what Martha calls his "dead reckoning"—staying on course, heading in the right direction.

In addition to being a bank director for more than twenty years, Kasler has served on the Ganeer Township Board as a trustee. He sits on various boards related to Riverside Hospital, including the Finance Committee and Riverside Trust, which raises money for the hospital. Since 1993, he has been active on the Senior Living Board, including its three subdivisions for Alzheimer's disease, total care, and senior living. He hosts an annual Pro Am (professional and amateur) golf tournament at Kankakee Country Club that is a major fund-raiser for Riverside and its community programs. Martha helps Jim with it and directs an annual fund-raiser of her own—the Ladies Riverside Tournament at South Shore.

For his contributions and tireless effort on behalf of several charities, Jim received the 1999 Good Samaritan award in Kankakee. It was a complete surprise that touched him deeply. His daughter Nanette and her husband were there for the awards ceremony as special guests. When soup was served as the first course, Martha and Nanette exchanged looks. Martha said, "I think this is pumpkin soup," which Jim detested because he had eaten it almost daily as a POW. Later they learned it was actually carrot soup, but Jim hadn't complained; even pumpkin soup couldn't have spoiled that special occasion for him.

In 2002 the Riverside Medical Center Foundation further honored Jim by naming him to the Chairman's Circle—an elite award given for exceptional service to the fund-raising arm of the hospital. But Jim doesn't see the award as a crowning achievement. It is an impetus to further effort toward building Riverside into one of the finest health centers in Illinois, including a heart center that he intends to help make one of the best in the country.

THE LEGACY OF FAME

Kasler is gracious with people who cultivate his fame and commemorate his accomplishments. He answers every one of the several letters he receives each week asking for an autograph, a personal note, or a signed picture (see fig. 25). He corresponds with authors who have used some of his exploits in studies of aviation or warfare, often volunteering to review materials for accuracy before publication. Ever since his return from Hanoi in 1973, various projects and commemorative events—large and small—have occupied Jim's time.

For example, Jim was among twenty-six conferees at the Former POW Conference held in Washington, D.C., on March 25, 1985. President Reagan had said in 1984 that an "end to America's involvement in Vietnam cannot come before we've achieved the fullest possible accounting of those missing in action." The conference concerned past efforts and future plans to account for these MIAs. Jim had told the press some years before that he strongly doubted North Vietnam was still holding Americans as slaves in their labor camps because "Americans make lousy slaves." Yet he was fully committed to accounting for MIAs because, for the Fourth Allied POW Wing the prisoners had formed in Hanoi, that was part of the mission: return with honor. He continues to oppose trade and diplomatic relations with Vietnam until this accounting is complete.

In 1993 Jim was honored at the twelfth annual "Gathering of Eagles" in Montgomery, Alabama, for his lifetime contributions to aviation history. He was recognized in particular as "one of the sky's greatest" and the only person in history to receive three Air Force Crosses (see fig. 26). Fellow honorees included Charles "Chuck" Yeager, the first person to break the sound barrier; Konstantin Treshchov, a Russian World War II ace who often flew four to five sorties a day during the Battle of Stalingrad; and Joshua Shani, who flew the lead plane into Entebbe to rescue Israeli hostages (see fig. 27). More than sixteen hundred dignitaries, international students, and graduates of Maxwell Air Force Base's Air Command and Staff College attended this weeklong event. The gathering was a tribute to aviators from all nations who helped to steer the world into the jet age.

Although many events Kasler attends call for a serious public face, he enjoys them and discovers humor wherever he goes. For example, during the fall of 1999, he visited the United States Air Force Academy in Colorado Springs, Colorado, where he spoke to cadets and attended what turned out to be a "snow bowl" football game at Falcon Stadium. Retired Air Force colonel Fred Kiley (co-author of *Honor Bound*, the definitive book on Vietnam POWs) arranged for three cadets to escort Jim to the game. Despite severe back pain aggravated by sitting for hours in the icy stadium, Jim demonstrated his famous Hoosier wit as the group got up to leave in a blinding snowstorm. He fixed the cadets with a determined gaze and said seriously, "Let's save a bus trip. Let's just walk back to the dorms!" He let the cadets squirm a while before telling them, "Oh, hell. I guess we can ride."

That same year, Olivet Nazarene University in Kankakee, Illinois, presented their third annual Leadership Award to Jim as part of the Reed Institute for the Advanced Study of Leadership. Virtually the entire student body looked on as he received the award and then gave him a standing ovation, even though most of them hadn't been born when he was shot down in 1966. After the university's president introduced him with a long list of his many awards and decorations, Jim quipped, "After that introduction, it might be sufficient for me to just stand here and let you stare at me." He told them his ambition had always been to be a warrior and revealed that in music class he had routinely requested "Onward Christian Soldiers" because he thought it was a battle hymn. At one point, he said, "I hope you never have to experience a war, but if you do, the values you're learning at Olivet will carry you through." Privately, he reflected that warriors had never needed to look far for employment because human history made their participation in a war all too likely.

In 2000, Kasler was inducted into the Illinois Military Aviation Hall of Fame for his contributions to military aviation in peace and war. The award paid tribute to his service in three wars and his exceptional courage in Korea and Vietnam. It also recognized his foundational work on the F-100 fighter plane, his achievements in precision aerial gunnery, and his years of instructing young pilots in flying and gunnery tactics. Attendees were startled to learn that this famous aviator didn't continue to fly airplanes after his retirement in 1975. Had they known how important Martha was to him, however, they wouldn't have been surprised.

Jim admitted he had never considered how much Martha had worried about his flying, and she didn't reveal her concern to him until after he retired. When they arrived at South Shore in Momence, he wanted to build a hangar on the land next to the fifth fairway and put in an ultralight plane. But one night, while watching the television program *20/20* with Martha, he saw a story about the developer of the ultralight, who had lost two sons to fatal crashes in his own ultralights. Martha looked at Jim as if to ask, Need I say more? She didn't want him to fight in three wars, return from Vietnam, and then get killed in a little ultralight pond jumper. Once he understood her anxiety over his flying, he promised he wouldn't put her through it again.

Kasler still attends several public ceremonies each year. On Father's Day in 2002, Jim and Martha traveled to Indianapolis to meet with Tyson Tilland, a young man whose Boy Scout Troop 41 refurbished the "Martha Lee," an F-86 Sabrejet painted to replicate the plane in which Jim had become a jet ace. It stands outside VFW Post 7119 on the property that was Fort Benjamin Harrison (see fig. 6). Jim actually had flown this plane in Korea, but not while shooting down his six MiGs. Tilland coordinated the refurbishment to earn his Eagle Scout badge, but all troop members joined the project after looking Jim up on the Internet and finding out what he had done. For Jim, it was a chance to talk to young people about the heritage of fighter aces and others who have given themselves to the defense of their country. As an added bonus, Nanette and Suzanne—who drove up with her family from Atlanta, Georgia— were there to help Jim celebrate Father's Day and his reunion with the plane.

The stand-in for Jim's "Martha Lee" was dedicated originally at the post in 1972, while he was still a POW, but he hadn't seen it since 1973. He was very pleased with the jet's shiny new aluminum skin and boldly painted markings but was a bit concerned that it had a metal canopy. The original, authentic glass canopy was found in a plane boneyard in Arizona after a lengthy search, but vandals shot it out. After several tries with Plexiglas, which vandals also destroyed, the post gave in around 1992 and fashioned a canopy of more durable metal. Fortunately, Bill Shields, an Indiana businessman and owner of Form/Tec plastics, volunteered to fit or design a virtually indestructible polycarbonate canopy to the F-86's specifications. Once the plane was fully restored, Post 7119 rededicated it in a public ceremony near the end of 2002.

THE LEGACY OF TORTURE

Jim tries to keep himself in good physical condition, but he has fought a war of attrition against ever-present injuries and deterioration over the past two decades. In particular, he regrets the loss of his golf game, which was very solid before Vietnam and still passable in the first few years after the war. In the early 1980s, however, his knee started walking out on him, and his golf swing became flatter and flatter, until he lost it completely. Also, the osteomyelitis flared up so badly in his leg that he couldn't function because of the drainage. He had to wear huge bandages and change them seven or eight times a day. Until the 1980s, there was no antibiotic to cure osteomyelitis. Yet, the doctors said they wouldn't operate on Jim's knee until they could stop the infection in his leg. Finally, he couldn't tolerate the pain and incapacitation any longer, so he consulted doctors in Indianapolis.

Dr. Thomas Slama, who was one of the finest doctors working on infectious diseases in the United States, had just come up with a new medication (Cipro, or ciprofloxacin, used to treat various bacterial infections, including exposure to anthrax). Dr. Slama and his medical team opened Jim's leg one more time, scraped everything out, and gave him the Cipro pills. That stopped the infection—nearly a miracle to Jim after suffering all those years—and enabled an operation on his knee. The doctors thought his knee operation would last only about five years, but it carried him into 2002. He had trouble with it, though, stemming from the original damage to his right kneecap that occurred when, as a teenaged B-29 tail gunner during World War II, he struck it on the ladder leading to his weapons station.

As noted earlier, Jim's right leg is shorter than his left because of the way the femur was shattered during his ejection, the ensuing poor medical treatment, and the abuse of his leg during torture, all of which contributed to improper healing. That threw his hips and back out of alignment, leading to serious back problems from curvature of the spine. Jim assumed he eventually would need an operation on his back and knee-replacement surgery, which together might even enable him to regain some of the golf game he had lost over the years.

Another outcome of the years of torture in Hanoi is that Jim has a difficult time writing legibly. The damage to his wrists was so extensive he can't move them precisely enough to control his penmanship. That troubles him, but he doesn't dwell on it. Also, he has painted scenes and landscapes well enough to hang several pieces in his house and to have sold others over the years before the Vietnam War (see figs. 28 and 29). (Although this artistic talent often surprises people, coming from a fighter pilot, many of the Kaslers' fighter-pilot friends are artists or musicians, or both.) Jim hasn't painted for years, but he wants to go back to it as a way of relaxing and expressing his artistic impulses. Yet, he knows the restriction in his wrist will affect the finer strokes that characterize some of his earlier work, so he has more adapting to do. He is sanguine about this continual need to accommodate physical limitations, observing that many of his friends and former colleagues no longer have that option because they've moved on to the next world.

In 2000 Jim took his son's advice and underwent successful back surgery in Birmingham, Alabama. Because the younger James had similar surgery to correct a back injury suffered in the Navy, he knew how effective it could be. So he badgered Jim into getting the operation, which resolved much of the daily back pain he had been suffering for two decades.

In 2002 Jim finally scheduled the knee-replacement surgery he had been putting off for several years because his leg had undergone so much earlier trauma. The knee-replacement specialist at Riverside Hospital in Kankakee is renowned nationally, and the postoperative care for a member of the hospital's Chairman's Circle could be nothing less than perfect. Jim attacked the regimen of physical therapy and rehabilitation with his usual focus and determination. Some back pain has returned because of his adjustments to the new knee, but he's still optimistic that a return to the links and the sweet echo of a birdie putt dropping into the middle of a cup are only weeks away.

Although Jim's physical life after Vietnam has not been a "tap-in putt," he shows no evidence of the posttraumatic stress exhibited by some of the younger enlistees captured in South Vietnam. He has surprisingly few psychological "quirks" as a result of his confinement, although Martha notes that he won't abide having a "POW sliver" of soap in any tray, and they stock enough toilet paper to supply the county. He also wants a large spoon for everything he eats that doesn't require a fork, refusing especially to use a little spoon for ice cream and soup. Of course, he won't eat anything that resembles pumpkin soup, no matter what size spoon accompanies it.

When Jim first came home from Vietnam, he hated to see his family in neutral colors, especially khaki or brown. He always wanted vivid colors around him because he had lived so many years surrounded by the dullness and gloom of prison cells. That aversion has mellowed over the years. Also, at Jim's insistence, both Kasler homes have high ceilings, large flow-through living areas, light wood trim, white walls, no basement, and no locks on interior doors—evidence of his response to six and a half years of imprisonment in low, dank, dark rooms. With a wry grin, Jim allows that years of deprivation may have made him a touch peculiar on certain issues.

Jim talks candidly about his years as a POW—so freely that one might mistakenly believe the terrors of his imprisonment no longer affect him. But his eyes take on a glint and begin to swing rapidly in their sockets as he relates some of the most vicious torture sessions, almost as though he is edging toward the trancelike state he had to enter in order to withstand them years ago. The muscles in his back and shoulders tense as well, perhaps shuddering against the memory of ropes and chains. At some point, he may even say, quietly, "I don't want to talk about that anymore." Jim has tucked the pain into the recesses of his mind, but his involuntary reactions reflect what he spent to retain his self-possession and honor.

THE LEGACY OF PARENTING: CHILDREN AND FAMILY

Jim and Martha have passed on their strong, independent way of thinking to their children, Suzanne, Jimmy, and Nanette. In particular, Jim's wanting them to be the best that they could be has guided all three in their professional lives.

Being first born, Suzanne believed it was her role to be perfect and correct. At the same time, she inherited Jim's drive to excel and to lead. As a teenager, she made lists of what she wanted for herself. At the top of every list was "to be famous in my chosen field." When she went to college, she already knew she wanted to study interior design. The first firm for which she worked did commercial design interiors and made her successful—one of the top one hundred designers in the country. Then she branched out to residential work and built her own business, the award-winning *Suzanne Kasler Interiors*, in Atlanta, Georgia. Like Jim, she is a true entrepreneur who makes things work, no matter how much effort it takes. Suzanne Kasler Morris now lives in Atlanta with her family.

Jimmy and Nanette, being younger, were less driven than Suzanne and probably had more fun. They became more focused with age, but Jimmy had difficulty finding himself for several years. He went to college in Bloomington on an athletic scholarship for wrestling and tennis. He dropped out of sports but maintained high grades and eventually graduated with a degree in environmental biology. Having always loved the sea and watched *Sea Hunt* religiously as a child, Jimmy wanted to be an oceanographer. But one day he dropped into the Navy's recruiting office to get some information and walked out forty-five minutes later enlisted in the Navy. Like his father's decision to enter aviation training in 1949, Jimmy's decision was impulsive but perfect for him. The Navy guaranteed he could join the newly formed Special Operations branch, which involved salvage diving. He discovered his calling as a Navy diver and director of diving and recovery operations. Among other significant events in his career, he was executive officer of the USS *Opportune*, a ship involved in recovering the space shuttle *Challenger* when it exploded and crashed into the sea.

Today, Jimmy is a retired Navy commander. As a contractor, he manages the Navy's Business Intelligence System. This system aggregates dozens of disparate databases into an integrated database "warehouse" and allows decision makers throughout the Navy to query data in previously unimagined ways. Kasler and his son have become very close in the last ten years because of shared interests, backgrounds, and personalities. Jim (the younger) is great at verbalizing, has Kasler's understated sense of humor, and is well read.

After her teenage years, Nanette also took an individual route to her true calling and present success. She knew from an early age that she wanted to be in the dental field, took a two-year college program in dental assisting, and was an orthodontic dental assistant and technician for eleven years. But by October 1982, sister Suzanne had become a successful interior designer in Indianapolis. She was just beginning *Kasler At Home* to focus on residential design, with a retail store of accessories and furnishings for the home. Nan went to work for Suzanne and found a talent she didn't know she had. She worked for *Kasler At Home* for nine years before establishing her own design business. Today, she is a well-known interior designer and has been owner of *NKL Designs* in Zionsville, Indiana (near Indianapolis), for nearly thirteen years. She lives in

Zionsville with her husband of eight years, Allen Valenti, but takes frequent forays to their second home in West Palm Beach.

Although independent and successful in their own right, the Kasler family members remain close. They have congregated as often as possible, especially in recent years. They assembled for Jim and Martha's fiftieth wedding anniversary in April 1999, when the siblings gave their parents a surprise dinner party in Florida. Jim was deeply touched by their effort and depth of feeling, showing emotion in a way that was rare before he went to Vietnam. In August they all got together again at South Shore, and in December, they gathered in Florida to celebrate the millennium. For that occasion, Suzanne, Jimmy, and Nanette rented two houses on the beach in Destin, Florida.

Jim and Martha weren't too sure bringing the entire volatile Kasler family together for the millennial New Year's Eve on the beach was a good idea—but they had a wonderful time. At midnight, they all collected at the water's edge to watch Jimmy ignite the impressive fireworks he had arranged. Try as he would, however, he couldn't light the matches. He kept striking one after the other, but they either wouldn't light at all or extinguished immediately in the wind. The family kibitzed continually, telling Jimmy it was the most anticlimactic thing they had ever seen. But he persisted. Finally, he lit a bottle rocket and yelled, "Oh ye of little faith!" The rocket climbed bravely a few feet into the air before it fizzled and plummeted to the sand. Everyone rolled on the beach, laughing and exclaiming that it was a perfectly typical Kasler outing.

Jimmy relives his ignominy every January because the Kaslers never miss an opportunity for a good-natured jibe. For instance, when he called Martha in January 2002, she said, "Didn't you just have a fine New Year's Eve?"

He said, "Oh, it was great, Mom, just wonderful. Some of the neighbors and all the kids came in. We cooked hot dogs and hamburgers, and I took all the kids over to the golf course to light fireworks."

Unable to resist, Martha said, "Oh God, Jim. Did they go off okay?"

After a pause, he replied with a sigh, "They went great, Mom!"

A WARRIOR LOOKS TO THE FUTURE

Although Jim and Martha have lived enough experiences for several lifetimes, they give every impression they're just getting started. As Jim says, he's the type of person who can never really retire, and he and Martha have too much to accomplish to slow down now.

Despite the wearing down of bone and sinew as Jim approaches his seventy-ninth birthday, he still has a warrior's walk, with torso erect, shoulders squared back, and piercing eyes that continually survey the scene, as though seeking an adversary on the horizon. When the Gulf War came along in 1991, he truly regretted that he wasn't still in the Air Force. He was the warrior who wanted to go back one more time—to be part of the strategic planning team that would win, and win decisively. He had many thoughts about how to conduct that war, based in part on lessons learned from Vietnam. He was glad another Vietnam veteran, Gen. Norman Schwarzkopf, had the opportunity to lead a successful campaign.

Jim has had equally strong opinions about the Balkans, Somalia, Afghanistan, and the 2003 war against Saddam Hussein. Like any good military strategist, he has evaluated each conflict in terms of its purpose, its military plan and objectives, and its exit strategy or intended outcome. Although he believes overthrowing Hussein was justified on humanitarian grounds and because of the dictator's potential for endangering allies in the Gulf region, he frets over the lack of a clearly defined (and quick) military exit. In particular, he was surprised the United States didn't have immediate plans to reconstitute the Iraqi police force and army. Without them, he believes U.S. forces will be there for a long time. His major concern for future conflicts is that they minimize loss of life—especially American lives—while achieving objectives as swiftly as possible. Today, he remains deeply interested in how the military will operate and progress in an increasingly fractured political landscape.

Keen as Colonel Kasler is about the future success of his country, he is almost completely unconcerned about personal glory and recognition. He doesn't bask in his own accomplishments, although he did say at a recent ceremony that one of the most exciting things ever to happen to him in the Air Force was becoming a jet ace in

Korea. He also is reticent about combat reminiscing and drinking with crowds of fellow fighter pilots, preferring quiet get-togethers with close friends. For example, he attended only one "Red River Rats Reunion" at Las Vegas, Nevada, in August 1973. Named for the fliers who followed the Red River on bombing runs into North Vietnam, the group met that year to ring the POW/MIA Freedom Bell as a joyous welcome home for the POWs and a tribute to the MIAs. Kasler also went to the first NAM-POW reunion that year but didn't attend another until the twenty-fifth. Furthermore, he wore neither his uniform nor a single decoration to the silver anniversary reunion in 1998.

Kasler is not unaware of his place in history. His bookshelves hold the volumes in which his daring deeds appear, and he has retained a few videotaped interviews and other memorabilia. He just doesn't wear it. Many of Jim's trophies, medals, awards, and correspondence from famous people probably belong in a museum, but he has them stored in his crawl space, stuffed in a closet, or slipped under his bed. Letters from President Nixon and from Nguyen Cao Ky (President of South Vietnam) reside cordially in folders with yellowed Air Force promotion orders, speech notes, the children's old report cards, and other routine papers.

Jim's son has more of his memorabilia exhibited on the walls than Jim does, although a visitor to Jim's home in Momence can spot a framed set of his Air Force wings and medals, the 1993 Gathering of Eagles poster commemorating his status as a jet ace in the Korean War, and—prominently displayed on his dining room wall—the portrait Maxine McCaffrey created for him after his return from Vietnam. It is a striking work of art: part drawing, part painting, and part collage (see fig. 30).

Little vignettes populate McCaffrey's work: Jim strapping himself into the F-105, Jim in POW garb and torture ropes, Martha and the children running out to meet him when he returned from Hanoi, and so forth. In the foreground is a central portrait of Jim in his Air Force colonel's uniform, sitting tall and gazing clear eyed out at the viewer—no, past the viewer, through the far window, out into the sky, and toward the future. It captures the essence of James Helms Kasler—ace pilot, resistor, survivor, husband, father, ever the warrior . . . ever seeking the next challenge, anticipating the next victory.

AFTERWORD

As this biography documents, Jim Kasler is an indestructible man who persevered in the face of death through years of wartime combat flying, massive injuries in Vietnam, and vicious, continuous torture at the hands of his captors at Hoa Lo prison. Colonel Kasler can thank his tremendously strong character for his miraculous survival.

Jim's status as a Korean War ace speaks for itself. In Vietnam he was one of the Air Force's top fliers, lauded by fellow pilots as "the Destroyer" for his effectiveness in the F-105 Thunderchief. Despite being junior in rank to many in his wing, he planned and led the June 29, 1966, Hanoi POL (petroleum, oil, and lubricants) strike. It was the most effective major attack of the Vietnam War, save perhaps the great B-52 bombardments that shut down the war.

The tough breaks ahead would have defeated a lesser person. During his captivity, Jim Kasler was in a painful and hopeless mess, squeezed between the disciplinary arm of the prison and the severe needs of his grotesquely wounded body. Several attempted "operations" never repaired him properly, but rather left him with debilitating infections that would haunt him for many years, even after his return. During numerous torture sessions, he suffered a ruptured eardrum, broken rib, broken teeth, multiple flayings of his buttocks and legs (which left his skin hanging in shreds), and a reinjury of his poor leg when his attackers repeatedly kicked it and jumped on it. Still, Jim refused to cooperate with his torturers, showing spectacular resistance and admirable integrity.

Insiders said that, had the Cuban program not wound down by the end of the summer of 1968, Jim Kasler might have been the

other American to die at the Cubans' hands. But he survived, returned home, and continued serving his country. I greatly admire
his courage and tenacity.

> JAMES BOND STOCKDALE
> Vice Admiral, USN (Retired)
> Medal of Honor recipient
> NAM-POW

APPENDIX A

Personal Reflections

ALTHOUGH much of this book owes its spirit and content to Colonel Kasler's statements or opinions, it doesn't often allow him to speak directly in his own voice. This appendix captures his direct observations on a range of issues, from Vietnam, to aircraft and military development, to leadership and politics, to personal dignity, ethics, and honor. His remarks reflect the views of a concerned, involved citizen, whose passion for duty, country, family, and friends has not dimmed over the decades.

QUALITY OF THE UNITED STATES'S ARMED FORCES IN VIETNAM

I learned a lot about the quality of our troops there when I talked to Al Sones in 1973. He was an Army major stationed at Fort Benjamin Harrison and a two-time veteran of Vietnam: his first tour was in 1966, and his last was in 1971. His unit was a typical combat outfit. He commanded an Air Cavalry troop of 128 men, and in his words, he had "combat patrols being shot up all over III Corps area twenty-four hours a day." Al's troop was based in a fairly secure outpost called "Dian" only about six miles northeast of Saigon. In 1971, the word came that the troops were going home. The pullout was under way, but not for Major Sones's unit because they were designated to remain for the rest of the war. What made this situation especially difficult was that Dian was the mustering point for units on their way back to the States.

When the cavalry troop returned to Dian after a day of engaging "Charlie" on patrol, they were tired, hot, and trudging along with fewer comrades than they started the day with. Yet, they had to endure seeing many other men holding a cold beer in one hand and waving with the other—from the back of five-ton trucks whisking them off to depart for the States. If ever the ground were fertile for unit problems, this was the time. Major Sones made the point that even under these extreme conditions, with very few exceptions, the troop's performance was outstanding. They were a credit to themselves and to this country.

PRESS COVERAGE OF THE VIETNAM WAR

I strongly believe in the media's right to report the truth and to keep the public informed. After all, our freedom depends on this flow of information. But the reporting of the Vietnam War rarely focused on the good, loyal men and women who gave their all. Where were reporters like Ernie Pyle in Vietnam—reporters who would convey to the American people and to the soldiers themselves that we had outstanding people there who were doing a whale of a job in the face of untold adversity? I maintain that the average American back home in the States received an unfortunate and warped view of this aspect of the war.

Our press exploited to the fullest everything bad that happened in Vietnam: every unfortunate incident and many incidents that weren't even true. Certain papers and newsmen here in the States, for reasons I find difficult to understand, seemed determined to discredit or undermine the morale of our armed forces and the faith of the American people in our government. I would think the least we could expect from our press when our country is involved in armed conflict is an unbiased view of it, but certainly never a biased view that favored our enemy—that reported and, in fact, supported our enemy's propaganda. During the last two years of the war, one of our wire services released as fact (and verbatim) the press releases from Hanoi.

THE ANTIWAR MOVEMENT

I know others disagree, but I believe the Vietnamese propaganda would have fallen far short of its mark had it not been supported so actively by the antiwar groups here in the States. The same people who plugged for a Communist victory during the war pushed amnesty for the deserters and draft dodgers, saying the latter were forced to break the law because they were so idealistic. But 98 percent of those men were no different from the deserters and draft dodgers of the other wars we have fought. They were cowards and malcontents who were trying to hide behind a moral issue to cover their crime. They wanted to live in this country and enjoy the fruits of our society, but they weren't willing to contribute anything toward its maintenance or survival.

WHAT MADE THE PRISONERS' SURVIVAL POSSIBLE

Some people think it was patriotism and love of country. Those elements are important, but it isn't enough to have a blind, faithful obedience or allegiance to one's country without understanding or scrutinizing her problems and virtues. Just being a flag waver on the Fourth of July won't do. This shallow patriotism wasn't durable enough for some of our prisoners in Korea when they were confronted with Communist indoctrination teams.

But Vietnam was a different story. Because the military learned from our experiences in Korea, the Code of Conduct provided moral guidelines. In addition, the prisoners were far better prepared to face a captivity situation because our training emphasized the possibility of becoming a prisoner. One can never predict the circumstances of captivity because in each war the enemy has reacted differently toward prisoners. But we suspected the POWs in Vietnam would be exploited for propaganda as they had been in Korea, and we were trained to negate the value of this propaganda as much as possible.

Also, the prisoners in North Vietnam were a unique group. Most were rated officers, most had college degrees, many had master's degrees, and most were career officers who believed in the Vietnam War. The education and training these men received over the years developed character, citizenship, and responsibility. They understood that despite the difficulties in this country and all its social problems, the United States has provided a blessed and rewarding existence for more people with more real freedom than any other country on earth. We all had a clear, realistic knowledge of our country's assets and knew our form of government can best correct its liabilities.

TREATMENT OF RETURNING VETERANS

For most of the men who returned from Vietnam, there was no welcome home as there had been after previous wars. Worse than that, many servicemen and women suffered rejection and insult for having served. It is one thing to oppose the actions of our government—that is our right as free Americans—but it is quite another matter to turn against the men and women who are called upon to serve our country.

I'm sure some who went to Vietnam did not go enthusiastically, but they went and did the jobs our government asked them to do. They certainly deserved better treatment upon returning home. One POW committed suicide after his return in the face of the rejection he felt for his service and sacrifice in Vietnam. I hope those who turned against our own people are ashamed of their actions. They should be.

FUTURE CONFLICTS AND KEEPING
OUR MILITARY STRONG

In a lot of my speeches, I've said people who aspire to be young warriors need not worry because in the history of the world, there will always be a war, and they will be involved in it. I've been giving that speech ever since WWII and, unfortunately, it's true. . . . It's too true.

But some farsighted planning has gone into the total-force concept, for leaders have recognized that the reserve forces are an effective fighting force at a bargain price. We talked for many years about achieving true combat-ready status for the Guard and Reserve, but never has there been so much action to achieve that goal. Congress has authorized improvements in military and technical manning, and extensive modernizing of equipment is well under way.

It is absolutely essential that the Reserve and Guard achieve and maintain a meaningful state of readiness. I don't believe the training of our National Guard units needs to change drastically. They certainly performed well during the Korean War, Berlin crisis, Cuban crisis, Vietnam War, and both Gulf wars, as well as in the Balkans and Afghanistan. In less than a total war, the Reserve Forces can respond, and they are now designated as the primary source for augmenting the Air Force. In the future, when there is a grave, national emergency, the Reserve Forces will be called to active duty and excel.

I hope we never enter another war we don't intend to win, with half the force it takes to do the job. But if we must fight again, we'll have a hell of a good team to put on the field. In the first place, we have an all-volunteer force of dedicated young men and women. The ones who aren't dedicated are being put out, and we don't need them. Also, many people want to go into the service, where they learn great skills and often straighten out their lives. I'm very proud of our armed services; they've done a fine job.

AIRCRAFT DEVELOPMENT

Today, airplanes are fantastically expensive, and we don't have the money to resupply. In 1952, the F-86 "A" models cost $178,000 apiece, which was relatively inexpensive. The price nearly doubled for the "D" model, rising to well over $340,000. Starting with the Century Series—the F-100 through the F-106—the prices went up dramatically. For instance, the "D" model of the F-105 Thunderchief, the most common variant, cost well over $2 million per plane.

Republic Aviation developed proposals to upgrade the F-105 with a more powerful engine, wider wingspan, and stronger landing gear. Those design changes would have made a finer airplane out of the Thunderchief for missions in Vietnam, but they never happened because we ran out of money. The assembly lines at Republic Aviation were shut down even as the war was being fought and aircraft were being lost. All told, Republic built only 833 Thunderchiefs from the two test-flight "A" models through the two-seater "F" models (including those later converted to "G" model Wild Weasels). We lost nearly half that number in Southeast Asia. They were the best strategic bombers available to use against North Vietnam, but we simply used them up.

Today's B-2 stealth bombers cost between $1 billion and $2 billion dollars each, depending on how much of the research and development for new stealth technology gets factored into the twenty-one actually built. Spreading that cost figure over a larger fleet of airplanes would cut the per-airplane cost enormously. At the same time, special-interest groups are fond of showing how their pet program could be fully funded by cutting just one more B-2 bomber from the budget. Fact is, that has already happened: we have just twenty-one B-2s and will never have more. The production lines and subassembly suppliers are already long gone. To order even one more B-2 would require prohibitive start-up costs. The Air Force would have to cut deeply into other programs, and it cannot afford to do so.

Our entire bomber force will soon be down to 175 airplanes: 94 B-52s, 60 B-1Bs, and only the 21 B-2s. It's absolutely mind-boggling to think that we're still using the B-52. It's like they say: the pilots are younger than the airplane. The B-52s are ancient; yet, their expected service life has been extended. Losing a single B-2 would be devastating, a truly irreplaceable loss of a national asset. Then, too, the cost of training each pilot now runs to more than $7 million, so our pilots are more expensive than the famous Six-Million-Dollar Man (or woman) on television years ago.

When I went down to Seymour Johnson Air Force Base in 1997 for a reunion, I had a chance to sit in an F-15. That airplane is still a frontline fighter, but it is more than twenty-five years old. Ten years used to be the expected service life of a fighter plane. When I sat in the cockpit, I could see the F-15 was a bit worn. Don't get me wrong. They are still maintained in great condition, but they're old airplanes. Metal fatigue has to be setting in with all the stress they go through.

People keep asking, why build these new fighters? First of all, we need new airplanes to replace the ones that are wearing out. The F-22 Raptor is expensive, to be sure, but it is a magnificent airplane, and we must have it for future conflicts. We need the stealth technology of this new generation of fighters and bombers to give our fighting people an edge. We were very lucky during

Desert Storm, but I hope we aren't lulled into a false sense of security based on that experience. Remember, we had hundreds of B-52s in our arsenal for Desert Storm. Today, as I said, we have fewer than one hundred. Based on the history of the world, and despite the prevalence of individual terrorism, we have to assume conflicts will continue that require capable airplanes and armament.

Still, I definitely think we're going in the right direction. Now we have the F-22. It's coming out. We have another fighter . . . they're looking long range to 2014 or 2015 for that development. It's something we have to do. But the big development is in weapons, and the satellite technology is going to be unbelievable as far as weapons delivery is concerned—it already is to the Afghans and other people around the world. To bring our bombers all the way from Arkansas and back to hit targets over there is amazing. I think the Russians are looking at what we did in Afghanistan with intense envy and thinking, "Maybe we could've done something like that, too." And maybe they could—two old bombers in and they could've pounded those caves, too.

So, I think air power has a solid future, and smart people are running the Air Force.

LEADERSHIP

Leadership is a big topic, so anyone reading this better eat a high-energy bar and dig in. Above all, regardless of the size of the force or the impact of a mission, leadership is the art of dealing with humanity. One day, when one of President Eisenhower's staff brought up this subject, the President took a small piece of string and laid it on his desk. "Look," he said, "If I try to push it, I don't get anywhere. But if I pull it, I can take it anywhere I want." As a leader I must dedicate my thoughts and actions to those under my command and then lead by example—leading is impossible if I'm running behind. To lead by example, I need a set of guiding principles, so I consider leadership a combination of character, influence, discipline, effective evaluation, empathy, and flexibility.

Character: The single identifying feature of a true leader is personal integrity. All great leaders have it and recognize it in others, as a little story I like illustrates: An Army private enjoyed his furlough and wanted more time off. Resourcefully, he wired his commanding officer: "No death, no emergency. Request extension of furlough. Having a wonderful time." Having heard all the usual alibis, his commanding officer responded: "Reward for honesty: extension of five days on present furlough granted."

A high moral standard universally complements personal integrity. The strength of character that enables a person to live a clean, open life is the same strength that guides all successful leaders toward their goals. The straight and narrow path is never congested, so that way becomes clear for a person with integrity. Or, as the poet Robert Burns said, "One may be better than his reputation but never better than his principles."

Character also means overcoming adversity and holding oneself to the highest standards of performance. Leaders are people who have the physical stamina to work twelve hours or more a day, as well as the ability to get those under them to do the same with no loss of effectiveness. Leadership means seizing every opportunity, but the trouble with opportunity is that it usually comes disguised as hard work!

Influence: Any military unit, or any other homogeneous body, with proper training should learn to tune themselves to the voice of their joint experiences. Out of uniformity of environment comes uniformity of character and spirit. From moving and acting together, people grow to depend on and support each other, as well as to subordinate their individual wills to the will of the leader.

Good leaders quickly recognize the group dynamics in the units they lead. They recognize that every group will covertly or overtly choose a leader, so no one can afford to ignore the fact that reputation and peer approval in the group sometimes carry more weight than the designated leader's influence. Shakespeare said, "Reputation is an idle and most false imposition, oft got without merit and lost without deserving." I tend to agree with him, but effective leaders raise a group's standards to meet their own through continual contact with its members. Another way of saying this is, People who wake up and find themselves a success haven't been asleep.

Discipline: Discipline requires common sense, but everyone knows there is nothing common about common sense. For all too long, officers and noncommissioned officers (NCOs) at all levels have abdicated their positions as disciplinarians because they lacked the proper self-discipline necessary to do the job. Leaders must have self-discipline and they must require self-discipline from their subordinates. Leaders have a disciplined hold on their positions only when, like a pilot before takeoff, they have personally checked every critical point for potential failure. A personal faith in the military value of discipline is the difference between military maturity and mediocrity. A salute from a proud person who feels privileged to wear the uniform is the epitome of military virtue.

Disciplined units have been the most effective and capable in combat or in peace. But if one person successfully pushes a limit, soon the group extends a rule to fit its own desires. Allowing the rules to change past the prescribed limit undermines the group and stymies one's effectiveness. Members of the armed forces have only three legal and moral options. They can obey the rules and be silent. They can obey the rules even if they disagree, but try to change them through the provided legal channels. Or they can get out.

Because leaders often must impose discipline, they must be wary of abusing it. The most obvious abuse—punishment too severe for the offense—will destroy a unit's confidence in a leader's judgment and wisdom. But the opposite—punishment too lenient or no punishment at all—will almost always entirely destroy one's effectiveness as a leader and undermine control over the group. If leaders establish a precedent that this rule infraction isn't worthy of punishment, they open the door for more flagrant violations of that rule and of others with more severe consequences.

Young people today are no different from what they were twenty years ago. They will test the rules to learn limits, so they can see exactly where they fit in. They do so, psychologists say, because people draw comfort from knowing the exact boundaries of conduct they must stay within to be accepted by society. Discipline helps everyone understand those boundaries.

Effective evaluation: Great leaders recognize and appreciate good work. No lotion relieves tired, overworked muscles or brains like hearing that one's efforts were successful. Most people, regardless of their rank, want to do a good job. What makes a finished job worthwhile is the feeling that everyone knows it is a good job.

Encouragement and a word of praise are sweet music to most of our ears, so saying a kind word doesn't cost leaders much but pays rich dividends.

As a complement to recognizing good work, however, effective leaders also are quick to spot and cull anything less than the best a person can do. This evaluation calls for an acute awareness of varying abilities, even for people who hold the same rank and skill level. In other words, good leaders must chastise sloppy efforts as quickly as they reward effective ones. To keep myself on track, I often remind myself that the Creator didn't arrange the joints of my bones so I could pat myself on the back.

Empathy: I like to use an old acronym—TCOOO—take care of our own. Nothing earns a group's confidence and respect faster than their knowing that someone in their organization is concerned about their welfare. Young people today, and yes, even some of their seniors need someone they can go to for guidance and advice—someone who knows them as individuals and is looking out for them.

During one large military exercise, while I was still in the Air Force, I participated as the forces commander and encountered one of the finest examples of leadership I have ever seen. A chief master sergeant was up at 4:30 A.M., before any others in his unit, making sure there was hot water for them to shower and shave with before they began their long, tiring workday. He lived in the tents with the men despite flooding rains and freezing weather. He ate with them daily. He inspected every tent each day: a large task because more than one hundred tents accommodated five hundred men. He scrutinized the area for cleanliness, sanitation, and safety.

During the day, the chief was there to help solve the million and one individual problems that arise when that many men are put together away from home. Each evening, he was back ensuring hot water was available for showers. He closed his day by visiting the NCO Club—not to drink but to be on hand just in case any problem might arise. On his way back to his tent, he stopped by the security police headquarters to see if anyone had gotten into trouble. After one last safety check through tent city, he turned in for his four hours of sleep before beginning the same routine the next day.

The three-week exercise involved thirteen hundred men from

fifty-two different units. They flew three thousand sorties with no accidents and only one incident. In my thirty-one years in the Air Force, I had never seen a man more involved with the welfare of his men, and it paid off. This man was a true leader. He was concerned, alert to the needs of his men, and willing to work hard to do his job well. He believed in TCOOO.

Flexibility: Even in an autocratic society such as the United States Air Force, I found that flexibility is a key to successful, outstanding leadership. No two wings or other Air Force units can be managed in the same way. Most units can operate—and many do—without dynamic leadership. The fact is, units themselves change because personalities and goals change. Therefore, leaders must tailor their approaches by continually reevaluating their organizations and being willing to admit that a change is necessary.

Too many leaders want to rest on their laurels. They take it as a personal affront when someone suggests a policy they devised and used well at one stage has outgrown its usefulness. No doubt, one of the reasons our military has become so mobile is to prevent the stagnation that seeps into long-term managers and to infuse new ideas into our units. We all tend to admire leaders such as Patton, whom we think of as having had a goal and never wavering from it. We tend to overlook that, despite their advertised toughness and inflexibility, these leaders' operating techniques are much more flexible than they seem.

FREEDOM AND RESPONSIBILITY

We fought the Vietnam War because of commitments to our allies in the free world. We fought so that one of our allies could remain free. Our commitments throughout the world are no less valid or vital today than they were decades ago. We cannot shrink from our responsibilities abroad. Too many nations depend on our strength and support for their survival.

Over the years that this country has been a nation, millions of people from every country in the world—of every race, creed, and color—have immigrated to the United States seeking freedoms this nation has to offer. We are the greatest, most powerful nation the world has ever known because our forefathers knew the value of freedom and were willing to sacrifice, to fight, and to die for it.

An overwhelming majority of Americans today know the value of freedom. They're willing to fight and die for their country, if necessary. This country united is unbeatable. That unity is our goal for the future and our destiny.

At the same time, we must take responsibility to protect and encourage the freedom of others. For example, issues such as desecration of the flag can be complicated because of our First Amendment rights and freedoms. As another example, I think one of the worst blunders the United States ever committed was interning the Japanese during World War II. Franklin Roosevelt did that against the advice of a lot of people in the Senate and Congress, and I think it was shameful.

Of course, during times of war or conflict, it can be tough to contain our feelings about denying people freedom just because they're different. For example, some people today are desecrating mosques or attacking Jews because they have lost sight of their responsibility to all of the human race. Being responsible means not jumping to the conclusion that, to keep our freedom, we have to suppress somebody or do something wrong. And that takes a great deal of thought.

CHARACTER AND CITIZENSHIP

I think the United States needs more emphasis on character development and citizenship education. Millions of dedicated Americans are working with thousands of groups and organizations on this very subject, but that training must begin in the home. We have just gone through decades in which far too many parents were so concerned with being liked by their children that they were afraid to correct or discipline them. They failed to teach them their responsibilities as citizens, and in the process of this misguided love, lost their respect and did their children a grave injustice.

On the other hand, over the thirty years since I returned home from Vietnam, I have received thousands of letters from young men and women telling me of their pride in the Vietnam POWs and in their country. Receiving these letters and their words has been one of the most gratifying experiences of my life. Because many of these young people are now guiding our nation, I feel reassured about our future.

YOUTHFUL EXUBERANCE AND MELLOWING WITH EXPERIENCE

I'm still exuberant but I've mellowed and gained a little wisdom (some say very little) over the years. For one thing, it's been a long time since I've been in a fight, so I guess my temper has softened. But even during my flying days, I never picked a fight. I just found that when somebody confronts you, and you know they're going to start something, the best thing to do is get in the first punch. So I would whack them right in the mouth or break a nose, which usually ended the situation.

In one case, I was down at Eglin Air Force Base during a fire-power demonstration. A captain came up to me and said something smart to me. (I don't know why because I had done nothing to him.)

I said, "I don't even know what you're talking about."

And he growled, "Yeah, well I don't think you're telling the truth, you sumbitch." So I just went smack and dropped him right there. And I didn't have any more trouble with him.

During the Vietnam War, many fights started in the bar because men were drinking and letting off steam. I rarely drank with the guys and, when I was in combat, I never touched a drop. But one night I joined some friends there when I had the following day off from flying. Wouldn't you know it, a couple fellows who didn't like my looks confronted me, and we mixed it up a bit. I was pounding one guy into the ground, so he tried to wrestle me. I wrestled him down and said, "All right, you son of a bitch, that's enough." I let him up, but he came at me again, and I smacked him in the mouth and dropped him. He was in another squadron, so I didn't see him after that. But some of his mates told me he didn't come out of his room for a week.

BUSINESS AND COMMERCIAL SUCCESS

I've been asked where I got my business sense. Probably, in large measure, it came from my father. He was a successful insurance-office manager for Commonwealth Life Insurance Company. No doubt, I also learned a lot from my years in various schools and command positions in the Air Force. I've always said a commander doesn't have to be the smartest guy in the unit. Good commanders are those who pick smart people to work for them. And that's exactly what our President and Commander in Chief has done—pick the right people to run key organizations. A successful commander chooses the right people for a job and is not jealous of subordinates. I've seen many commanders destroy themselves and others' careers because they were jealous of the people who worked for them.

This idea carries over to business leadership. I don't think you have to be the smartest guy in the room. CEOs have to be intelligent, but it's more important to know how to pick subordinates—people who run the shop from day to day. For example, I'm afraid of computers, so I have a computer expert sitting in the office with me to do all that stuff. (Now, Martha has a computer at home, and she frightens me sometimes because she keeps calling in these outside experts to straighten things out.)

Of course, as a businessman, I have the "disadvantage" of being unable to threaten people the way a commander can in the Air Force. You know, it's hard to tell someone, "Do it or else, you bastard!" [laughs] But I treat my people very well. They're good workers and they stick with me.

CERTAINTY IN DECISION MAKING

A good leader—or any individual—has to be decisive in order to live and progress in the world. But I've probably made mistakes in my life because I tended to jump to conclusions. I think when you get an idea in your mind, you ought to sleep on it and say, "Okay, let's examine this from all aspects." Of course, had I done that concerning South Shore, I probably wouldn't be in the golf business. I most likely would have stayed in the Air Force.

But I can relate an anecdote that proves my point about thinking before you act or talk. Often, the *Kankakee Journal* calls me for my opinion on national and international events. On September 11, 2001, I watched on the clubhouse's big-screen television as two airplanes hit the twin towers. When the first one hit, I thought some idiot had tried to fly between them. Later I learned the awful truth and discovered those responsible were Muslim terrorists.

The *Journal* then called to ask my reaction to the attacks, but fortunately, I was out doing something on the golf course. Had they reached me, I probably would have said, "I'm not sure that people of the Muslim religion can ever become loyal to our country." Later that day, I heard a Muslim man on television crying and saying, "How can they do that? This is my country." Thank God the *Journal* didn't reach me earlier. That extra time enabled me to correct an inaccurate judgment and recognize what I should have known: in this country, religious beliefs don't preclude good citizenship and loyalty.

ART, PAINTING, AND BOOKS

I've always been fascinated with art and admired artists. We had a neighbor in Las Vegas, Joyce George, who is an artist. She has a studio in Albuquerque now and is very good. I was enthralled with her work. But I've always visited museums and love to look at art, so it has been a release for me.

I painted all the time when I was in Las Vegas (1952–1953) and continued for a number of years. I would have to be up at 5:00 A.M to fly, but I'd still stay up painting until 2:00 A.M. I am self-taught, but I think I've done a couple pretty good things. I have painted some Civil War stuff with horses and cavalry, some rural or farm scenes, that sort of thing (see figs. 28 and 29). I kind of moved away from it after Vietnam, but I intend to get back into it one of these days.

I also love to read, especially when I'm in Florida, where I don't need to focus every day on running the golf course. There, I go through a book every couple of days and enjoy many kinds of books: histories, biographies, and lots of mysteries. My favorite book is *Lee's Lieutenants*, which I've read many times. But then, I've always favored the South because I spent much of my life there. In a book I'm reading now, a young kid says, "That's the first time I realized the South didn't win the war." I guess I identify with that.

KNOWLEDGE AND UNDERSTANDING

These two conditions are tough to bring together because we can know without understanding, which I consider to be the key to relationships between people and societies. If people believe you understand and appreciate their position or their nature, you've overcome 90 percent of the challenge. But understanding calls for an amalgamation of so many talents: wisdom, tact, sincerity, honesty, and many others. Few of us can consistently exhibit all these attributes, so understanding doesn't come easy.

Perhaps one path to understanding is first to gain knowledge and then to suspend judgment until what we know leads to empathy for others. I'm not sure I'll ever attain complete knowledge or understanding of even a few things in this world, but I believe the quest for knowledge requires us to learn at least twelve things: the value of time, the need for perseverance, the pleasure of serving, the dignity of simplicity, the true worth of character, the power of kindness, the influence of example, the obligation of duty, the wisdom of economy, the virtue of patience, the nobility of labor, and the teachings of He who said, "learn of me."

FRIENDSHIP

True, close friendship is absolute gold—and it's rarer than we sometimes recognize. For example, some of our friends reflect the same ideals and principles that I believe in but aren't the people I would turn to in a crisis. The difference is hard to explain. We're close friends with dozens of couples, but I'm especially drawn to some of them because I know they're absolutely loyal to Martha and me in a wonderful, profound way.

This deep, true friendship has nothing to do with how much money people have or their position in society. So, if I had any financial problems—or any other troubles—these are the people I know I could turn to and they would immediately respond. I can think of a number of friends who don't have a lot of money, but I know they would do anything they could for me if I asked them to—and I would do the same for them.

Of course, in many ways and without question, Martha is my

best friend. We've had a lot of togetherness over the last thirty years, which is wonderful. She says that she can't even imagine not being around or with me anymore, and I feel the same way about her. To us, friendship is probably what it is to everybody—being really comfortable and at ease with someone you know you can totally trust. And you know, even if you get upset with them, it doesn't matter because it's going to be fine the next day. That's how Martha expresses it, and I agree. By that definition we're fortunate to have many people we can call friends.

FAMILY

Well, my family is Martha and my children. I have the best family relationships of anybody I know, including those with my kids. Even though we may go for long periods when we don't see each other, we're very close. I'm extremely proud of that because a lot of families don't have this closeness. The children also are highly successful and confident—all of them—in what they do. So when we get together, everybody is kidding everyone else, and we have a ball. As Martha says, the most fun you can have is a great time with your children.

I'm especially happy that we get along so well because I was pretty tough with my kids when they were growing up. Martha jokes that my being gone during their teenage years may have been for the best because they reached the point of chaos and rebellion that drives all parents crazy. Of course, Suzie always says, "I was never any trouble, but those twins ruined my life!" It's true: Jimmy and Nan were a handful—particularly Jimmy, who took special delight in tormenting his older sister. In any case, I was strict with my kids and sometimes I felt bad about it, but I think it has paid off in our case.

One little story will reveal a lot about our family relationships. Years ago, Suzie was already a world-renowned designer, so her house in Indianapolis was fashion-magazine perfect. A well-meaning acquaintance had given us something that was meant to commemorate a family event, but it was garish and funny to look at. Still, we didn't want to hurt the person's feelings by just getting rid of it, so we humorously passed it on to Jimmy. He immediately sent it to Suzie for a joke, but she assumed it was sincere. She obviously couldn't make this oddity fit into her perfectly decorated house; yet, she couldn't just throw Jimmy's gift away. Instead, she hid it in a back room.

That Christmas, the whole family was visiting Suzie's house, and she invited a lot of people to a party. Jimmy nosed around, found his "gift," and put it right in the middle of all her decorator stuff. She would come in, go into shock, and snatch the thing up to hide it again. But Jimmy was watching her. He saw where she put it every time, retrieved it, and put it somewhere else in the house. It drove her nuts but cracked up the rest of the family. Suzie has loosened up a lot since then—in self-defense, I guess. As for that special gift, every few years it will turn up under someone's Christmas tree. It's always good for a laugh. We can never remember who got it last, but it is becoming a family heirloom.

Concerning families and family values in general, I think September 11 has united a lot of people and brought many families back together. Among our club members or those in Kankakee, I've seen families mend. Couples our age or a little younger have daughters moving back in with their two or three children. Or they're taking care of children a daughter abandoned, so at least the grandchildren have a home and family to call their own. Our country has trouble assimilating some of our citizens, but I think building family relationships would make that job easier. For example, I admire the Asians because of the respect they have for their families, their intelligence, and their emphasis on learning. Dedication to our families is a great foundation for commitment to our country.

HONESTY AND INTEGRITY

I rank these qualities number one on my list of personal attributes. If people lie to me, I lose respect for them. Naturally, I have to temper this view. When a kid lies about something, for example, I know there's room for forgiveness. We've probably all said, "I don't know how that got there!" when a parent or teacher asked about something we took without permission. And some lies—a bit of dishonesty—may be necessary for the greater good. I've seen occasions in which a little white lie might save a marriage or a friendship, or something even more significant. So there may be an occasion when you could compromise on honesty, but not integrity, which is what holds a person's character together.

HONOR AND DIGNITY

People have asked me how I endured imprisonment, especially the torture. I remember one night lying in irons on the floor of the cell that we called the "Ho Chi Minh Room." I was in great pain after a three-day torture session with the Vietnamese. I knew they would soon be back and I was very lonely. I wondered to myself, What the hell is a 43-year-old man doing lying in this filthy hole letting these animals beat the life out of him?

I asked myself, If I do what they are asking me to do, would my family forgive me? Sure they would. They love me.

How about God? Would He forgive me? Of course. He knows what I'm thinking right now and yes, He would, for ours is a merciful God.

Would my country forgive me? Certainly. No government in the world is more forgiving than ours.

They would all forgive me because they would all know, or at least would all want to believe, that I had done my best. Then why not end the suffering and the unending anxiety of waiting for them to come after you again?

It was a tempting thought. But there was another party I hadn't thought about yet: myself. One has to live with oneself, and as long as I possessed the strength and the mental faculties to resist, surrendering was out of the question. Nothing can destroy a person more completely than the loss of pride and honor.

Robert Louis Stevenson said, "Anyone can carry his burden, however hard, until nightfall. Anyone can do his work, however hard, for one day." That was the pattern of our lives in Hanoi during those early years of terror. We lived to endure each day, hoping that nightfall would bring a few hours of relief. We easily could have compromised our beliefs and made our lives much easier by cooperating with the Vietnamese. But our goal was to return home with our honor intact. Some brave men did not survive the early years, but those who did came home with honor and dignity.

I hope people who read this account of me will recognize that these two attributes—honor and dignity—are my most important legacy, as well as guiding principles for our country's future.

APPENDIX B

Military Decorations

A COMBAT veteran of World War II, Korea, and Vietnam, Col. James H. Kasler has a total of seventy-six military awards for valor and service (see fig. 31). This total places him high among the one hundred most decorated soldiers or airmen in U.S. history.

THREE AIR FORCE CROSSES

Congress created the Air Force Cross (AFC) in 1960 to match the Army's Distinguished Service Cross and the Navy Cross. It ranks just below the Medal of Honor as an award for extraordinary heroism in combat. Thousands of aircrew members flew against the enemy in Southeast Asia from 1960 to 1973, but fewer than three hundred officers and airmen earned the AFC. A handful earned two. Only Colonel Kasler has earned three.

Colonel Kasler earned his first AFC as mission commander of a perfect F-105 strike on the heavily defended Hanoi petroleum storage complex. This strike occurred on June 29, 1966.

Kasler earned his second AFC as leader of a formation hit by antiaircraft fire while evaluating low-level delivery against a priority target. When his wingman, Fred Flom, was hit and ejected, Kasler located the downed pilot, flew cover at low altitude until his fuel was almost gone, refueled at an airborne tanker, and returned to direct rescue operations. Flying at treetop level to locate his wingman, he was shot down and captured by the North Vietnamese on August 8, 1966.

Kasler's third AFC was awarded for his heroic, almost inconceivable resistance to abuse by the North Vietnamese during his incarceration from August 8, 1966, to March 4, 1973. His extraordinary heroism and strength of character were an inspiration to his fellow POWs.

OTHER MAJOR AWARDS

Two Silver Stars
Legion of Merit
Nine Distinguished Flying Crosses
Two Bronze Stars, one with the "V" device for valor
Two Purple Hearts
Eleven Air Medals

SELECTED BIBLIOGRAPHY

Alvarez, Everett, Jr. with Anthony S. Pitch. *Chained Eagle*. New York: Donald I. Fine, 1989.

Basel, G. I. *Pak Six*. New York: Jove/Berkley, 1987.

Broughton, Jacksel M. *Going Downtown: The War against Hanoi and Washington*. New York: Orion, 1988.

———. *Thud Ridge*. New York: Bantam, 1985.

Blakey, Scott. *Prisoner at War: The Survival of Commander Richard A. Stratton*. New York: Anchor Press/Doubleday, 1978.

Denton, Jeremiah, Jr. *When Hell Was in Session*. New York: Reader's Digest Press, 1976.

Dorr, Robert F. *Air War Hanoi*. London: Blandford, 1988.

———. *F-86 Sabre: History of the Sabre and F J Fury*. Osceola, WI: Motorbooks, 1993.

———. *Vietnam: Combat from the Cockpit*. Osceola, WI: Motorbooks, 1989.

Dorr, Robert F., and Warren Thompson. *The Korean Air War*. Osceola, WI: Motorbooks, 1994.

Dramesi, John A. *Code of Honor*. New York: Warner Books, 1975.

Drendel, Lou. *F-105 Thunderchief in Action*. Carrolton, TX: Squadron/Signal Publications, 1974.

Frisbee, John L. "Valor in Three Wars." *Air Force Magazine* 69, no. 11 (November 1986): 119.

Gaither, Ralph. *With God in a P.O.W. Camp*. Nashville, TN: Broadman Press, 1973.

Guarino, Lawrence. *A POW's Story: 2801 Days in Hanoi*. New York: Ivy Books, 1990.

Harvey, Frank. *Air War: Vietnam*. New York: Bantam, 1967.

Howes, Craig. *Voices of the Vietnam POWs: Witnesses to Their Fight*. New York: Oxford University Press, 1993.

Hubbell, John G. *P.O.W.: A Definitive History of the American Prisoner-of-War Experience in Vietnam, 1964–1973*. New York: Reader's Digest Press, 1976.

Johnson, Rick. "Kasler Exploits under A. F. Lid." *The Indianapolis Star*, October 30, 1966.

Johnson, Sam, and Jan Winebrenner. *Captive Warriors*. College Station: Texas A & M University Press, 1992.

Keating, Thomas R. "Kaslers' Thanksgiving Great." *The Indianapolis Star*, November 23, 1973.

———. "POW Yule No. 6—And Holding." *The Indianapolis Star*, December 22, 1972.

———. "Waiting Getting Harder Now." *The Indianapolis Star*, February 7, 1973.

Knebel, Fletcher. "Red Jets Can Rule the Skies." *Look* 17, no. 7 (April 7, 1953): 31–35.

McCain, John S., III, with Mark Salter. *Faith of My Fathers*. New York: Random House, 1999.

McDaniel, Eugene B., with James Johnson. *Scars & Stripes*. New York: J. B. Lippincott, 1975.

McGrath, John M. *Prisoner of War: Six Years in Hanoi*. Annapolis, MD: Naval Institute Press, 1975.

Mulligan, James A. *The Hanoi Commitment*. Virginia Beach, VA: RIF Marketing, 1981.

Nixon, Richard. *The Memoirs of Richard Nixon*. New York: Grosset & Dunlap, 1978.

Penner, Diana. "Plane Is Tribute to Former POW." *Indianapolis Star*, June 17, 2002.

———. "Reader Will Help Restore Fighter Jet." *Indianapolis Star*, June 18, 2002.

Plumb, Charlie, and Glen H. DeWerff. *I'm No Hero: A POW Story*. Mechanicsburg, PA: Executive Books, 1973.

Purcell, Ben, and Anne Purcell. *Love and Duty*. New York: St. Martin's Press, 1992.

Risner, Robinson. *The Passing of the Night: My Seven Years as a Prisoner of the North Vietnamese*. New York: Random House, 1973.

Rochester, Stuart I., and Frederick Kiley. *Honor Bound: American Prisoners of War in Southeast Asia, 1961–1973*. Annapolis, MD: Naval Institute Press, 1999.

Rowe, James N. *Five Years to Freedom*. Boston: Little, Brown, 1971.

Rutledge, Howard, and Phyllis Rutledge. *In the Presence of Mine Enemies, 1965–1973: A Prisoner of War*. Old Tappan, NJ: Fleming H. Revell, 1973.

Salter, James. *Burning the Days: A Recollection*. New York: Random House, 1997.

———. *Cassada*. Washington, D.C.: Counterpoint Press, 2000.

———. *The Hunters*. Washington, D.C.: Counterpoint Press, 1956, 1997.

Scott, Robert L. *God Is My Co-Pilot.* New York: Ballantine, 1943, 1971.

————. *The Day I Owned the Sky.* New York: Bantam, 1988.

Sharp, U. S. Grant. *Strategy for Defeat: Vietnam in Retrospect.* San Rafael, CA: Presidio, 1978.

Shelton, Isabelle. "Kisses and Cheers for Bringing Them Home." *Washington Evening Star,* May 25, 1973.

Shortridge, Norm. "The Hardest Part of Being a POW Wife Is When You're Alone." *Indianapolis Magazine* 10, no. 2 (February 1973): 26–32.

Smith, Lawrence S., ed. *9th Bombardment Group (VH) History (1st, 5th, and 99th Squadrons): A B-29 Superfortress Unit in World War II.* Princeton, NJ: 9th Bomb Group Association, 1995.

Stockdale, James Bond. *A Vietnam Experience: Ten Years of Reflection.* Stanford, CA: Hoover Press, 1984.

————. *Thoughts of a Philosophical Fighter Pilot.* Stanford, CA: Hoover Press, 1995.

Stockdale, James, and Sybil Stockdale. *In Love and War,* 2nd ed. Annapolis, MD: Naval Institute Press, 1990.

Szulc, Tad. *Fidel: A Critical Portrait.* New York: William Morrow and Company, 1986.

"The Prisoners Return." *Time* 101, no. 8 (February 19, 1973): 12–20.

Toliver, Raymond F., and Trevor J. Constable. *The Blond Knight of Germany.* Blue Ridge Summit, PA: AERO, 1985.

Veith, George J. *Code Name Bright Light: The Untold Story of U.S. POW Rescue Efforts during the Vietnam War.* New York: Dell, 1998.

Yeager, Charles, and Leo Janos. *Yeager: An Autobiography.* New York: Bantam, 1985.

INDEX

ABOUT THE AUTHORS

Perry D. Luckett retired from the U.S. Air Force in 1990 after twenty years of service as a communications officer and professor of English. He holds a Ph.D. in English and American studies from the University of North Carolina, Chapel Hill, and has taught writing and literature at the University of Colorado and the U.S. Air Force Academy. Dr. Luckett is the author or language editor of several books, including *Charles A. Lindbergh: A Bio-Bibliography* and nine volumes of NASA's Space Technology Series, as well as articles on military women in popular culture, Vietnam War literature, and early powered flight. He lives in Colorado Springs, Colorado, where he is president of Executive Writing Associates, a firm that specializes in professional writing, editing, and training.

Charles L. Byler is a retired English teacher with twenty-seven years of service in Pennsylvania's public schools. He served in the Air Force as an F-105 weapons loader at Bitburg, Germany, from 1963 to 1966 and under Colonel Kasler's command during the AIRCENT NATO tactical weapons meet at Chaumont, France, in June 1965. Mr. Byler holds an M.Ed. in English from Slippery Rock State College, as well as an M.A. in writing from Vermont College of Norwich University. He is the author of several magazine articles and a novel, *After Nam: A Police Story*. He lives in Boyertown, Pennsylvania.